Rain To My Roots

A Pastor Among The Psychologists

RAIN TO MY ROOTS

A Pastor Among the Psychologists

BY

Derek Osborne

©2015 Derek Osborne

ISBN: 978-0-9927642-8-9

PUBLISHED BY
WHITE TREE PUBLISHING
BRISTOL
UNITED KINGDOM

wtpbristol@gmail.com

ABOUT THE AUTHOR

Derek Osborne is a retired Church of England minister and an Honorary Canon of Norwich Cathedral. He is married to Hilary, and together they have worked in a variety of parishes. They also served on the Chaplaincy Team of Lee Abbey, the Christian Community in North Devon which welcomes thousands of guests each year, and have made annual return visits there to lead Bible teaching weeks. Derek and Hilary have three children and seven grandchildren, and live in Cromer. Derek is an enthusiastic supporter of the Canaries — Norwich City Football Club.

Copies of this book — and copies of *Roddy Goes to Church* also by Derek Osborne — can be purchased from websites of major internet booksellers, or from:

Norwich Christian Resource Centre (P&P extra)
St Michael at Plea
Redwell Street
Norwich
NR2 4SN
Tel: 01603 619731
norwichcrc@btconnect.com
www.norwichcrc.co.uk

In grateful memory of
J Stafford Wright
(1905-1985)

Enlightening biblical scholar
Stimulating teacher
Encouraging mentor

CONTENTS

PREFACE

Acknowledgements and Thanks

My warmest thanks are for my wife Hilary: for her constant love and support through the years; for accepting, in our retirement, my long absences in the study producing this book; for correcting and improving my written English.

My thanks also to –

Bishop David Atkinson for his Foreword. His own writings have included contributions to the literature on pastoral theology, as well as Bible commentaries, and he writes regular reviews of newly-published religious books; he has also been a visiting lecturer at Wycliffe Hall, Oxford. I have, therefore, greatly valued his comments and suggestions having read my original MS: the substance of these has been incorporated in the final product — though, needless to say, this present work, with any remaining imperfections, is all mine!

Chris Wright, of White Tree Publishing, for his encouragement and expertise. Bishop David, in his Foreword, has expressed warm appreciation of Chris's father, the late J Stafford Wright (our past College Principal) to whom this book is dedicated. It is he who first sparked my interest in the interface between biblical theology and pastoral psychology and encouraged me to pursue my reading through the years following ordination.

Caroline Clipsom, a member of our church — particularly for her expert typing and patient revision re-typings.

Gita Dickenson, whose painting is on the front cover. She is a local artist who also is involved in the life and witness of our church.

The origin of this publication is a paper prepared, some years ago, for a month-long Mid-Service Clergy Course at St George's House, Windsor Castle. I remain grateful to the Course leaders for urging me to expand its contents into book form.

A book like this is bound to reflect much that has been learned from fellow Christians. For me, these have included, particularly, those outstanding college lecturers recalled by David Atkinson; colleagues who have shared ministry with Hilary and me, and so many other friends who have enriched our lives by their example of compassion and courage, and by living out the truth and grace of Jesus. We thank God for them all.

With regard to quotations, rather than cluttering end-of-chapter pages with detailed references, I have sought simply to indicate brief sources within the text. I apologise for any omissions.

Finally, and supremely, thanks and praise and glory be to the Lord of life for the root-refreshing rain of his Word and Spirit.

Derek Osborne

FOREWORD

Bishop David Atkinson

We used to call him 'Prin'. J Stafford Wright was Principal of Tyndale Hall, Bristol when Derek Osborne trained there for the Anglican priesthood — and he was still Prin for my first term there some years later. My 'year' felt ourselves very fortunate: Colin Brown taught philosophy and church history, Anthony Thiselton helped us to find a pathway through hermeneutics, J I Packer taught us doctrine. Denis Tongue travelled in to teach New Testament. Alec Motyer joined and taught us Old Testament and Hebrew; John Wenham, Greek. And what of 'Prin'?

In my term with him, he taught Old Testament, but also led a seminar on human biology and the Incarnation; he had critically explored his way into some of the teachers of the occult; he read scientific journals; he had written on baptism policy, on theological anthropology, on sects, on the date of Ezra's return to Jerusalem. His pastoral preaching drew on philosophy and psychology. No area of knowledge seemed off limits. Prin's great gift to us was to show us that, with the Bible in one hand and with modern scholarship in the other, there was nothing that could not be explored. God is truth — and all truth is God's truth, wherever we may find it. 'God' — he was fond of quoting from Ecclesiastes — 'has put eternity into our minds'.

Derek Osborne follows in Prin's footsteps. Derek is a pastor of forty years' experience, and still active in a long retirement. He does not claim to be a frontline theologian, let alone a professional psychologist, but with Bible in one hand and the writings of psychologists and therapists in the other, he explores a creative conversation between the two in a way that helpfully illuminates the pastor's task.

Derek engages both with those who think that psychology and Christian theology are sworn enemies, and — at the other extreme — with those whose theology so dissolves into humanistic psychology that Christian identity is lost. He is willing to draw insights from wherever he can find them, and measure them in the light of the biblical Gospel. So he develops a rich conversation with 'depth' psychologists such as Freud, Adler and Jung; with 'lateral' psychologists such as Carl Rogers, Gestalt, and Brian Thorne, and with the great 'height' psychologist Victor Frankl with whose logotherapy Derek finds himself having considerable sympathy.

Throughout, Derek has the biblical Gospel centred in Jesus Christ firmly in his sights. The depth psychologists are explored particularly in relation to the biblical doctrine of regeneration; the lateral psychologists in conversation with the doctrine of redemption; the logotherapy of Frankl in dialogue with the doctrine of revelation. Derek has a warm, evangelical and joyous tone that culminates in his closing chapter, bringing all things together in Jesus Christ our Lord.

Illuminated by apt quotations from poets such as George Herbert and Gerard Manley Hopkins, verses from hymns and some contemporary anecdotes, Derek has walked fearlessly among some of the giants in the history of psychology, sometimes finding resonance and sometimes grounds for criticism, in the light of the biblical Gospel. His work will be an encouragement to other pastors in exploring God's truth wherever we may find it.

David Atkinson

INTRODUCTION

"Mine, O thou lord of life, send my roots rain."

Winter is past. Gerard Manley Hopkins, Jesuit priest and poet, surveys the loveliness of a rural scene now bursting with new life under a cloudless sky. Exuberant verse celebrates the freshness and beauty of the season — a glory which seems to replicate, faintly and fleetingly, the perfection of God's original creation.

Nothing is so beautiful as Spring —
      When weeds, in wheels, shoot long and lovely and lush;
      Thrush's eggs look little low heavens, and thrush
Through the echoing timber does so rinse and wring
The ear, it strikes like lightnings to hear him sing;
      The glassy peartree leaves and blooms, they brush
      The descending blue; that blue is all in a rush
With richness; the racing lambs too have fair their fling.

What is all this juice and all this joy?
      A strain of the earth's sweet being in the beginning
In Eden garden.

In sharp contrast, ten years later (March 1889), a similar scene feeds very different feelings, of bleak dejection. At painful variance with the juice and joy of Springtime, his own life seems barren. Immersed in sombre self-depreciation, it seems to him that nothing he has produced lives; his poetic creativity has run dry:

> See, banks and brakes
> Now, leavèd how thick! lacèd they are again
> With fretty chervil, look, and fresh wind shakes
> Them; birds build — but not I build; no, but strain,
> Time's eunuch, and not breed one work that wakes.
> Mine, O thou lord of life, send my roots rain.

Dogged by such mood swings, Hopkins' periodic bouts of depression were often very severe indeed. The "terrible" sonnets, written mainly in 1885, provide poignant evidence of this: only someone who has been there knows the vertiginous horror of such mental anguish:

> O the mind, mind has mountains; cliffs of fall
> Frightful, sheer, no-man-fathomed. Hold them cheap
> May who ne'er hung there. Nor does long our small
> Durance deal with that steep or deep.

The last line of this poem draws comfort from the thought that death will end all suffering and, in the meantime, nights bring temporary oblivion: "All life death does end and each day dies with sleep". But in the darkest of the six "sonnets of desolation" he laments the bitter isolation of a despair unrelieved even by sleep:

> I wake and feel the fell of dark, not day.
> What hours, O what black hours we have spent
> This night! What sights you, heart, saw; ways you went!
> And more must, in yet longer light's delay.

Many of the distressing states of mind so vividly de-scribed may well indicate a depression which was *endogenous* — that is, derived from within, having no apparent external cause; but it is likely that *reactive* depression also played a part in the poor self-esteem expressed in the Spring sonnet of 1889 quoted earlier. General ill health towards the close of the previous year had culminated in typhoid. But whatever its concomitant causes, no doubt partly explicable in psychoana-lytic terms, melancholy, in Hopkins, was always connected with his religious feelings. Just as his joyful delight in crea-tion sprang from the felt immanence of the Creator, so dark moods were associated with a sense of God's absence. His poems were written primarily for God: a sense of divine withdrawal causes them to seem like unreceived, useless missives. Perhaps the metaphor also applies to his prayers:

And my lament
Is cries countless, cries like dead letters sent
To dearest him that lives alas! away.

It is this impression of spiritual desertion (like the mystics' "Dark night of the soul") which is the bitter core of his heaviness of heart and which can lead him to remonstrate with God over his feelings of poetic sterility, which contrast with the burgeoning life of nature in Spring. Echoing Jeremiah's complaint (see *Jeremiah 12:1 and 2a*) he ex-presses hurt and bewilderment at God's attitude towards him, which seems to be one of capricious displeasure:

Thou art indeed just, Lord, if I contend
With thee; but, sir, so what I plead is just.
Why do sinners' ways prosper? And why must
Disappointment all I endeavour end?

Wert thou my enemy, O thou my friend,
How wouldst thou worse, I wonder, than thou dost
Defeat, thwart me? ...
Mine, O thou lord of life, send my roots rain.

For those with eyes that see, it is evident that the flame of faith in him, which can flicker and burn very low, is never extinguished. He never ceases to relate to God and to address him; a note of hope is never entirely absent; the leaden echo is accompanied by the golden echo, however faint; and underneath the weakness is a steel-like self-surrender to the divine will — the essence of his religious vows.

That faith sustained him and held him during his last days on earth. On April the 29th of that same year (1889) he wrote to his friend Robert Bridges, "I am ill today, but no matter for that as my spirits are good".

His last words on the day he died (June the 8th) were "I am so happy, so happy". And clearly, the fertile beauty of the very sonnet in which he lamented his dryness, as well as the totality of his poetic productions preserved to us, demonstrate that his cry was heard, his prayer answered: the Lord of life had nourished his creativity; the rain from heaven had refreshed his soul.

Theology and Psychology

Reflections such as these have led me to the title of this book — *Rain to my Roots — A Pastor Among The Psychologists*. They also serve as a way-in to my theme, which is the interface between biblical theology and human psychology. What, precisely, does Hopkins mean by "roots"? What is the "rain"? Crass questions; "We murder to dissect." However, it is surely legitimate, if prosaic, to understand "roots" as a poetic metaphor signifying the depths of his innermost being, where the springs of his creativity are located.

In psychological terms we are in the area of the Unconscious, or essential Self, which, it is argued, largely determines the individual each one of us uniquely becomes, and our continuing potential. For the Jesuit Hopkins, this deep-down centre is also where the union of his human spirit and the divine life is found.

The heaven-sent root-refreshing "rain" for which he longs echoes a metaphor which is found in the Bible. Significantly, when "rain" is used there to picture the divine blessing it is associated with *God's Word* descending from above and producing spiritual life and fruitfulness (e.g. *Isaiah 55:10-11*). This rain, this Word, is life-giving because it is imbued with the Holy Spirit's fertilising, reviving power.

The Ignatian emphasis upon the imaginative contemplation of Holy Scripture as a means of grace and renewal would have been a central part of the poet's spirituality. God does refresh us by means of his Spirit in his Word. Thus, by a logical extrapolation, "rain" can be interpreted as the whole subject-matter of biblical studies — God himself revealed, understood and experienced by the Holy Spirit's ministry in accordance with his Word.

On this understanding, "Rain to my Roots" signifies a *rapprochement* between theology and psychology where, consistent with the analogy, the latter is dependent upon the former; juxtaposing the two in this manner must not imply equality of status. Theology as the queen of sciences should be normative, and indeed, formative for other areas of learning. This is especially true of psychology which is, by definition, anthropocentric — its focus is the human personality.

Theology is theocentric — that is, interpreting and evaluating all learning in the light of God's self-revelation. The key question, What does it mean to be human?, could seem to call for a response expressed in psychological terms. The Bible's answer, however, is always framed in terms of our creatureliness and dependence upon our Creator. True humanness is to be defined in relation to the image of God in us as delineated in Holy Scripture and demonstrated supremely by Jesus, the incarnate Son of God. "In the gospel records he stands out above other people as unique. He provides a pattern against which all other humanity may be assessed.... We are intended to see in Jesus a perfect picture of what man should be." But even Jesus "is never seen by the synoptic writers as totally self-sufficient. His perfect humanity is always seen in relation to God. The Johannine portrait, with its constant reference to the communication between the Father and Son, brings this out more vividly, but it is not absent from the synoptics, as *Matthew 11:25ff* shows" *(New Testament Theology — Donald Guthrie).*

Thus God's written Word with its focus upon his incarnate Word becomes the grid through which psychological theories, models and values in regard to humanness must be filtered. John White, Christian psychiatrist and author, has expressed dismay that so many pastors succumb to the "seductive lure" of counselling which is derived from the human sciences, notably psychology, rather than from the Word of God.

"I could not hide the sense of betrayal and alarm I felt that those to whom I looked for a better understanding of my faith (Christian ministers) were tasting the latest tidbits from my own area of expertise, sometimes finding more significance in them than in revelation" (*The Shattered Mirror — John White*). Christians, especially those in positions of influence within the Church, demean themselves and diminish their ministry if ever they trim their sails to catch the prevailing psychological, sociological (or philosophical) wind.

This is not to "dismiss what the human sciences have to contribute". A right understanding of the Christian gospel depends largely upon a correct view of the human condition; it would be foolish to ignore the conclusions arrived at by psychologists and sociologists. "But" to quote John White again "they are deficient not only in failing to deal effectively with the human problem, but in failing to see its essential nature. Though they give us valuable insights of which we should avail ourselves, they are unable to offer more than a partial solution to the dilemma we find ourselves in." Unless, that is, those solutions resonate with revealed truth. As it is vital for roots that the rain reaches them, psychology needs to be permeated by Christian doctrine or it will prove brittle, and barren. This principle gives a subtle twist of meaning to the term "*radical* theology".

The Botanical Parallel

In the natural world healthy roots are of first importance for vigorous plant growth. In addition to rain, growing shoots are affected by the soil in which their roots are embedded, their proximity or otherwise to other plants, and their exposure, above ground, to light and air. Productive development is both "pushed" from below by nourishment from soil via roots, and "pulled" from above by light and air (hence phototropism — plants grow towards the light). In a reverse process, light and air reinforce life in the roots — by photosynthesis, and respiration, through leaves. Botany and horticulture deal with all three aspects of plant culture: roots, soil and other plants, light and air access.

To apply the parallel with psychology: the deep-lying hidden origins (roots) of an individual's distinctive personality are probably perceived by most people as its proper subject-matter. However, two other assumptions are shared in one

7

form or another by all psychologists: the development of personality as influenced by the individual's circumstances and interpersonal relationships (soil and other plants); and the goal-directed nature of behaviour, including the drawing-power of ideals (light and air).

Scheme

Obviously, these three broad orientations overlap. But they suggest a useful three-part scheme for dividing an overview of psychological insights and the different approaches to psychotherapy which are derived from them. More importantly, this scheme helps us more easily to identify biblical themes having the sharpest relevance to the three emphases. In the following chapters, with the botanical parallel in mind, I have labelled these three main "schools" of psychology, with blatant over-simplification, "Depth", "Lateral", and "Height" psychology.

The first adjective (Depth — Chapter 3) obviously describes the classic, foundational psychoanalytical approach of Freud, his associates and followers, exploring the *roots* of personality: and the following chapter (4) explores the apposite biblical doctrine of regeneration (or New Birth). By the second psychological category (Lateral — Chapter 5) I mean the emphasis on the formative influences of a person's cultural context, especially relationships (the soil and other plants). This is followed (Chapter 6) by a consideration of the corporate aspects of redemption drawn from Holy Scripture. Height psychology (Chapter 7) will be recognised by some readers as Victor Frankl's term positing, as a necessary complement to Depth psychology, a spiritual and noological dimension — the upward drawing power of Meaning (air and light); revelation (Chapter 8) is the theme considered most relevant here — the biblical key which unlocks all else. A final chapter (9) has as its focus the perfect Man, who was also divine — our Lord and Saviour Jesus Christ: Emmanuel.

But the first two chapters, which follow, are intended to prepare the ground. They form a general approach to psychology and theology respectively as they impinge upon each other, but affirming the primacy for both of revealed truth, Holy Scripture.

I am aware of two possible weaknesses inherent in the approach outlined above. The first relates to the fact that biblical theology is a cohesive body of truth rather than a collection of doctrines. Regeneration, redemption and revelation, along with all other *foci* of scriptural teaching, are aspects of a unified whole. But I have tried to bear this in mind and let the interconnection between these emerge as an important factor with regard to psychology. A second weakness, it may be considered, lies in an apparent attempt to fit theological themes into a psychological frame of reference, thus diluting the antecedent, formative nature of biblical truth. This is certainly not intended.

My concern is to critique psychological models and paradigms by exposing them to the light of revealed truth; to do this it seems sensible to focus that light upon the areas under consideration *having first identified them* — but not thereby asserting their priority status. "Holy Scripture containeth all things necessary to salvation: so that whatsoever is not read therein, nor may be proved thereby is not to be required of any man, that it should be believed as an article of the Faith, or be thought requisite or necessary to salvation" *(Article 6 of the Articles of Religion of the Church of England).*

A Pastor Among the Psychologists

Here, belatedly, I must come clean: I have received no formal training in psychology nor am I an academic theologian. I write as a common-or-garden clergyman. However, as the great Baptist preacher, C H Spurgeon, once said to his students, "If, in your pastorates you are not theologians, you are nothing". Through the years I have enjoyed the stimulus of trying to keep up-to-date in a non-specialist way with both theology and (pastoral) psychology, through reading, and consultation with professionals. I have sought to submit such knowledge as I have gleaned to the touchstone of Holy Scripture and then to integrate it into my ministry — with what degree of effectiveness those who know me will judge. But I have been encouraged to take the view that this amateur status in both fields may, just possibly, be advantageous: perhaps I can avoid that "tunnel vision" which academic theologians and professional psychologists have both in-formed me, with cheering honesty, is a constant danger among them and their colleagues. And, after all, "amateur" has an honourable meaning: "one who loves ... the subject".

As to method, I have employed broad theological and psychological brush strokes rather than finely etched detail — which I lack the tools for, anyway. This approach runs the risk of seeming to be too generalised. Having read, for example, a variety of books and articles dealing with subjects like depression and anxiety, and listened through the years to not a few sufferers, I am fully aware that my depiction of such afflictions in the following pages may seem cursory. In alluding to them rather than describing extensively their symptomatology I am assuming that my readers will *know* what I am talking about — from personal experience, or from involvement in the sufferings of others, or from reading one of the many relevant books which are readily available.

For similar reasons I have eschewed the inclusion of umpteen anecdotal case-studies which are characteristic of books dealing with pastoral/psychological issues. There is a place for these. But the present book has no pretensions to be any kind of contribution to the Christian Counselling Handbook genre (though, as I say, I have benefited greatly from reading many of these). My concern is to explore the interface between the two approaches to the human condition — theological and psychological — and help my readers to do the same. It is quite possible that *particularisation* in the interests of demonstrating relevance could be self-defeating. Distracted by individual trees we may lose sight of the wood. Precise, person-focused illustrations may actually detract from the relevance-factor by their narrow singularity; specific examples of personal situations can have the effect of excluding others which would more accurately reflect those of the reader. The Holy Spirit is the Communicator *par excellence* and he can illuminate truth from God's Word, or consonant with God's Word, and apply it with transforming power to specific persons or groups.

God-Centred Perseverance

Numerous poignant human problems have no obvious solutions. The "thousand natural shocks that flesh is heir to" can raise painful questions to which there are no satisfactory answers. About many such issues we have to remain reverently agnostic, trust in God, walking with Jesus hour by hour — sometimes through the darkness of doubt and painful bewilderment, yet confident that what is hidden to us is known to him and that hereafter we shall understand. Dietrich Bonhoeffer's counsel was "to pray and do right and wait for God's own time".

Such a course is possible because even during the worst of times, when God's purposes seem incomprehensible, there is so much in his revealed truth which can penetrate our minds, bringing light and hope and purpose to our lives. "The secret things belong to the Lord our God, but the things revealed belong to us and to our children forever that we may follow all the words of his law" (*Deuteronomy 29:29*).

And by grace we may yet perceive and praise his glory, and creatively enjoy him.

We can learn from Hopkins. In this profoundly theocentric poet we find a fusion of persevering Christian devotion, scholarship, perceptive love of nature, and innovative verse — using words as an artist uses colour and form, and as a composer uses musical notes and rhythm. But supremely, he reminds us of the glory of God — the grand theme which permeates all his writing, both poetry and prose. For him, that glory is discernible in the intrinsic beauty of nature (despite the Fall and man's smudge and smell); secondly, in our senses, by which, though warped by sin, we may perceive the divine power in creation; and thirdly, in the correlation between these two (the objective form and the subjective apprehension) which can be expressed in poetry (and, of course, in art and music). All three aspects reflect divine glory. Thus, whether producing word-pictures of nature on a broad canvas or describing a single bluebell, he can see "The grandeur of God" and say "I know the beauty of our Lord by it."

This central, Christ-centred philosophy concerning the glory of God is expressed by Hopkins in an address entitled "The Principle and Foundation" based on the opening of a work which profoundly influenced him — *The Spiritual Exercises of St Ignatius Loyola*. It begins "Man was created to praise, reverence, and serve God our Lord.... And the other things on the face of the earth were created for man's sake, and to help him in the following out of the end for which he was created". He adds that we therefore need to repent of the sin which makes us purblind and self-centred, in order to see and extol God's glory. "What we have not done yet we can do now, what we have done badly hitherto, we can do well hence forward, we can repent our sins and BEGIN TO GIVE GOD GLORY. The moment we do this we reach the end of our being, we do and are what we were made for."

Moreover, we are also reminded by Hopkins that the darkness which can, for a time, hide God from us and obscure his glory, and thereby seem unbearable, cannot totally eclipse his love. The Christian will sometimes feel, in life, the downward and destructive drag of death (a principle akin to Freud's "*Thanatos*"?) but always Christ will "easter in us". His poems emphasise the hope-dimension in Christianity much more than the suffering. In this strange co-mingling of distress and joy, anguish and peace, producing something of beauty which glorifies God (in the case of Hopkins, inspired poetry), we may see a fulfilment of Paul's well-known words in his letter to the Romans (*8:28*): "And we know that in all things God works for the good of those who love him, who have been called according to his purpose".

The "all things" must include both the painful and the pleasurable. Pain is never less than pain; darkness does not cease to be darkness. But God's love penetrates the pain, his light begins to throw a pattern onto the darkness, so that something good, something beautiful, gradually takes shape and is then strengthened in us. Above all, Jesus, "The man of sorrows and familiar with suffering" becomes known to us in intimate companionship; the forming of his image in us is advanced; and new hope, peace and energy (creativity) may be gently, progressively released to his glory. Michael Ramsey writing about the power of the transforming love of Christ to redeem suffering quotes a comment of Karl Barth on *Romans 8:35 and 37*, "Thus our tribulation without ceasing to be tribulation is transformed. We suffer as we suffered before, but our suffering is no longer a passive perplexity, but is transformed into a pain which is creative, fruitful, full of power and promise. The road which is impassable has been made known to us in the crucified and risen Lord" (*Be still and Know* — *Michael Ramsey*).

God's rain can reach and revive our roots however dry they are, however hard the soil.

"*Mine, O thou lord of life, send my roots rain.*"

Writing this book has been part of my own spiritual journey. This explains why its title, derived from Hopkins' "Rain to my Roots", retains the personal pronoun. Mercifully, the dreadful "black hours" and "cliffs of fall" described so vividly by the poet have been comparatively rare in my own life. Nevertheless, what I have written is motivated by an unshakeable certainty forged by personal experience, and confirmed through forty-plus years of pastoral ministry to others, that God does speak, healingly, in and through his Word.

I have found many psychological and theological works heavy-going: they demonstrate an off-putting tendency to be wordy, abstruse, and self-reverential. Oliver Edward (1711 to 1791) is famously quoted, in Boswell's *Johnson*, as declaring "I have tried too in my time to be a philosopher: but, I don't know how, cheerfulness was always breaking in." My forays into psychology and theology have often been cheered by the breaking in of light from Holy Scripture. If what is written in the following pages brings spiritual refreshment to the reader, to God be the glory. To revert to this book's central metaphor: the rain is from heaven; my aim has been simply to dig a few irrigation channels.

CHAPTER 1

Psychological Roots

"The unexamined life is not worth living" Socrates

"This above all, to thine own self be true:
Thou canst not then be false to any man."

Polonius's fussy farewell words to his son Laertes (*Hamlet*) include (above) just about the most problematic piece of advice a young man (or anyone) could be given. It may have made sense in Shakespeare's time but what on earth does it mean — today? According to the psychologist Winnicot the adolescent is "engaged in trying to find the self to be true to". Maybe Laertes was out of his teens but at what age could he, or any of us, be expected to have solved that adolescent problem?

When can we know who we really are — what it is that makes up our unique identity, the core reality which distinguishes us from others? What do we mean by selfhood? Polonius makes a connection between personal authenticity (being true to "yourself") and honourable, positive relationships: "Thou canst not then be false to any man." Fine — in theory. The trouble is, as Winnicot pointed out, we can all too easily develop what he termed a "false self" and this, by the same token, will undermine genuine *rapport* with other people.

Perhaps early experiences have made us somewhat fearful of, say, authority figures, leading us into avoidance strategies, or belligerence or over-compliance, any of which are likely to falsify relationships in adulthood. The "self" we exhibit may have been over-conditioned in some way by the perceived expectations of others and does not correspond with our deep-down nature. But such a line of thought serves only to bring us back to the fundamental problem: how can we know and understand our own basic nature — both in the general sense of the characteristics we share with all other human beings and, in particular, in relation to our individuality.

So, is there any practical usefulness in Polonius's counsel? How can his advice about being true to others possibly make sense in a society where spin and hype determine what is to be believed about others? In a post-modern world where "image" is everything, truth about a person is what is *projected*: the way his or her actions and words are presented. We are into an age of "designer-personality". This determines not only the making of a President: lesser mortals also are too often defined and "known" by their roles and carefully tailored public persona: so many "empty suits".

The way we come across to others becomes all important. All of us are tempted to conform, and slip into the techniques of "impression management". To this end we, also, can so "compartmentalise" our lives that aspects considered detrimental to our image are sectioned off, and ego-boosting "lies" are lived out.

"To thine own self be true" — which self? And with which selves are people relating to each other?

It was Carl Jung who spoke of the "presenting self" as the *persona* — which is mostly determined by the role we fill in life (husband, wife, father, mother, business person, teacher, artist, pastor, doctor, etc). Arguably, in this general sense, the *persona* is socially desirable, even necessary, for although we are not defined by function alone, the fact is that we do relate more easily to each other on the basis of "the part we play" in life and the way we choose to comport ourselves. It is not helpful to wear our heart on our sleeve, or bluntly to express every thought, or bare our soul, all the time. The obvious danger though, as indicated above, is that the role, the *persona*, becomes the "reality" obscuring the real person — even to himself or herself — and takes over so that a genuine, congruent response to other people becomes difficult, if not impossible. Thus the "self" is falsified. Perhaps this line of thought approaches Polonius's meaning: authenticity is needed, rather than self-deception.

But does any of this really matter? It is possible that to some people such explorations amount to pretentious nonsense and can only lead, if taken seriously, to a kind of narcissistic, angst-ridden introspection: "Who am I?" "Who should I be?" "What do people think of me?" etc etc. Others, though, will concur that social cohesion *is* inevitably undermined when the principles of personal integrity and mutual respect (Polonius-style) are cynically disregarded. And whether we care or not, we are immersed in a global culture where it can seem that mendacity smears every part of life, and even the masks worn are often suspect. (This is, of course, a generalisation: probity is not altogether absent in public affairs or personal relationships. There is a Christian perspective on this matter which will be considered later).

In the meantime, the relevance of psychology to these issues is surely apparent, for it is the science of the human soul or mind (the psyche): the study of the nature and presentation of the essential "self". No psychological school would claim to have the subject wrapped up — nor ever will. Thomas Carlyle (1795 to 1881) wrote, with typically incisive wit, of "the folly of that impossible precept, 'know thyself': til" he added "it be translated into this partially possible one, 'know what thou canst work at'". Perhaps psychology can help us to "know what thou canst work at". In particular, it may expose to us some of those accretions (often distressing) which, for one reason and another, have become part of the "false self", and indicate ways through to a more authentic and happier selfhood (sometimes described, paradoxically, as "self-transcendence") and thereby into richer inter-personal relationships.

Psychology

Some areas of psychology are limited to the task of observing and recording human behaviour — measuring and classifying the responses and reactions of people under different conditions. Such studies, often resulting in tables, graphs, and statistics, can be useful in determining practical steps to improve the well-being and effectiveness of men and women in all kinds of day to day situations — e.g. the workplace, the school or college, the armed services, the home, the sports ground, the roads and motorways.

This broad field of research is designated by such descriptions as *academic psychology, experimental psychology* and *applied psychology*. Other psychologists may specialise in possible links between personality and biological factors such as genetics, brain chemistry, and the endocrine glands. In University Courses in psychology the subject of *cognition* looms large — that is, study of the various modes of knowledge: perceiving, remembering, imagining, conceiving, judging, reasoning: and the *cognitive function* in relation to the place of feelings and will in the conscious life is also explored. Human development generally is considered, with the help of sociological findings. The genome project will increasingly affect research in these areas.

A further branch of psychology has its focus in psychiatry

— the study and treatment of mental, emotional, and behavioural disorders, including psychoses. The treatment of these conditions and of debilitating neuroses calls for advanced training and specialist skills which include a knowledge of psycho-pharmacology, for many sufferers are provenly helped by medication. The distress of less serious conditions can also be alleviated by antidepressants and mood-enhancing drugs which may be prescribed by a General Practitioner.

For obvious reasons the present book does not attempt to enter such specialised departments: its subject matter is the more commonly-experienced symptoms of mental and emotional unease, and the light which psychology can shed upon these. Many of us, without verging on psychotic illness, know what it is, for example, to be floored by depression for a time, or gripped by anxiety. In other words, various common neuroses have, temporarily, got the better of us and perhaps returned periodically in the form of enervating moods, sharp fears or exhausting obsessiveness. And yes, some will be helped by medication to surmount these.

Many will also benefit from the skilful, compassionate counsel of a trained psychotherapist. Often, though, the listening ear of a good friend, the shoulder to cry on, the genuine, congruent affirmation and advice of people that know us well, and care about us — these will be a healing source of comfort, correction and encouragement. As Christians we can also be open to the wonderful ministry of the Holy Spirit permeating our conversations and our prayers for each other. He will help us to recall, and will apply to our hearts, appropriate truths from Holy Scripture: thus reinforcing healthy habits of God-centred trust and obedience.

But arguably such mutual support will be much more effective if we learn from psychology to understand more clearly the nature and source of inner dissonances, how we can come to terms with them and deal with them, and how we can move forward with renewed self-respect into more fulfilling relationships and purposeful living.

It is important that well-meaning but uninformed friends avoid platitudes — not least, pious platitudes; these are best left unspoken.

Not everyone is called to train as a psychotherapist or counsellor but each of us can become better equipped, through psychological insights, to know ourselves and to help others. For example, most of us will readily agree with the interesting, if obvious, conclusions of *developmental psychology* that changes in our perceptions, feelings, attitudes and behaviour take place as we grow through infancy, childhood, and adolescence into adulthood, so that each of us becomes a unique person.

The questions arising from this basic truth are even more interesting. What has determined that development? What factors have influenced the formation of the person we have become — and will become in the future? How much is nature? How much is nurture? Will psychology be rendered obsolete by the successful completion of the genome project or does the person we become depend more on how we respond to what our genes prompt us to do? In psychological/ethical terms: what is the relationship between "is" and "ought" — the way we are and the way we could and should be? The debate continues.

But (to begin at the beginning): the fact is that all of us have known the helplessness and vulnerability of infancy and a consequent dependence upon the security of loving care. Some, sadly, have experienced the absence or cruel opposite of such love, and as a result, have grown up feeling dis-equipped in some measure to form mature relationships — or really to enjoy life. None of us has known such love in perfection, for no parents, however mature, can be perfect in their care. Inevitably, therefore, to a lesser or greater degree we all develop personalities with some inner insecurities and disharmonies. In adult life these can emerge as feelings of inferiority which show themselves in anxiety, depression, aggression ... leading to all sorts of compensating behaviour patterns (varieties of the "false self") which can complicate personal relationships. Such problems are more painfully present for some than for others. Why?

Some of us come to terms with our own nature, both inherited and conditioned, as we grow older, and develop a modest self-esteem which benefits others. Others find this much more difficult. What makes us differ? Some grow into loving relationships with parents and with peers which heal, to a significant extent, the felt vulnerabilities and separation-fears inherited from childhood. Others seem unable to lose that feeling of non-acceptance, and seek to compensate in immature ways. How are the variations explained?

No psychologist would suggest that there are definitive answers to such questions, nor that complete integration of the personality is attainable. But psychological insights can perhaps uncover some causes of emotional fragility and invalid thought-patterns, and point ahead to positive, healing readjustments.

Or can they?

Psycho-babble?

Not everyone gives credence to such claims for psychology. To some people they are emperor's clothes or psycho-babble. This is partly because the vocabulary of psychology can indeed come across as gobble-de-gook which conflicts with earthy common sense. Moreover, there are different schools of psychology representing different approaches to the understanding of personality and, compounding this confusion, they can use the same terminology to mean different things: the old word *ego*, for example, has various nuances of meaning. Even introductory courses in Psychology and Psychotherapy can be dauntingly involved and perplexing, often complicated by intricate charts and diagrams and esoteric terms. It is not altogether surprising that to many people psychology "is like a blind man in a dark room looking for a black cat that isn't there". In recent years the fog has thickened. New therapy-movements have proliferated. It has been claimed that disturbingly inadequate regulatory controls mean that almost anyone can set themselves up as a Counsellor or Therapist: what credentials should they need?

On top of all this, we can be left bewildered by a jumble of mysterious acronyms: PTSD, RMT, FMS, CBT, AD/HD, DID, MPD, PLT etc etc. (Post-Traumatic Stress Disorder, Recovered Memory Therapy, False Memory Syndrome, Cognitive Behaviour Therapy, Attention Deficit/Hyperactivity Disorder, Dissociative Identity Disorder, Multiple Personality Disorder, Past-Life Therapy. And we can feel unsettled by exhortations to "get in touch with your inner child", engage in "deep process work", recognise "learned helplessness" in yourself, and so on. Bookshop shelves become clogged with numerous self-help volumes and pop-psychology titles which can induce moods of self-doubt and lead us to buy the lot.

One Big Con-Trick?

A Canadian psychologist, Tana Dineen, has written a book arguing with dismay that her profession has become a huge self-serving industry which dupes large numbers of people into becoming dependent "users" of its services, in the interests of profit. The title of the volume says it all: *Manufacturing Victims*: exploiting our vulnerabilities, the "industry" persuades us that we are all "victims" — any feelings of unhappiness, boredom, anger, sadness, and guilt or whatever, can now all be interpreted as signs of prior trauma of which we are victims. In fact, such "psychologising" has, she suggests, taken over virtually every aspect of human existence. There are psychological experts in death and dying, obesity and eating disorders, being married and being single, sexual pleasure and sexual dysfunction, being fired and being successful, mid-life crisis and growing old, childcare and eldercare, and so on.

In this way psychologists become the new, self appointed, omnicompetent pastors and doctors: "our social problems are all human problems and we are the experts in this". Their expertise and skills, it is claimed, equip them to discern the causes of "stress, distress or trauma" at the root of our unhappiness; and they possess the superior status and power which enables them to "know what is best". As a result "people … are turning more and more to psychology for relief. Some do this through weekly appointments; others by frequenting seminars and workshops; others by endlessly buying books on "abuse", "trauma", "stress" and "recovery"; all in pursuit of an illusive experience held out like a carrot or a pot of gold by the Psychology Industry."

Thus "society is becoming more and more filled with people who consider themselves victims of one sort or another." The author's claim is apparently borne out by recent statistics in America which indicate that the psychologists' PR seems to work: "in the early 1960s, 14% of the US population (25 million) had received some psychological service. By 1976 that number has risen to 26%; by 1990, to 33%. And by 1995, according to the APA, 46% (128 million) had seen a mental-health professional. Some predict that by early in the 21st century, users will be the majority — constituting 80% of the population!".

Arguably, Dineen overstates her case, though, in fairness, she does not consider all psychologists to be tarred with the same "arrogant" brush! Nevertheless, her impressively-documented criticisms are all the more thought-provoking because she writes from within the profession. Her motivation is to unmask what she sees as an abandoning or corrupting of psychology's foundational qualities of objectivity and compassion, in the interests of self-aggrandisement and profit; and she wishes to see its integrity restored. I am not a psychologist: others, who are, must assess the validity of the charges she levels. However, with two important principles we may readily concur.

First, any inculcation of emotional hypochondria or self-pitying "victim mentality" is reprehensible when we recall that there is so much *real* suffering. A great many live with emotional wounds and personality damage inherited from genuinely traumatic events in their past. It is undesirable that others of us, more fortunate, should be pressured into ransacking our unreliable memories for hypothetically baneful causes of that unease which prevents us being as happy as we imagine we could, or should, be. Too many fight daily against the formidable reality of anxiety and depression and obsessional states, whatever may be their cause, without the attempt to "manufacture" more victims.

Secondly, trouble-free happiness is, in any case, a chimera, the search for which is self-defeating and self-diminishing. It should never be dangled as a carrot or a pot of gold. Happiness, when experienced, is a by-product of pursuing higher aims than self-equilibrium and self-actualisation. The fact is, that to develop any kind of maturity (and authenticity?) there is a sense in which we need problems more than we need solutions. I do not, of course, mean those severe problems which can be seriously debilitating; as we shall acknowledge later, sufferers will protest that there is nothing whatsoever ennobling or "romantic" about clinical depression (for example) in itself — it is known to them as simply a vile, destructive horror. But many emotional crises which are not incapacitating can bring out the best in us in a way that an easy life does not. A journey of personality-development is never completed. It is not the business of psychotherapy to remove all the obstacles encountered on the way. Jung wrote "In the last resort it is highly improbable that there could ever be a therapy which got rid of all difficulties. Man needs difficulties: they are necessary for health. What concerns us here is only an excessive amount of them."

Examples of difficulties and problems which all individuals face at some time are: facing up to fears, reacting to developments beyond our control, making some kind of sense of painful complexities, accepting responsibility for decisions and actions.... If psychology promises escape from these it does not serve our best interest: if it helps us to face them with self-understanding and practical wisdom it is a useful friend. Arguably, psychology can do this best when its approach is informed by biblical teaching, through which God communicates guidance, encouragement and resilience, which in turn inculcate overflowing hope by the power of the Holy Spirit, as we trust in him (*Romans 15:4-5 and 13*).

But can there be any integration of psychological principles and practice with biblical teaching?

Friends or Enemies?

Some Christians take the view that the two approaches cannot mix: they have validity in their own spheres but no attempt should be made to employ them in combination. The pastor, if he or she is wise, will stick to areas of spirituality, Christian belief and practice, and resolve not to meddle in mental and emotional problems, which are the province of psychology. Conversely, it is held to be the psychotherapists' wisdom to leave spiritual matters to the pastor and concentrate on psychotherapeutic technique. This attitude is obviously untenable, for it discounts the huge amount of biblical teaching applicable to well-known causes of human stress and misery, including anxiety, depression, guilt, resentment and bluntly, the sin-principle which complicates all these.

A more serious objection to psychology sometimes raised by Christians is that the two approaches are inimical. To stand by biblical truth will inevitably mean jettisoning the findings of psychology: their starting points, their value-systems, their aims, are poles apart. Psychology can have nothing whatsoever to offer to biblical Christianity, which in itself, alone, contains the answers to all human problems.

There are factors which make such a position under-standable. It is true, for example, that psychology is a fairly new science compared with theology, and resonances be-tween the two are not readily seen; the premises and deduc-tive methods of the former can indeed seem alien, and contradictory, to the familiar and (to Christians) sacred truths and principles found in Holy Scripture. Moreover, it is undeniable that many professional psychologists and psychia-trists (and others involved in the theory and practice of the Behavioural Sciences) have discounted a spiritual/religious dimension altogether.

Dorothy Rowe, in her best selling book *Depression,* writes: "to a great many psychiatrists and psychologists the presence of a religious belief is, at its best, evidence that the person is naïve or stupid and, at worst neurotic or even psychotic.... When I advise (clinical psychologists) that in therapy with a depressed person it is a good idea to discover what that person's religious beliefs are, many of my colleagues look at me strangely and think that I have ceased to be a rational person, having discovered religion in my old age. I have been shocked to find that some of my colleagues whom I have always regarded as the most open-minded of people have shown themselves to be so against religion that they refuse to take seriously the religious belief of other people." She adds that without this openness concerning the relevance of religious convictions "the therapeutic enterprise must fail, since the therapist and the client are travelling on different paths and not hand in hand."

Some psychologists betray a spirit of actual antagonism towards a religious dimension, preferring to adopt a "purely scientific", reductionist, approach dismissive of any factors which cannot be quantified and labelled, as in a laboratory. Religion for them, including orthodox Christianity, is a non-verifiable, fanciful intrusion worse than Carlyle's "transcendental moonshine": it serves not only to muddy the psychotherapeutic water but actually causes or exacerbates some of the painful complexes that bring people for treatment. It is therefore necessary at this stage to grasp the nettle of atheistic, or secular, psychology.

Secular Psychology

The first point to make is that views dismissive of Christianity, based on psychological pre-suppositions, can become boomerangs. If it is claimed, for example, that faith in God represents a "wish-fulfilment" dynamic; if we say, with Freud, that "God" is the projection of a felt need for a Father-figure; it is obvious that such claims are double- edged. An individual's atheism may, by the same token, demonstrate an emotionally-determined need (wish) to disprove the existence of God; and Freud's personal antagonism towards religion and its Father-God can also, on his own theory, be accounted for by his bad relationship with his father. Hence, if the atheist says to the Christian, "you only believe in God because you find some personal, psychologically-explicable comfort in so doing, or because of your social conditioning" the believer can retort with logical justification, "And how about yourself and your non-belief?"

In a well-known exchange a reckless young student who had a smattering of psychology once attacked Archbishop William Temple after a lecture with the charge, "You only believe what you believe because of your early upbringing". The Archbishop promptly dispatched him with the reply, "You only believe that I believe what I believe because of my early upbringing because of *your* early upbringing". Thus the boomerang returns.

The "secular" psychologist can say nothing about the reality of the divine Being to whom a person responds.

But to pursue the issue more deeply: we cannot ignore the effects of early conditioning upon later religious belief and behaviour. And serious attention must be given to Freud's claim that hidden factors in the Unconscious greatly influence a person's view of life and meaning. These considerations raise the matter of objectivity: is objectivity possible in assessing religious truth-claims? Can we truly *know* the true import of biblical statements? Or will our interpretations inevitably be coloured and shaped by presuppositions formed by sociological/psychological factors?

Theologians acknowledge these and other forms of "pre-understanding" as problems in establishing the intrinsic validity of biblical revelation. Some years ago a Church of England Doctrine Report (*Christian Believing*) stated, "No-one expounds the Bible to himself or to anyone else without bringing to the task his own prior frame of reference, his own pattern of assumptions which derives from sources outside the Bible" (from the section *The Christian and the Bible*).

However, the problem of pre-understanding does not necessarily invalidate the Christian's claim to have discovered objective truth revealed in Holy Scripture. Two points can be made. The first is that the "boomerang" principle still applies: objections to religious truth-claims on the ground that they are formed by "pre-understanding" are themselves disqualified by the same argument. Secondly, and much more importantly, although it is true that we unavoidably come to the Bible with personal and culturally-determined presuppositions, this does not mean that our understanding of what we read is irrevocably determined by them.

The process can take place in reverse. As Anthony C Thiselton writes: "There is an ongoing process of dialogue with the text in which *the text itself progressively corrects and reshapes the interpreter's own questions and assumptions*" (my italics) *(The Two Horizons — Anthony C Thiselton)*. I would add that it is foolhardy to discount the ministry of the Holy Spirit in this process: it is he who opens the Word to the mind, *and* the mind to the Word.

A second charge levelled at Christianity by some secular psychologists is that "conversion" signifies intellectual and emotional immaturity. People become Christians for rudimentary, "childish" reasons which are psychologically explicable. This claim takes no account of those who are first drawn to Christianity by the cogency and relevance of biblical theology, and are attracted by the moral perfection and redeeming love of its Founder: consequent allegiance to him has involved self-sacrifice, not only solace.

For such converts, the sanity and transforming power of faith in Christ contrasts with the empty wisdom of current world-views. But conceding for a moment that there may be some truth in the imputation that religious faith begins as a compensation for inner emotional dissonances, it cannot then be inferred, logically, that such beginnings *continue* to characterise, and therefore confute, Christian faith. The charge may be valid, from a psychological point of view, that a person initially turns to God for apparently immature reasons. After all, the origins of the religious quest are varied. Schleiermacher, for example, wrote of the need for "a feeling of absolute dependence" as fundamental to human self-consciousness, which led him then to talk about God. Other felt needs seeking relief in religion relate to the dissolving of fear, the assuaging of grief and sorrow, the removal of guilt-pangs, the healing of loneliness, the search for meaning — as well as, more positively, being "surprised by joy" and "lost in wonder, love and praise".

Someone has cynically interpreted religious experience as "a thinly-veiled sublimation of the aim-inhibited sexual impulse". Returning to a more elevating line of thought: Rudolph Otto emphasised human longing for contact with an intuited "numinous" — the holy. But a spiritual experience entered upon *at whatever level* can grow far higher than its simple, even "infantile" roots. Gordon Allport comments "were we to gauge our evaluations by origins we would disparage the eloquence of Demosthenes because his oratory served as a compensation for his tendency to stammer. We would depreciate Schumann's music because it may have been touched by his psychosis.... And the fact that many psychologists take up their science because of personal maladjustments would make psychology worthless" (*The Individual and his Religion — Gordon W Allport — and below*). The eminent psychiatrist and Oxford don Anthony Storr who died in 2001 "acknowledged that it was his own difficulties in forming relationships with people, and his own depressive tendencies that impelled him towards psycho-analysis; like his father before him (a former Sub-Dean of Westminster Abbey) he was chronically subject to vacillation and anguished self-doubt". Far from invalidating his achievements, this background arguably enhanced the very considerable comfort and self-understanding which he brought to a great number of people, not least through his books. I count myself among them.

Allport comments, "the mistaken view that higher mental operations, originating in personal motivation, are therefore rationalisations and untrustworthy is called by logicians the 'genetic fallacy'. Unlike other modes of doubting, it is basically illegitimate, and cannot be permitted a part in any discussion of religion."

Clearly, Christ did not regard as "infantile" the frailties, common to all men and women, which often prompt spiritual hunger. With divine insight and compassion he addressed the human condition and invited to himself the anxious and fearful, the weary and burdened, and those longing to find God (*John 14:1, and 16:33; Luke 12:7 and 32; Matthew 6:25-34; Matthew 11:28*).

Carl Jung asserted, in opposition to those psychologists antipathetic towards religious experience, that the most fundamental requirement for the healing and wholeness at the heart of human longing is "the integration of the inner life with God". In a frequently quoted statement, he wrote: "Among all my patients in the second half of life ... there has not been one whose problem in the last resort was not that of finding a religious outlook on life. It is safe to say that every one of them fell ill because he had lost that which the living religions of every age have given to their followers, and none of them has been really healed who did not regain his religious outlook" (*Modern Man in Search of a Soul*). The personal declaration made in a BBC interview concerning his own religious position is well-known: "suddenly I understood that God was, for me at least, one of the most certain and immediate experiences.... I do not believe, I know. *I know*".

We shall return to Jung later and consider some important caveats concerning his theistic belief. But other, more biblically orthodox, psychologists also claim that without a spiritual dimension, psychology (in all three of its main emphases: depth, lateral and height) becomes "cabin'd, cribbed and confined" and therefore will prove to be inadequate for those needing psychotherapy. They argue that an approach to personality problems which takes no account of spiritual core beliefs and values, and religious experience, and which models itself exclusively on the natural sciences, will be seriously deficient.

For example, a "laboratory" approach to the understanding of mental and emotional distress which seeks a cause-and-effect mechanism akin to biological and physiological processes is, surely, chilling and ultimately dehumanising. Clearly, psychiatrists using a "scientific method" may accurately deduce some causes of mental illness in this way; but the danger is that all cases will be made to fit the same Procrustean bed. Such a reductionist approach to personality problems, whatever form it takes, is likely to trivialise or by-pass the often complex character of inner distress and its determinants. Human beings are not biological machines whose functions and dysfunctions can be explained in purely technical terms.

Mary Stewart van Leuwen (former Associate Professor of Psychology at York University, Toronto) comments sadly: "It is not an exaggeration to say that psychologists are in danger of becoming a collection of mere research technicians" *(The Person in Psychology — Mary Stewart Van Leuwen — and below)*. In the light of this, Christian Psychologists, guided as they are by a set of control beliefs derived from Scripture, should counteract such a reductionist attitude by being "constructionalist" in their psychology of the person. "Christians should be challenged to greater activity in the field.... Our acceptance of Scriptural authority should be an advantage, not an impediment, to such a task — but not because Scripture gives us a complete anthropology that can substitute for a systematic psychology; Scripture does not do this, although some Christians have tried to force this kind of systematic completeness into their reading of it. But Scripture does tell us enough about the ultimate origin, nature, and destiny of human beings to give us a set of control beliefs by which we can critically evaluate existing psychological theories and help to formulate more adequate ones.

As *Christian* constructionalists, bound to Christ by the grace of God, we are uniquely aware of human themes that are still considered puzzling or irrelevant to psychology as a whole — themes such as pride, guilt, the search for an object of worship, and the transcendent origins of human creativity." Therefore "we can and should be pursuing our understanding of Scripture on an intellectual as well as a confessional level if we want to mine its resources effectively for psychology".

Paul Vitz, quoted by Mary Stewart van Leuwen, deplores the person-centred psychology which discounts spiritual realities, ignoring the existence of God: "the acceptance of God enlarges and enriches psychology by making religious life relevant and interpretable ... a Christian psychology would be both a bigger and better psychology — that is, a broader, deeper, and truer psychology." Such a psychology is not merely desirable: it is essential. For ironically, when we settle for a reductionist view of human nature which excludes any spiritual dimension, materialism or biologism take over and a terrible sense of meaninglessness and futurelessness is likely to ensue, leading to worse neuroses. The worst kind of unhappiness is that which is without the hope that the God of hope gives "filling us with all joy and peace as we trust in him". That hope, as we have seen, is communicated from the pages of Scripture by the "power of the Holy Spirit" (*Romans 15:4 and 13*).

A humble reliance upon revealed truth will give insights that lead to a truer understanding of personality, including the problems and pains which cause distress. Christian psychotherapists and counsellors, who are guided in their work by personal core-beliefs and values and insights into human nature drawn from the Bible, allied to their interpersonal counselling skills, should enhance their effectiveness by becoming channels through which the rain can reach the roots.

The Psyche of Psychology

If the human soul is the soul of psychology (the "psyche") it is difficult to see how spiritual instincts and the religious quest, found in human beings everywhere, can be ignored by psychologists. Back in 1953, Pope Pius XII in his address to the Fifth International Congress of Psychotherapy and Clinical Psychology held in Rome stressed the illegitimacy of separating the sphere of psychology from the soul in a religious sense: "You psychologists and therapists ought to take account of this fact — the very existence of each faculty of psychological function has its warrant in the purpose of the whole.

What makes a human being to be such is principally the soul, which is the essential form of his nature. It is from this that flows, in the last analysis, the whole of human life: in it are rooted all psychological processes, with their particular structures and organic laws". Certainly, in the New Testament, echoing the Old Testament, the "soul" denotes the fountain of the inner life, the uniting essence of personhood, the seat of the emotions, the location of the personality's motivations. Most significantly, it is where spiritual consciousness and a believer's relationship with God are rooted.

These considerations throw up an interesting question: can a secular, atheistic psychotherapy be an instrument of divine healing?

Psychotherapy and Common Grace

The biblically-derived doctrine of the "general" or "common" grace of God reminds us that his goodness and kindness can be experienced irrespective of the spiritual faith, or non-faith, of its human agents or the recipients. There is much in human life, in the gifts and talents possessed by men and women, in their creativity and compassion, which is good and true and beautiful, reflecting the nature and purpose of the divine Creator — even though there may be no conscious dependence upon him, or even acknowledgement of him.

This common grace of God does not necessarily lead on, in individuals, to an intimate encounter with him bringing forgiveness and redemption — this is the effect of "special" or "saving" grace; it is, none the less, a source of blessing from God himself which may well elicit personal faith in him later. Many Christians will feel deeply grateful to God for the skilled, wise, and compassionate counsel and support of a "secular" psychotherapist. Through such a person they may have been helped to make coherent sense of their life-situation; others will have experienced a significant degree of relief from mental and emotional pain, release into a greater enjoyment of life, an improved ability to manage roles and relationships *and* they have become more effective channels of God's love to others.

Such believers would no doubt acknowledge, after due reflection, that it is only by the grace of God communicated by the Holy Spirit to the deepest recesses of our being that any of us can begin to experience growth towards true healing and wholeness. But this divine process does not necessarily preclude the sensitive application of psychological insights by a non-Christian therapist — any more than God's healing power necessarily circumvents the skills of non-Christian physicians and surgeons in the case of physical illness or injury.

Anthony Storr, himself a Christian, pointed out that the key factors determining the efficacy of any psychotherapeutic approach are integrity and compassion within a *developing relationship* between patient and therapist. "It is the attainment of a new kind of relationship with others and with himself which ultimately heals the patient.

The changing relationship with the therapist becomes a bridge which leads to the formation of more adult ties with people outside the therapeutic situation, and it is this changing relationship which constitutes the transference." "Therefore" Storr writes "it has long seemed to me probable that in selecting a psychotherapist, it is more valuable to know whether he is capable of the right attitude to the patient than to know which theory of personality he holds." (The above quotations are from *The Integrity of the Personality — Anthony Storr.*)

We recognise, on the basis of common grace that appropriate compassionate expertise such as this is not the monopoly of psychotherapists and counsellors who are Christians. God can use all kinds of channels for his healing power.

In this chapter I have considered some of the pros and cons of psychology from the point of view of a Christian pastor. In the following chapter there is a shift of focus from the roots to the rain — to biblical theology, in a broad sense, as it interfaces with psychology. But as we move on, it is our wisdom to acknowledge with respect and gratitude the contribution made by psychotherapists and associated practitioners to the alleviation of mental and emotional suffering and the promotion of well-being — whether they are Christians or not.

I have read no tribute more moving than that which emerges from a book written by Kay Redfield Jamison; at the time of writing she was, herself, a Professor of Psychology; her book is entitled *An Unquiet Mind — A Memoir Of Moods And Madness.* Hopefully, few of those reading the pages I am writing will ever know the terrible depths of psychotic illness which she has endured and which she describes with such courageous candour. But the following quotations are all the more powerful because she does write out of her own experience, in order to help others.

The paragraphs are an affirmation of the value of psychotherapy coupled, in her case, with medication. It is important to stress that Jamison's sickness was severe and acute. But the value of "tablets and talk" in combination, which she underlines, may often be applicable to much less serious symptoms of stress. It may well be that a milder medication, when appropriate, can, by moderating mental and emotional pain, "make psychotherapy possible"; and psychotherapy can indeed heal.

This is her testimony to that fact:

"At this point in my existence, I cannot imagine leading a normal life without both taking Lithium and having had the benefits of psychotherapy. Lithium ... clears out the wool and webbing from my disordered thinking, slows me down, gentles me out … and makes psychotherapy possible. But, ineffably, psychotherapy *heals*. It makes sense of the confusion, reigns in the terrifying thoughts and feelings, returns some control and hope and possibility of learning from it all. Pills cannot, do not, ease one back into reality....

"Psychotherapy is a sanctuary: it is a battle ground: it is a place I have been psychotic, neurotic, elated, confused, and despairing beyond belief. But, always it is where I have believed — or have learned to believe — that I might someday be able to contend with all of this....

"The debt I owe my psychiatrist is beyond description. I remember sitting in his office a hundred times during those grim months and each time thinking, What on earth can he say that will make me feel better or keep me alive? Well, there never was anything he could say, that's the funny thing. It was all the stupid, desperately condescending things he *didn't* say that kept me alive; all the compassion and warmth I felt from him that could not have been said: all the intelligence, competence, and time he put into it; and his granite belief that mine was a life worth living.

"He was terribly direct, which was terribly important, and he was willing to admit the limits of his understanding and treatments and when he was wrong. Most difficult to put into words, but in many ways the essence of everything: he taught me that the road from suicide to life is cold and colder and colder still, but — with steely effort, the grace of God, and an inevitable break in the weather — that I could make it."

CHAPTER 2

Biblical Rain

"Truth is for people" (J I Packer)

There is, of course, ample biblical precedent for making the connection between the truth of God's Word and life-giving rain. Consider two examples:-

First, from *Isaiah 55*:

The Israelites had endured many long, weary years of exile in Babylon, as a consequence, it has to be said, of unfaithfulness to God. Chastened, they are now heavily oppressed by the decadent idolatry and gross materialism of the scornful foreigners among whom they lived. Desolate and homesick, they have no heart for singing the songs of Zion, for Jerusalem itself, with its Temple (God's dwelling place), is in ruins. So they hang their harps on the willows, and weep. Was God's covenant with them also in ruins?

But in Chapter 40 of Isaiah, new hope is in the air: promise of an end to their captivity, of a return home, and of a coming glory far greater than anything in the whole of their previous history, for it will be shared, in time, by people from all nations. In order to revive their spirits it is as if they (and we, with them, as we read) are led out of the claustrophobic surroundings of pagan temples, towers and trade-centres into open country, to look up into the immense sky and be reminded by God that "As the heavens are higher than the earth, so are my ways higher than your ways and my thoughts than your thoughts". He is their Creator and Redeemer, and will rescue, revive and restore them (see *Isaiah 40:26-31*).

Let them, therefore, seek him afresh with repentance and expectant trust, for with him there is mercy and pardon (*Isaiah 55:6-7*). Let them raise their heads and feel the soft rain on their faces, the rain which "comes down from heaven and does not return to it without watering the earth and making it bud and flourish, so that it yields seed for the sower and bread for the eater". And let them be reassured, afresh, that "so is my word that goes out from my mouth: it will not return to me empty but will accomplish what I desire and achieve the purpose for which I sent it". The cheering purpose of God is to lead them out with joy and peace amidst great celebration and rejoicing, shared by the natural creation, to a new corporate life of fruitfulness which will glorify him (*verses 12-13*).

These wonderful promises do reach far beyond the immediate circumstances of the Jews in exile. They have resonances with those glorious eschatological passages of the New Testament which speak of a new heaven and earth, an eternal homeland, which will be the heritage of all believers at the end of time. But the promises are never irrelevant during this in-between period.

Here is hope for us, caught up in *our* culture's strange, sad mix of deadening secular materialism, empty hedonism, and a sterile New Age spirituality which has spawned clusters of desiccated new deities and DIY religions. The rain will not cease to fall: it can still reach our roots, bringing revival and new resolve in the present *and* reassurance about that future renewed sinless community of the redeemed when we will be together forever with the Lord.

And for individual believers there can be, in the here and now, a new springtime, however many years of spiritual exile lie behind, however advanced our age, however long a winter has passed, however depressed we may have been. As another

(Anglican) poet, George Herbert, expresses it: (from *The Flower*).

> How fresh, O Lord, how sweet and clean
> Are Thy returns! ev'n as the flowers in spring;
> Who would have thought my shrivell'd heart
> Could have recover'd greenness? It was gone
> Quite under ground; as flowers depart
> To see their mother-root, when they have blown;
> Where they together
> All the hard weather,
> Dead to the world, keep house unknown...
> And now in age I bud again,
> After so many deaths I live and write;
> I once more smell the dew and rain,
> And relish versing: O, my only Light,
> It cannot be
> That I am he
> On whom Thy tempests fell all night.

Secondly, a further occurrence (among others) of this rain-metaphor for the Word of God is found in an earlier reference — *Deuteronomy 32:2*.

Moses knew all about hard experiences: despite dramatic miraculous reminders of God's presence and power, forty years in the wilderness leading a vast rabble of demoralised ex-slaves had been a long winter to endure. Still fresh in their memory was the trauma of their Egyptian misery, when even cheering news of imminent divine intervention on their behalf had fallen on deaf ears "because of their discouragement and cruel bondage". This negative state of mind persisted during their desert-wanderings. Moses frequently needed to castigate their rebelliousness towards God; and all too often he himself had been the butt of their defiant grumbling. Now, they all stand within sight of the promised land, and Moses lifts his voice in a narrative-song to the Lord "in the hearing of the whole assembly" — just as he had at the Exodus-crossing of the sea (*Exodus 15*). The opening words show his continuing compassionate realisation that the people remain shaken, weakened, subdued, and in need of hope and encouragement;

> "Let my teaching fall like rain
>> And my words descend like dew,
> Like showers on new grass,
>> Like abundant rain on tender plants"

Torrential downpours can wash away tender plants. Gentle rain, like dew, and showers, will reach their roots and revive them. It is not that Moses' ensuing words are bland or pietistic pitter-patter. "Teaching" means strong doctrine focused in the character of God (see *verses 3-4*): his song/sermon is punctuated with reminders of the Lord's faithful dealings with his people in justice and mercy, and his words contain both rebuke and warning.

But the fact is that the vulnerable and fragile — even the selfishly vulnerable and fragile — can be refreshed and heartened by receiving theocentric truth faithfully and sensitively proclaimed. Moses was, indeed, "a prophet mighty in word and deed"; flawed, certainly, but here he reveals that his zeal for God and his Word, though imperfect, and his God-given vision and wisdom, and his dismay over the nation's sins, was paralleled by a perceptive compassion for those he was called to serve. Perhaps it was this rare mix of qualities which helped to make him Israel's most revered leader — to this day.

Arguably, today's most effective Christian pastors will demonstrate the same double motivation: of faithfulness to God and his truth, and empathic concern for those committed to their charge.

Back to Isaiah: the great Servant of the Lord who features so prominently in his prophecy as God's Agent of revival and restoration, is pre-eminently, such a person: the supreme Model for ministers. For example, from *Isaiah 42:1 (f):* "Here is my servant, whom I uphold, my chosen One in whom I delight: I will put my Spirit on him and he will bring justice to the nations. He will not shout or cry out, or raise his voice in the streets. A bruised reed he will not break, and a smoulder-ing wick he will not snuff out."

The Servant's ministry described here, comments Alec Motyer *(The Prophecy of Isaiah),* is "quiet, unaggressive, unthreatening.... To this Servant nothing is useless, even the *bruised reed* (however it came to be crushed is not the point), which is useless as a support for anything else. Neither is anything (e.g. *a smouldering wick*) too far gone towards extinction ... here is quintessential service ... exemplified perfectly in our Lord Jesus Christ" (who was full of truth and grace in equal measure) "and is to be reproduced in all who would serve the Lord with true service." Precisely.

It is the pastor's solemn responsibility faithfully and sen-sitively to communicate both the objective validity of biblical truth and its subjective appositeness; his, or her, calling is to be a servant of the Lord's people by being a servant of the Lord's Word — *a channel for the rain to reach the roots.*

The Two Books

Preaching at an ordination service in Edinburgh Cathedral, a Puritan Minister, David Dickson, counselled the candidates: "You must seek to know two books supremely well — the book of Holy Scripture and the book of the human heart."

Three and a half centuries later, a contemporary theologian, J I Packer, often strikes the same note in relation to Christian ministry; for example; "Revealed truth is for people, and must be studied in terms of what it is meant to do for them". Future ministers must therefore "be equipped to know people as well as enabled to know Scripture", and develop "an instinct for relevance as well as a love for the truth itself."

"The question that informs and shapes a training course must be, not just 'what is God's truth?' but the bigger question, 'how should the truth of God be impinging on people'?" (quotations from *Training For The Ministry, in Ministry in The Seventies Ed. Clive Porthouse*). More recently: "It is vital to realise that truth is for people, and therefore, the pastoral function of theology is ultimately primary. Professional theologians should be winning their spurs as pastors no less than as scholars" *(in "Evangelical Futures")*.

Sadly, this pastorally-focused theology is not always found in our seminaries. The American New Testament scholar Walter Wink issues the following disturbing indictment: "The outcome of biblical studies in the academy is a trained incapacity to deal with the real problems of actual living persons in their daily lives" (quote from *The Two Horizons — Anthony C Thiselton*).

The present book is not about theological colleges and the training they provide for would-be pastors — an area I am not qualified to comment on.

But I do seek to address, with some conviction, the pastoral-relevance factor: the *connection* between revealed truth and people. Thirst for an experience of the living God will never be quenched by an abstruse, academic theology which is unrelated to the current human situation and the plight of individuals within it.

Not that our daily lives are full of heavy problems. We do not spend *all* our time (*pace* Hamlet) dodging the slings and arrows of outrageous fortune, grunting and sweating under a weary life, nor quailing before a menacing conscience; some of the time, indubitably — maybe a lot of the time.... But pleasure and delight, happy memories, high hopes and exciting aspirations, also mark our days. God has provided richly so much for our positive enjoyment. Human love and friendship, the natural creation, music and literature, poetry and art, drama ... are not totally "soured with sinning" and can yet reflect what is "true, noble, pure, lovely, excellent, admirable, *praiseworthy*" (*Philippians 4:8*).

In the light of this, is there no such thing as "Christian hedonism"? Christian teaching which fails to evoke and enhance grateful wonder and delight in response to beauty, truth and goodness, and to all God's blessings, is doubly a turn-off: it neither corrects or comforts us in our troubles, nor deepens our joys; it makes no *connection* between God and our experience. J I Packer again: "The supreme skill in the art and craft of theology is to link the theoretical and cognitive aspects of God's revealed truth with its practical and trans-formative aspects in an unbreakable bond. For God shows himself to us and tells us about himself so that we may not just know of him but know him relationally in a life-changing way and taste the full joy of that knowledge in our fellowship with the Father and with his Son Jesus Christ" (from *Evangelical Futures*).

Within the Church

Congruence between doctrine and every-day life is a pastoral priority for another reason. Returning to the theme of life's dissatisfactions and hard times: Christians themselves, in periods of bleak honesty, can find themselves questioning the reality of their knowledge of God. Their experience does not seem to match the divine promises they read in their Bibles.

Consider, for example, one of the invitations of Jesus Christ: "If anyone is thirsty, let him come to me and drink. Whoever believes in me, as the Scripture has said, streams of living water will flow from within him. By this he meant the Spirit, whom those who believed in him were later to receive" (*John 7:37-39*).

Common sense tells us, as do all the rules of straightforward exegesis, that Jesus is speaking of actual spiritual experience. Not an ego-trip, not a beaming-up to a religious cloud 9, but an intimate encounter with himself by which he brings about a radical change within us: he claims to satisfy spiritual thirst.

More: he states that, in response to faith in him, the Holy Spirit's refreshing presence will be known in the deepest recesses of the soul like a springing-well of living water, permeating the whole personality and flowing out to others.

Now there will be times for followers of Christ when this promise does not seem to have experiential fulfilment. An inner spiritual dryness persists. Usually such periods are relieved by a fresh ministry of the Holy Spirit: scriptural truth again clears our minds and we are led into green pastures by quiet waters where our soul is restored.

But suppose the sense of spiritual unreality continues? "Most men live lives of quiet desperation"; is it possible that religious people sometimes validate Thoreau's aphorism as much as others? It has been claimed, by some detractors of religious faith, that it can (apparently) exacerbate emotional unease. One cynic has unkindly said that conversion merely means exchanging one bunch of neuroses for another; and the new can be worse than the old.

Not a few of the "psychological" problems referred to in

the last chapter, especially those linked to feelings of anxiety and guilt, become all the more depressing and debilitating if they are judged to be culpably inconsistent with the new life of faith.

If, as can be the case, these feelings are then repressed, and camouflaged by a pious *persona* or bogus religious *joie-de-vivre* they will undermine spiritual authenticity, and perhaps break out with alarming inappropriateness. Relationships may thus become governed by the games that religious people play, resulting in an absence of "awareness, intimacy and spontaneity" *(I'm Ok — You're Ok — Thomas A Harris)* among them.

It could be that in our churches there is a degree of unreality beneath all the trappings of church membership. Perhaps some have given up the search for a relationship with God which really does have healing relevance for their inner world of fears and sorrows; instead, they have taken refuge in conforming themselves to a corporate ecclesiastical correctness, which fools most of the congregation most of the time.... Even "going through the religious motions" can give temporary relief.

What changes *can* believers properly expect to ensue from faith in Christ? Can the experiential credibility-gap be bridged? *Psalm 107 (verses 19-21)* states "They cried to the Lord in their trouble, and he saved them from their distress. *He sent forth his word and healed them;* he rescued them from the grave. Let them give thanks to the Lord for his unfailing love and his wonderful deeds for men."

The truth-is-for-people approach seeks to forge a link between God's healing Word and the human condition — including, that is, both the total person, and his or her relationships. In short, it is a ministry which channels his rain to our roots and revives them.

47

Theism

The theological stance involved here could be described as a healthy *theism* in that it represents a coming together, by means of his Word, of God's transcendence and his immanence. As the passages from *Isaiah 55 and Deuteronomy 32* make clear, the source of the rain is indeed the sovereign, holy Lord who reveals his will and his ways in Holy Scripture. But by those same Scriptures he *draws near* to us with refreshing, life-giving power.

This juxtaposition of God's numinous otherness and his intimate closeness is epitomised in a beautiful statement from *Isaiah 57 (verse 15):* "This is what the high and lofty One says — he who lives forever, whose name is holy: 'I live in a high and holy place, but also with him who is contrite and lowly in spirit, to revive the spirit of the lowly and to revive the heart of the contrite'".

The transcendent origin of Holy Scripture ("God-breathed" and "Spirit-inspired" — *2 Timothy 3:16 and 2 Peter 1:21*) means, significantly, that whilst emerging from different historical milieux, and revealing the personalities of the writers, they (the Scriptures) are supra-mundane as to their true source. They stand over us and above us, but speak *into* the world's changing fashions of thought, which come and go through the centuries. This is their value: they will always shed a corrective and/or creative light on current world-views — not least on prevailing opinions about the human condition generally and on perceptions of the problems of individuals.

The Bible will reveal non-negotiable absolutes having profound practical importance for every-day living, in every age, including its psychological aspects. Such absolutes need to be identified and appropriated in each generation — this is the task of hermeneutics, which can be defined as bringing together the two horizons, of the biblical writers and contemporary society. It is an essential exercise, for without the recognition and heeding of biblical absolutes we sink into a relativism which leads to intellectual confusion, amorality and/or immorality, emotional discord, the coarsening of our culture and the decay of social cohesion — in a word: destabilisation.

> Things fall apart: the centre cannot hold;
> Mere anarchy is loosed upon the world (*Yeats*).

As Fyodor Dostoevsky expressed it, in *The Brothers Karamazov*: if there is no self-revealed God, to whom we are accountable, and no future life "nothing would be immoral any longer, everything would be permitted." If God is dead, Hopkins' view of poetry's function (and that of all true art) as glorifying him, is meaningless; the inevitable result is that human creativity turns sour and may well produce ugliness, in the deepest sense of that word: base, degraded, morally repulsive. Science may be misused, with destructive results. Society is likely to become threatened by moral melt-down and a descent into irrational anarchy; and human relationships increasingly unravel.

Theism, then, safeguards an essential connection between the God who is there and who speaks in Scripture, and us. A connection, without which, I contend, there can be no true and lasting psychotherapy. What has gone wrong if there is no such *connection*? Put simply, this absence indicates that theism has been displaced by one, or both, of two theological aberrations: deism and/or "meism".

Deism has the effect of distancing God; meism, of domesticating him. The former cuts off God from our experience; the latter identifies him with our experience. One makes no connection with the divine, holding that no connection is needed; the other posits a spurious connection: we are, by nature, deified.

Deism

Deism puts God at a distance. His existence is not denied but he is regarded as a remote, impersonal deity who does not involve himself in his creation or in human affairs. He is absent. It is as if his transcendence rules out any possibility of his immanence; therefore he cannot be known in any personal sense. It is difficult to see how such a view can be derived from the Bible, but this does happen. How?

Wink's charge against some theological teaching of dissociating theological studies from present human concerns pointed up, in his view, the seriously deadening effect which *historical criticism* can have, in interpreting the Bible. "Historical criticism" refers to the exercise of establishing the original meaning of what is written in its original context. Such an approach is clearly of crucial importance and enormous value.

The danger is that it can become an end in itself: merely an academic task. The biblical horizon is scanned but there is no attempt at an engagement with our horizon. The Bible's meaning for today, and its contemporary power, are ignored. "The historical critical method has reduced the Bible to a dead letter. Our obeisance to technique has left the Bible sterile and ourselves empty." "The biblical writers", he argues "addressed concrete situations in life; but the biblical scholar who adopts the methods of historical criticism suppresses the very questions which are most fruitful to ask in order to arrive at an understanding of the text." "The text of the Bible speaks to more practical issues about life, especially life within communities. These are not always the same as the questions which win a hearing from the scholarly guild." (Quotes from

The Two Horizons — Anthony C Thiselton).

It is as if the rain is channelled off, through academic conduits, away from the roots which desperately need it (and for which it is sent from heaven); it is then stored in antiseptic glass tanks where it is endlessly analysed and categorised by scholars. Inevitably, it goes flat; it can even become stagnant; no longer is the life of God communicated. Thus theism, rendered null and void, is reduced to deism.

Deism is not only encountered in recondite theological journals, or academies. It percolates through to street-level. (Just as the bizarre styles of the cat-walks fetch up later in the chain-stores and on the streets as a recognisable, if modified, trend).

At a "popular" level, deism is discernible when there is a vague belief in the existence of God which is unaccompanied by a relational knowledge of him arising from personal trust resulting in commitment and obedience. Deism can invade churches. Even a high regard for Scripture found in churches which emphasise preaching can lead to bibliolatry rather than to the knowledge and worship of God; this too is deistic religion.

Evangelical theology which majors on the "propositional", and ignores the practical; where proclamation becomes the conveying of biblical information in a take-it-or-leave-it manner with no regard for the pastoral needs of the people-hearers; which neither connects with current issues nor engages the prevalent world-view; such theology is more deistic than theistic. Emil Brunner uses a striking image to describe some aspects of such Protestant orthodoxy as a "frozen waterfall": mighty shapes of movement, but no movement"!

Megaphone theology, no less than megaphone diplomacy, is unproductive. Worse: it keeps people away from the God who made them and loves them and desires to communicate with them. "Too many of us preach messages that suffer from what might be called 'doctrinal overload' … there is little sense of God's authority where so much of the message is lecture and so little application is found" (J I Packer) (from *Honouring The Word of God – ccollected shorter writings Volume 3).*

So any kind of doctrinally exemplary Sunday service, traditional or contemporary, formal or informal, "high" or "low", can degenerate into formalism — defined succinctly by A W Tozer as "orthodoxy without the Holy Ghost". We may affirm and respond repeatedly "the Lord is here — his Spirit is with us" but if we do not actually expect him to draw near to us we are unlikely to draw near to him; and such affirmation becomes piously hollow. "Worship" wrote Carlyle "is transcendent wonder". But worship touched by deism is not really worship at all: it becomes spiritually dehydrated and joyless, lifeless "form", lacking wonder and transforming power.

"I haven't the faintest interest in theology which does not help us to evangelise" declared James Denney, the Scottish biblical scholar. But evangelistically, churches infected with deism are non-starters. From a pastoral/psychological point of view, too, deism is equally deadly. Useless. For it means that we cannot, in fact, know God at all. We are on our own. The Bible may contain truth but it is sterile truth: it has no relevance in the real world, here and now, except as a religious system of thought and practice, among many others. Spiritual thirst must remain unsatisfied. There is no point in approaching God in prayer with the words "please," "thank you," or "sorry", for as the impersonal First Cause he can neither hear nor respond. All this is light-years away from the glorifying of God and fully enjoying him forever which is "the chief and highest end of man" (*Westminster Confession of*

Faith: The Larger Catechism).

How does this stultifying religious mindset and attitude come about? What causes deism to become so widespread?

Carl Jung hinted at a process accounting for this which, it may be considered, has some truth in it — and has some similarities with Wink's point. He reminds us that after New Testament times, doctrines and dogmas and creeds were formulated by various Councils of the Church in order to fix, with semantic precision, the theological truths at the heart of the Christ-centred, Spirit-given, encounter with God. These Confessions state clearly and systematically truths concerning the three Persons of the Holy Trinity, and how these truths impact upon human society and individuals. Jung defined these credal statements as "crystallised forms of original religious experience".

In this, he was surely correct, for the writings of the New Testament (as of the Old Testament), on which the creeds were based, do reflect religious experience. Inspired by the Holy Spirit, the writers were putting into words what had taken root in their hearts and minds, what they now *knew* by experience, and were convinced of in their thinking, concerning the persons of the Holy Trinity, the relationship of human beings to this triune God, and its consequences. Their writings certainly have the nature of divinely revealed truth; "But that does not necessarily mean that they popped into apostolic minds ready-made. It is more natural to suppose that they crystallised out of the experiential-ethical transformation that those who received the Spirit, the apostles among them, underwent. The insights of the New Testament writers concerning the Spirit took their rise, no doubt, from the words of Jesus but were distilled into their mature form via experiential response to experienced deity" (*J I Packer — The Holy Spirit and His Work* from *Celebrating The Saving*

Work of God).

Now the subsequent hammering-out and condensing of these experienced, scripturally-expressed truths into orderly doctrinal statements ("crystallised forms") was clearly an expedient exercise. The fact is that Creeds and other Confessions of Faith can lead to clearer understanding, more relevant evangelism, and the safeguarding of the genuine against the counterfeit — truth against error, good against evil, the holy against the harmful.

But the obvious danger (and this is Jung's case) is that by this process of verbal refining which, largely because of recurring ecclesiastical controversy, has continued through the centuries, theology becomes separated from its experiential roots. It gets to be taken up with *words*, and nothing more. It develops into a predominantly academic, cerebral discipline. The glory of saving grace runs into the sands of intellectualisation. ("His theology was correct, down to the last icicle of doctrine").

In this way theology no longer communicates the reality of direct encounter with God. It ceases to meet the psychological and social needs of people; it does not speak to their hearts nor have relevance to their relationships. In a word, *it becomes deistic.* God is distanced. Jung saw this as a sad failure of Christian education, the prime task of which should be, in his view, that of conveying to the conscious mind the reality of God. "The western attitude", he wrote "with its emphasis on the object tends to fix the ideal — Christ — in its objective aspect and thus to rob it of its mysterious relation to the inner man. Creed and ritual have become so elaborated and refined that they no longer get through to the psychological state of the ordinary man and religion is congealed into externals and formalities." (From *An Introduction to Jung's Psychology — Freida Fordham).*

Christopher Bryant in his book *Jung and the Christian Way* writes: "All his life Jung was concerned with knowing God, with the immediate intuitive awareness of God. He believed that the religion of many Christians who like his father, relied on an intellectual faith, divorced from any experience of the realities believed in, was seriously defective. In a letter written in 1945 at the age of 70 he affirms, '*it is of the highest importance* that the educated and "enlightened" should know a religious truth as a thing living in the human soul and not as an abstruse and unreasonable relic of the past'".

Again, let it be said, there are serious problems about going along with Jung's total stance in relation to Christianity — a stance which it is, in any case, difficult to pin down. But it is possible to concede that he could be describing accurately here one way in which theology can become a barrier between the rain and the roots, rather than a channel....

St Paul goes further in delineating the negative effects of this kind of deism. He taught that in "the last days" flagrant amorality and immorality will, significantly, be connected to *empty religion*, described by him as "having a form of godliness but denying its power" (*2 Timothy 3:5*). Paul's words echo a similar expression used by Jesus Christ encountering the deism of the Sadducees. Attempting to ridicule the concept of resurrection they put forward a gross caricature of the biblical doctrine, clearly implying that any divine involvement with such "nonsense" was a derisory idea (they excluded God from all human history and human experience).

In unmasking the absurdity of their case, Christ begins by putting his finger on their basic error: "you do not know the Scriptures or the power of God" (*Matthew 22:29f*). The Sadducees' "knowledge" of the Scriptures was pathetically superficial; they were strangers to both their real meaning *about* resurrection, and this led to a closed mind regarding the power of God demonstrated *by* resurrection.

At the burning bush (*Exodus 3*) God identified himself to Moses as the God of *Abraham, Isaac and Jacob,* who were long since dead. But not dead!

For Yahweh, "I AM WHO I AM", is God of the living. When Jesus later declared, "*I am* the Resurrection and the Life", this was a revelation of divine truth, and power.

His own resurrection-life is a present possession of those who *believe* him and who put their trust in him.

Both kinds of knowledge are needed: intellectual understanding and openness to the experienced power of God. But deism negates both. There must be a flow-through of divinely-oxygenated rain-water: God's life-giving Word, to cleanse, revive, and empower our churches — and our souls.

"O Lord of life, send my roots rain".

When God Seems Out Of Reach

In exposing the serious deficiencies of deism, by which God is removed from us, we must be sensitive to the fact that surely no Christian unfailingly experiences God's intimate nearness; as with Hopkins, he is trusted in his felt absence as well as in his enjoyed presence.

This does not make deism correct: the view that communion with God is impossible because he is remote is utterly unbiblical. But in the Christian life, he will sometimes *seem* remote. A loyal believer may endure a time of spiritual darkness and dryness as an intrinsic ingredient of discipleship — that is, not necessarily as a consequence of disobedience. At such times, reliance on God is buttressed by a faith unaccompanied by any sense of God's proximity.

"Who among you fears the Lord and obeys the word of his

servant? *Let him who walks in the dark, who has no light,* trust in the name of the Lord and rely on his God" (*Isaiah 50:10*). During testing, perhaps painful, circumstances, God can seem distant rather than close; *but revealed truth concerning him is no less true.* He will always be true to his *Name* — all that he has revealed himself to be in his Word. The temptation to think deistically must be resisted. Better to find direction through the darkness by holding to biblical truth than by seeking the illusory solace promised by DIY remedies and the equivalent of self-kindled "light" — a "light" which only leads into increased grief and pain, or worse (*Isaiah 50:11*).

Deism, in denying the possibility of revelation and intimate experience of God's love, can only consign us to this fate, and leave us there. But the fact is that God's truth can engage the head, directing our steps and forming our attitudes, though the heart may seem, for a time, unaffected. By the grace of God the heart can catch up later — and be *sealed* again with an assurance concerning the Word of life and the personal possession of eternal life (*Ephesians 1:13 to 14*).

The light *will* return, brighter than before. In the meantime, it must be remembered that the objective validity of God's Word does not depend upon some kind of subjective endorsement. Neither joy-filled spiritual experiences, nor moods of bleak desolation in relation to God, affect the truth of his truth. The former, whilst lifting our spirits, do not actually enhance God's truth *as such*; by the same token the latter do not detract from it.

God's truth is one thing; our enjoyment or non-enjoyment of it is another. The central point here is that the theme of relevance in connection with Bible study is important for both darkness and light. The Holy Spirit, through Holy Scripture, has much to say about our felt emptinesses, when God seems far away, as well as speaking into "the joy of elevated thought" occasioned by his experienced immanence.

Often, it is in looking back upon difficult times that the realisation dawns: when our hold on God was perhaps loosened through inner weakness and/or the pressure of hard circumstances, he held us, and our faith, though battered, did not fail. We have been "baffled, to fight better." *(Oswald Chambers)*. We learn that we can even trust him for our trusting. His Word is the rock beneath our feet, even when it is not the song in our hearts; revealed truth is inspired, though we may not, for a period find it inspirational. It is our wisdom to go on taking it in.

And to cleave to Christ — the Christ encountered in Scripture. "Our understanding of God is forever marked by the fact that in Christ he has been 'fleshed out' at one point in our human history. Even if God seems distant, transcendent, 'from eternity to eternity', we are not in the dark about God and his character.

As Paul put it, the glory of God has been imaged for us in the one, true human who bears the divine image, Christ himself: and by beholding his 'face' we see the glory of the eternal God" (*2 Corinthians 3:18; 4:4-6*) (*Paul, the Spirit and the People of God — Gordon Fee*).

Deism can make no contribution to psychology. More importantly, deism shuts the door against God and keeps it shut; it makes the Bible a closed book which it is pointless to prise open. Most seriously, it diminishes Jesus Christ.

Theism affirms that, by the ministry of the Holy Spirit, the unfolding of his words *will* give light, and give understanding to the simple, and make Christ known to us.

Meism

A contrasting danger to deism, which is equally an obstacle to authentic Christian experience, is *meism* (closely related to *wannabeism*).

Meism, in contrast to deism, restricts God to the here and now. On a broad canvas this is sometimes manifested as pantheism, which identifies God and nature. But in relation to human beings, in particular, it limits God to being *inherent* in us; this leads to a kind of deification of the depths of the psyche. Some readers will be reminded of the views of the late Bishop John Robinson expressed in the early 1960s in such books as *Honest to God* — but views still held by many today. For Robinson "God" is not to be thought of as a divine person separate from ourselves but as the "ground of our being", the fundamental "reality" deep within us.

This echoes the teaching of the theologian Tillich and there are also strong resonances with the current New Age movement which, for all its bewildering diversity, is permeated by the common theme of self-divinization — self-is-God. Like the present-day variety of alternative medicines, there is a great number of spiritualities and religious practices with which people may connect for the purpose of finding inner wholeness — equivalent to the divine within us. Each one amounts to creating your own interior Reality: God in your image, a DIY god to fit your shape — after all, the self is divine anyway.

Numerous and diverse these forms of religion may be, but each one is considered valid and "true" — for there is no Absolute Truth by which to check it out. My truth and your truth, my god and your god, are equally the real thing. "God" is what makes you feel good inside. Meism rules, okay.

The same phenomenon is observable on the specialised theological canvas which considers the relation between the different religions — a canvas where we encounter a kind of corporate meism — (*weism?*). In contradistinction to the biblical doctrine of the uniqueness of Christ pertaining to salvation, three views are commonly promulgated: *syncretism, pluralism, and intuitionism.*

Syncretism means fusion: it claims that all religions are basically the same, they are simply different expressions of a common quest for "God". Each one is true but incomplete in itself (including Christianity), so the ideal is a coalescence of them all. Worship would mean reverencing the Essence of all religions.

Pluralism means, not fusion, but confederation, or the co-existence of different religions, which are all considered equally valid and complete as approaches to God. One protagonist of this view, John Hick, wrote a book called *God Has Many Names*: his title sums up the pluralist position. Religious variety is okay; rivalry is not okay. Pluralistic worship means people coming to God together in their own way, and Jesus Christ is one such way, among many others. Gandhi said, "The soul of religions is one but it is encased in a multitude of forms. I cannot ascribe exclusive divinity to Jesus. He is as divine as Krishna or Rama or Mohammed or Zoroaster".

(It should, perhaps, be added that pluralism, *in itself*, should not necessarily be seen as a threat to Christianity: arguably, it is preferable to totalitarianism or any kind of intolerant exclusion of morally legitimate views. In New Testament times the gospel had to win its way in the market place of competing ideologies. Paul's evangelism included dialogue — the exercise of what we now call apologetics: commending the truth and relevance of the faith within the context of a pluralistic society. Pluralism only becomes problematic for the church if Christians sell the pass by complying with the attitude that Christianity does have merely equal validity with the truth-claims of other religions.

Gandhi's position has no place in biblically-based theology. It is when pluralism becomes relativism that it does have to be opposed as a threat.

Thirdly, intuitionism as a philosophical term encapsulates the view that the perception of truth is by intuition (as are ethical principles). Its religious application implies that revealed, propositional statements are not needed: God can be apprehended and known by some kind of inner illumination ("spiritual" intuition) as self-evident.

The source of such "divine" enlightenment may be within the psyche, or outside — perhaps equated with Nature; more dangerously it could be found in the strange worlds resulting from mind-distorting drugs, or dabbling with the occult. (Perhaps we should add a fourth position described by the term *universalism*, which holds that all religious views are unimportant because everybody will be "saved" whatever their beliefs or non-beliefs).

Clearly, all these religious stances overlap and interweave; *all* of them sit comfortably within the mish-mash of New Age spirituality. All are aspects of meistic religion (introject the one that most grabs you). And all three are in inevitable conflict with orthodox Christianity.

The Bible teaches that Christ alone reveals God clearly to us (because in him, uniquely, dwells the fullness of God) and he alone reconciles us to God, by his atonement. To put the matter succinctly: Christo-centric revelation and Christo-centric redemption are indivisible. Jesus is God's divine king. He is the only Name under heaven by which we must be saved. God's Kingdom of Light is the Kingdom of his dear Son.

The pay-off, psychologically speaking, of meistic theology is, as indicated above, self-gratification: the spiritual quest becomes harnessed to the ultimate feel-good factor, which is virtually synonymous with "God-within".

When infecting Christianity, this attitude reduces divine grace to a mystical cure-all guaranteed to produce happy inner equilibrium (*homeostasis*) allied to enhanced self-esteem, and a wonderful unfolding self-fulfilment (actualised *wannabeism*). Within the church, this kind of ego-centric spirituality leads (at its best!) to pietism — a disproportionate preoccupation with interior religiousness; but this easily degenerates into a narcissism commonly manifested, corporately, in what J I Packer calls "Hot Tub Religion" — that is, "sensuous, relaxing, laid-back: not in any way demanding, whether intellectually or otherwise." So, "many churches ... are already offering the next best thing to a hot tub — namely, happy gatherings free from care, real fun times for all ... a warm, back-scratching use of words in prayer and preaching; and a warm, cheerful afterglow."

The irony of meistic spirituality is that it is self-defeating: it diminishes "me". The dumbing-down of biblical Christianity insulates "worshippers" from divine truth and grace — which alone, by the Spirit's power, can release personality potential, enriched by his fruit and gifts, to the glory of God. If deism *deflects* the rain from the roots, meism *saturates* them with rain-water so filtered and flavoured that any growth will prove to be limp, fragile, and distorted.

Personal Pronouns

Perhaps a further, modifying, reflection on meism and wannabeism is needed.

The quest, religiously, for a feel-good factor and for personal fulfilment is not all bad. In many ways it is natural, and understandable: the years bring pressures and pains, and problems of pointlessness, which can get us down and undermine enjoyment of life. Pleasure can seem very elusive, or short lived when it comes our way. Peace of mind is rare; a sense of purpose can prove to be delusive. And the Christian gospel is, after all, good news of great joy.

Jesus' heart went out to people because they were harassed and helpless, like sheep without a shepherd: he recognised their feelings of vulnerability and futurelessness. And he had come, he said, in order that they might have life and have it to the full, through *personal* belief and trust in him.

I think it was Martin Luther who declared that true religion is a matter of personal pronouns. That principle is borne out by Holy Scripture: e.g. "The Lord is my shepherd, I shall not be in want. He makes me lie down in green pastures, he leads me beside quiet waters, he restores my soul." Paul is equally personal in testifying to his Christian experience, "the life that I live in the body, I live by faith in the Son of God, who loved me and gave himself for me" *(Galatians 2:20).*

But this personal knowledge of God, which is the essence of "eternal life" (true fullness of life), has its focus in Jesus Christ, himself, *who is encountered in and through the Bible.* The Christ of Scripture is both the path and the prize. The search for a privatised (meistic) Christ, whose shape must fit individual demands and expectations, leads nowhere, for it ignores the sign-posts of Christian teaching (doctrine) erected by the Biblical writers — and succinctly expressed in the Church's creeds. We can't plot our own course, find our own way, to God. C S Lewis made this point, seventy years ago, in one of his broadcast talks of 1944 *(Beyond Personality).*

"Doctrines aren't God: they are only a kind of map. But that map's based on the experience of hundreds of people who really were in touch with God — experiences compared with which any thrills or pious feelings you and I are likely to get on our own are very elementary and very confused". Moreover, the dream-road that leads to an individualised, touchy-feely God is a dead end: "You won't get eternal life by just feeling the presence of God ... neither will you get anywhere by looking at maps without (travelling).... In other words, theology is practical.... If you don't listen to Theology that won't mean you have no ideas about God. It'll mean that you'll have a lot of wrong ones — bad, muddled, out of date ideas" (*Meistic ideas*).

In other words (let us say it again) there must be a correspondence between our experience of the divine life and the revealed truth of Holy Scripture concerning it. There must be a correlation between the subjective and the objective, the experiential and the doctrinal, aspects of Christianity. Not deism, not meism, but theism. William Temple writes about "the transcendence of the immanent" and "the immanence of the transcendent".

How is that correspondence effected? How is the correlation actualised? How are we enabled to relate to God as both transcendent and immanent; and to the Christ who both reigns in glory and lives within us and among us? (*Ephesians 1:19-23, and 3:17*). How may we both understand revealed truth, and be empowered to live it out as an experienced reality, in practical, joyful obedience?

By what agency does the rain actually reach our roots and revive us? The single answer to these questions is — the Holy Spirit, the "Go-Between God"; he is both the life in the rain and its channel.

Holy Scripture, the Human Heart, and the Holy Spirit

God's Empowering Presence is the title of a widely-acclaimed work authored by Gordon Fee, professor of New Testament at Regent College, Vancouver; it is a scholarly, exhaustive study of every reference made in the New Testament epistles by

Paul to the Holy Spirit and his activity. The book's title is his summation of the Spirit's distinctive role and ministry.

One foundational fact stands out a mile: in order truly to know the living God we do need the light of his given self-disclosure in his Word. But more: in order for his revealed truth to enlighten our minds, cleanse our consciences, comfort our hearts, energise our wills and forge us into a fellowship — in short, to be powerful in our total experience — we are also dependent on the ministry of the Holy Spirit. He it is by whom the God disclosed in the Bible becomes present to us and in us and among us. Under his influence the sovereign Lord who has spoken through prophets, psalmists and apostles and, supremely, through his Son, draws near and speaks to our hearts in the here and now.

And it is he, the Spirit, who through the Word written leads us to the Word incarnate, and links us intimately with him as Saviour, Lord and Friend, through the gift of faith. No-one has described this essential link between Scripture, heart-experience, and Spirit, more clearly than John Calvin: "As God alone can truly bear witness to his own words, so these words will not be given complete acknowledgement in the hearts of men, until they are sealed by the inner witness of the Spirit. So the same Spirit, who spoke by the mouth of the prophets, must pervade our hearts, in order to convince us that they faithfully passed on the message entrusted to them by God.

We cannot be sure of the Word unless it is confirmed by the witness of the Spirit." "The Lord has inter-twined the truth of his Word and his Spirit in such a way that we respect the Word when the Spirit illumines it, enabling us to see God's face, and we welcome the Spirit, with no risk of error, when we recognise him in his Word" (from *John Calvin: The Institutes of Christian Religion edited by Tony Lane and*

Hilary Osborne) Thus, it is by his influence that Dickson's two books (Holy Scripture and the human heart) come together.

What this amounts to is that our supreme authority in seeking both to understand and to enjoy Christian spiritual experience — including its healthy psychological consequences — is the Holy Spirit speaking in Holy Scripture to our hearts. It is in this way that the credibility-gap between truth believed and truth experienced — a gap which so often undermines Christian joy — is bridged. Oswald Chambers made this point in his book *Biblical Psychology*: "If we have not received the Spirit of God we shall never discern spiritual things or understand them; we shall move continually in a dark world, and come slowly to the conclusion that the New Testament language is very exaggerated. But when we have received the Spirit of God, we begin to 'understand what God has freely given to us' ... 'not in words taught us by human wisdom, but in words taught by the Spirit'. The Apostle Paul here is at the very heart of things — as he always is, because ... he is 'moved by the Holy Spirit' in a special manner to expound the basis of Christian doctrine".

The point made clear by these quotations from Lewis, Calvin and Chambers is the heart of the matter: in God's providence there is a wonderful continuum between the Spirit's inspiration of the Scriptures, which portray Christ, and our present Spirit-given experience of Christ communicated in response to faith. This echoes the teaching of Paul who, for example, reminds Christians (*2 Thessalonians 2:13-14*) how God's call to salvation was made effectual in their lives: it was *"through the sanctifying work of the Spirit and through belief in the truth"*. Which comes first? Dr James Denney comments "It is impossible to separate these two things, or to define their relation to each other. Sometimes the first seems to condition the second; sometimes the order is reversed. Now it is the Spirit which opens the mind to the truth; again, it is the truth which exercises a sanctifying power like the Spirit. The two, as it were, interpenetrate each other." Paul has preached the gospel, but "God has spoken to us all in his Word and by his Spirit — God, and not only some human preacher" *(The Epistles to the Thessalonians)*.

The Bible is not the terminus of faith: by it, God the Father leads us to his Son. The written Word points to the incarnate Word, and introduces us to him. Truth is a Person. It is the ministry of the Holy Spirit to make this connection — to make the Christ of Scripture known to us in our understanding, in our hearts, in our experience.

In evangelical circles particularly, much is made of the plea for preaching to be expository in style. Quite rightly so, for declaratory exegesis is of first importance. However, Scripture must not only be expounded but also internalised; only thus will Christ himself become personally known, as well as proclaimed. Only thus can preaching be truly "with a demonstration of the Spirit's power" *(1 Corinthians 2:4)*.

Openness to this dynamic principle of Spirit-and-Word making Jesus real to us will have healing, liberating consequences, not only for our relationship with God, but also with other people and with our inner self — those two areas so often undermined by fatigue and fraught with painful dissonances.

"Surely the reality that God (by his Spirit) is personally present in and among us should encourage us through the exigencies and weaknesses of our present life, not to mention revitalise us, when our shoulders droop and our hands grow weary.

The coming of the Holy Spirit in us and among us means that the living God, in the person of the Spirit, is indeed with us. And he is present ... as an *empowering* presence. Here, then, is one of the shifts that must take place in our thinking and experience if we are to be biblical, and thus more effective, in our postmodern world, we must not merely cite the creed, but believe and experience the presence of God in the person of the Spirit." These words of Gordon Fee represent a healthy theism in contradistinction to the spiritually debilitating effects of deism and meism (*Paul, the Spirit and the People of God*).

"Truth is for people." By the Spirit's power in us and among us, not least within our ministry of care and counsel to one another, God's healing truth can get through to us.

The rain can reach our roots.

CHAPTER 3

Depth Psychology

"We are lived by our Unconscious" — *Sigmund Freud*
(Summary by Georg Groddeck — German psychoanalyst
1866-1934)

"The present contains nothing more than the past, and what is found in the effect was already in the cause." (Henri Bergson, French philosopher).

Applied to human personality, Bergson's dictum makes an interesting subject for debate. Are we only the product of our past? From a Christian standpoint, that view is, surely, to be questioned. What about, for example, Paul's awareness of "future grace" — the upward pull of the divine purpose which had transformed his personality and was constantly leading him on towards maturity in responsive Christian zeal? (*Galatians 1:15 and Philippians 3:10-14;* see also Chapter 8).

Even without this future-factor, Christians can never view the present as a pre-determined package; it is not a manufactured box which encloses us. Such a reductionist, fatalistic attitude ("I can't help being the person I am for I have been conditioned and moulded by my past — or by my genes") is untenable. We can change in the here and now: new thought-processes, motivations and attitudes can break into the box — even spring up within us.

Nevertheless, it is obvious that each one of us *has* been largely shaped by past experiences, primarily in infancy (some would include pre-birth existence in the womb) but also as we have developed through childhood, adolescence and adulthood up to the present moment. This commonly acknowledged link between present effect and past cause in personality-development was not always obvious: we owe its acceptance in large measure to Sigmund Freud (1856-1939) who was not content simply to observe and record human behaviour, but sought to explain it in scientific terms by looking for its *causes*.

TH Huxley maintained that "causality is the first great act of faith on the part of a man of science". That statement may be under question today particularly in the field of physics; but it was Freud's genius that he was the first to apply *with thoroughness* this scientific principle enunciated by Huxley to the study of personality.

In the process Freud revolutionised the way of looking at ourselves.

Drawing on the natural sciences of his time he sought to apply similar methods of approach to psychology. Analogies were suggested between the functioning of the mind and the various reactions and processes observed in the laboratory by physicists and biologists. He could even refer to the human personality as an "apparatus" — an enclosed system of interacting psychological energies.

Supported by conclusions drawn from his clinical sessions with patients, he affirmed that it is not by accident, coincidences, or arbitrary decisions that any one of us becomes the person we are: our distinctive mental attitudes, emotional responses, and behavioural characteristics (all marked, to a lesser or greater degree, by inappropriate distortions) have their roots in early experiences and memories.

Put simply, idiosyncrasies (including neuroses) do have past causes.

These causes, he concluded, because they mostly have painful associations have been repressed into the Unconscious, but can be uncovered by psychoanalysis. Probing the Unconscious, though, reveals it to be not only a repository of repressed memories of past crises; it is also the seat of powerful instinctual drives and impulses, dominated by sex and aggression, which are interweaved with those accumulated memories. Outside influences and pressures serve both to inflame and to frustrate these buried energies.

One important way of uncovering the inner dynamics involved is through the analysis and interpretation of dreams. Freud described these as "the high road to the Unconscious", for in dreams all manner of buried impressions and repressed desires and fears emerge into conscious awareness (albeit during sleep) — hence "wish-fulfilment" dreams, and nightmares.

Freudian psychoanalysis, based on *Depth Psychology* (so called for obvious reasons) is universally recognised as one of the most significant landmarks of the Twentieth Century, and it is a sign of his great impact upon modern thought that many of the concepts, phrases and actual words which Freud invented are commonly known and used: for example, his terms for the three active factors in the mind — *id, ego,* and *super-ego*; and *defence-mechanisms*.

But not everybody is familiar with their meaning, so perhaps brief clarification is in order.

Id, Ego, Superego and Defence Mechanisms

The *Id* designates the contents of the Unconscious dominated by primitive, mainly sexual, urges with an interacting energy (libido) surging between them. This raw energy seeks an outlet through channels linked to sensual pleasure; but also present is a force made up of self-destructive elements which are, literally, "beyond the pleasure-principle".

The first was called the Life Instinct (*Eros*). The second

was referred to (though not by all Freudians) as the Death Instinct (*Thanatos*) — perhaps unconsciously aimed at finding nirvana: the ending of personal existence; the painful confusion caused by this inwardly directed destructive urge usually finds relief by being projected onto others; or it may be fed back into the libido, resulting in a dark potent mix of sex and aggression which can take the form of masochism or sadism.

In Freudian theory the Life Instinct is the dominant tendency but both impulses (sex *and* aggression) will constantly be seeking expression, pushing for an eruption into conscious life, and, if further repressed, can become hidden centres of increasingly volcanic emotional force. Such repression is common because the Pleasure Principle which impels the gratification of sexual appetite, and the break-out of aggression, are both opposed by the Reality Principle which governs the Ego.

The *Ego* (the "I" or "self") is the choosing part of us which seeks to restrain and organise the wild demands of the *Id* in the light of real life: gratification is delayed and control exercised in the interests of conforming to social acceptableness (the Reality Principle). The Ego, which is what we usually think of as the "mind", is the centre of conscious awareness, compounded of thoughts and feelings plus the ability to assess the cause and effect of behaviour and to regulate words and actions accordingly. Its control of the *Id* is complicated by pressures upon it from the conscience, called by Freud, the *Super-ego*.

The *Super-ego* is the policeman of the personality. Its moral attitudes are derived partly from up-bringing (the standards of parents and other authority-figures are introjected) and partly from the developing individual's wider moral environment — community, society, school, church etc.

The *Super-ego* with its "oughts" and "shoulds" — mainly of a prohibitive nature, strongly opposes the *Id* and its wild desires. Thus the *Super-ego* is, broadly, synonymous with conscience.

The *Ego* can be visualised, then, as caught between the untamed sexual and aggressive urges of the *Id* demanding immediate gratification, and the *Super-ego* which forbids such externalisation — sometimes with quite vehement authority. It is predictable that the *Ego* develops techniques to evade, or lessen the conflict: these are called *Ego defence-mechanisms*.

One of these has already been referred to: *repression* — pushing sources of painful tension back down into the cellar of the Unconscious (repression is usually resorted to without the person realising it). Other *defence-mechanisms* include *regression* (an immature escapism into a childish response to stress); *displacement*, also referred to earlier, when painful emotions perhaps arising from anxiety or depression are transferred to something or somebody else completely unrelated to the real cause — like kicking the cat or taking it out on a partner, or, infinitely more seriously, acts of violence, even war. (Blaming God is a common religious displacement phenomenon).

In *Escape into Fantasy* inadmissible demands from the *Id* can be indulged in the imagination and ugly facts turned into pleasurable day-dreams (hence the appeal of pornography and violence in books and films). *Denial* is common: a refusal to admit that there is a problem, and the assertion of untroubled control; this is perhaps related to *Rationalisation*, which has been defined as "giving good reasons for bad actions"!

Other techniques, arguably less retrogressive, for avoiding anxiety-signalled conflicts include *Identification* —

connecting closely with the values and status of esteemed individuals so as to share, vicariously, in their life-style (a kind of virtue-by-association); and *sublimation* — the substitution of socially-approved behaviour and achievements which win approbation, for prohibited sexual-aggressive conduct.

Psychoanalysis, in the view of its practitioners, can lead to an identifying of these defence-mechanisms and an understanding of the inner conflicts which give rise to them — particularly as exacerbated by outside vetoes fed into the *Super-ego*. This exercise can, in turn, relieve tension and suggest a re-ordering of attitudes and behaviour which produces greater happiness than is achieved by "playing games" — i.e. indulging in *defence mechanisms* and other cover-ups.

The psychoanalytical approach can also, it is claimed, shed helpful light on more common, every-day problems such as hyper-sensitive reactions to particular issues (getting hot under the collar), a fear of social contact, embarrassing slips of the tongue (or feeling tongue-tied), blushes, and repetition-compulsions (repeating certain courses of action even though these produce unhappy results). If the roots of such symptoms can be unmasked, their alleviation can be more easily put in hand, and even, in time, removed.

Because, according to Freud, we are all largely "lived by our Unconscious" (Groddeck's phrase), failure to come to terms with the dynamics of his "depth psychology" can lead to all manner of neurosis — a term summing up states of mental conflict which get out of hand and produce emotional pain and stress — sometimes becoming, in their intensity, very debilitating. Examples recognised by most of us are anxiety, depression, and obsessional impulses.

Anxiety, Depression, and Obsessional Impulses

Anxiety can be a chronically painful emotional state, with dread and apprehension as its most prominent features. Its focus is usually a sharp fear related to the future. Sometimes this takes the form of "catastrophic" thinking — some terrible calamitous development is always around the next corner. Perhaps this is seen as the "deserved" consequence of some perceived mistake or misdemeanour.

Freud identified three varieties of anxiety which he labelled *Reality, Neurotic,* and *Moral. Reality anxiety* obviously attaches to actual crises that may be facing us in the real world tomorrow; actually, even if these are in the imagination, the effect is no less real. *Neurotic anxiety* arises from the fear that we cannot control those powerful primitive drives — perhaps they will overwhelm us and lead us into terrible trouble; and we find it increasingly difficult to handle the associated fears and fantasies which we are repressing. *Moral anxiety* (the fear of our Super-ego) is about flinching from the pain of a guilty conscience; this is rooted in the tension between the demands of the Super-ego and the non-compliance of the Ego.

The same three-fold categorisation could be applied to *depression* which, as the word implies, is a low emotional state fed by feelings of inadequacy and hopelessness; commonly, other components are regret and remorse, even despair, because depression is usually associated with loss, whether real or imagined. Depression is sometimes brought on by aggressive feelings (from the *Id*) being "unsuccessfully" exteriorised and then re-directed inwards, resulting in self-blame and lowered self-esteem.

If anxiety is mainly a sharp pain of fear related to the future, depression is more like a heavy ache associated with some loss in the past. The equivalent term for *Reality* (anxiety) related to depression, is *Reactive* — signifying a response to an experience of actual loss as, for example, occasioned by bereavement — or a failure, or rejection. As with anxiety *some* losses may be imagined — but the resultant symptoms of depression are none-the-less real.

Endogenous depression is so-called because, like neurotic anxiety, it is derived internally: often the underlying cause cannot be identified — we are simply overcome, emotionally and mentally, by a nameless bleakness and blackness; sometimes this can be analysed as plummeting self-esteem associated with the ego's lack of success either in controlling the Id or in rising to the demands of the super-ego. This can link with *moral* depression which is associated with guilt feelings: along with the fear of consequences, guilt and anxiety can intertwine, producing emotional pain, and depression is likely to follow on as an enervating symptom of felt moral inadequacy and failure.

Both anxiety and depression can lead to *obsessional behaviour* as a desperate escape-route. It is as if their all-pervading oppressiveness results in an urge to attain relief by incessantly repetitive thought-patterns or by repeating certain compensating actions — rituals and routines — called, for obvious reasons, acts of neurotic compulsion. These can take such forms as frequent hand-washing, locking and re-locking doors and windows, avoiding cracks in the pavement whilst walking, or touching every lamp-post.

Other, minor, compulsions are commonly observed in the form of superstitions: for example, avoidance of walking under a ladder, and the little rituals which some professional sportsmen and women feel are necessary for success. Sometimes an over-scrupulous concern about the correct use of words and/or numbers, in ordinary conversation, indicates a neurotic obsessiveness. "Control-freakery" and any kind of excessive pre-occupation with what are, objectively, unimportant matters may signify an obsessional mind-set.

In reality, of course, the symptoms of anxiety, depression, and obsessiveness commonly flow into each other. Frequently, for example, depressive moods give rise to panic attacks which are more usually associated with anxiety; conversely, unremitting stress can lead, via anxiety, to the emotional exhaustion which is an ingredient of depression. Thus a mixed cluster of complaints can be voiced by the same person, separated by only short distances of time: and both, with tears — of exhaustion or anger –

> *"I am so tired ... constantly played out.... Anything, everything, is too much for me to handle. I'm running on "empty". Everything is such an effort, and pointless, hopeless anyway. I've been here so many times.... I've had it up to here.... There's nothing left.... I'm fighting, all the time fighting. Fighting my thoughts, fighting myself. I can't turn my brain off. Churning stomach. Waves of fear and panic. My head is all over the place. Why can't I be normal? The pain, the pain of fear.... Where can I find release?.... I just want to go to sleep and not wake up again."*

There is no doubt that depression, whether or not mixed with anxiety, can be very debilitating. A retired senior physician once expressed to me his personal view that no affliction is more distressing. The titles of two particular books on the subject of depression attest vividly to the same conviction: *Malignant Sadness* (Lewis Wolpert) and *The Noon Day Demon* (Andrew Solomon). My physician-friend's words also recall to mind other, opening, lines of Hopkins from a sonnet quoted earlier:

> No worst, there is none. Pitched past pitch of grief,
> More pangs will, schooled at forepangs, wilder wring.
> Comforter, where, where is your comforting?

(It seems to him that the word "worst" can never be used when even worse experiences are feared; "pitched" and "pitch" combines the thought of being tripped headlong — and blackness; "pangs" derive their learned power from "forepangs" — he fears yet greater anguish; "Comforter" is a cry to the Holy Spirit).

Spike Milligan, associated with the anarchic comedy of *The Goon Show* etc, suffered from severe depression. The following short poem recalls a spell in the Psychiatric Wing of a hospital –

> The pain is too much
> A thousand grim winters
> grow in my head.
> In my ears
> the sound of the
> coming dead
> All seasons, all same
> all living
> all pain
> No opiate to lock still
> my senses.
> Only left, the body locked tenser.

No Christian has written prose on this theme with more pertinent, helpful clarity than the great Baptist preacher C H Spurgeon. He describes, from his own experience, the

RAIN TO MY ROOTS

awfulness of depression, the reality of dependence upon the tender mercy of God, and of grace-given courage. Here is an extended quotation from a chapter headed *The Minister's Fainting Fits* from his *Lectures to my students*.

"Causeless depression is not to be reasoned with, nor can David's harp charm it away by sweet discoursings. As well fight with the mist as with this shapeless, indefinable, yet all-beclouding hopelessness. One affords himself no pity when in this case, because it seems so unreasonable, and even sinful, to be troubled without manifest cause; and yet troubled the man is, even in the very depths of his spirit. If those who laugh at such melancholy did but feel the grief of it for one hour, their laughter would be sobered into compassion. Resolution might, perhaps, shake it off, but where are we to find the resolution when the whole man is unstrung?

The physician and the divine may unite their skill in such cases, and both find their hands full, and more than full. The iron bolt which so mysteriously fastens the door of hope and holds our spirits in gloomy prison, needs a heavenly hand to push it back; and when that hand is seen we cry with the apostle, "Blessed be God, even the Father of our Lord Jesus Christ, the Father of mercies, and the God of all comfort; who comforteth us in all our tribulation, that we may be able to comfort them which are in any trouble, by the comfort where with we ourselves are comforted of God" (*2 Cor. 1: 3-4*).

It is the God of all consolation who can:
'With sweet oblivious antidote
Cleanse our poor bosoms of that perilous stuff
Which weighs upon the heart.'

When we are ridden with horrible fears, and weighed down with an intolerable incubus, we need but the Sun of

Righteousness to rise, and the evils generated of our darkness are driven away; but nothing short of this will chase away the nightmare of the soul".

Clearly then, such a darkness can be completely unrelated to any spiritual declension or moral failure, and to imply otherwise can be cruel in the extreme. God's people are not immune to depression or anxiety. But sadly, Job's comforters are still around, all too ready to impute culpable deserving-ness. Spurgeon, typically, points to the right way forward for the Christian: "The lesson of wisdom is, *be not dismayed by soul-trouble*. Should the power of depression be more than ordinary, think not that all is over with your usefulness.

Cast the burden of the present, along with the sin of the past and the fear of the future, upon the Lord, who forsaketh not his saints. Live by the day — ay, by the hour. Put no trust in frames and feelings. Care more for a grain of faith than a ton of excitement. Continue with double earnestness to serve your Lord when no visible result is before you. Any simpleton can follow the narrow path in the light; faith's rare wisdom enables us to march on in the dark with infallible accuracy, since she places her hand in that of her Great Guide ... be it ours, when we cannot see the face of our God, to trust under *the shadow of his wings*."

The sympathetic presence and persevering compassion, and prayers, of a Christian friend can help enormously. So can the company of a worshipping congregation open to the love of God released among them by the Holy Spirit. Hymns and songs can lift the heart.

And there are also "common sense" strategies which may bring some relief from depression — like long walks in the country (which Dickens, a sufferer found helpful and which Spurgeon advocated), writing down your thoughts, phoning a friend, being open to kindly advice, accepting invitations to meals out, perhaps "losing" your mood in the excitement and anonymity of being part of a crowd — at a football match or a concert or whatever. These straightforward steps are certainly more effective than those various obsessive behaviour patterns which can, in fact, worsen the underlying distress.

But, of course, it can happen that such home-spun measures are just too unrealistic: the problems and difficulties loom too large. The pain is all-consuming. At such times, a doctor may need to prescribe appropriate medication and/or the compassionate insights of a skilled counsellor may be needed.

Psychotherapy

Operating from a Depth Psychology stance, what psychotherapy techniques come into play in a counselling situation?

Gone are the days of the couch and the detached, dispassionate (out of sight?) analyst probing and prompting so as to make the Unconscious conscious.... Post-Freudians, whilst holding to Freud's basic model and theory of intra-psychic conflicts and their impact upon every day life, have downplayed the force of the libido and emphasised the importance of inter-personal relationships.[*]

Consonant with this, therapists will sit face to face with their clients in an informal atmosphere: counselling, *as a good experience*, is an essential part of the therapy, for this

---

[*]Freud's views have been modified by a number of well-known post-Freudians – notably his daughter Anna Freud, and Melanie Klein, Karen Horney, Erich Fromm, Harry Stack Sullivan, plus Bowlby, Winnicott, Fairbairn, Riviere, Eriksen..... All have made distinctive contributions to the exploration and understanding of psychoanalytical principles but it is beyond the scope of the present book to incorporate these. We are concerned with the presentation of Depth Psychology in broad outline. Suffice it to say that the variations from Freud are focused in an emphasis, complementary to his libido theory, upon the influence from the outside world of other people and their effect on the mental life – raising issues such as self-esteem, security, concern about social status etc.

helps to counteract the bad experiences which have produced distress. But the basic aim of Depth Psychology therapies remains the same: to *analyse* the problem, thus helping a person to be in touch with their feelings, identify the causes of tension, and make the necessary healthy readjustments.

Perhaps the key concept in this process is *interpretation*; that is, helping the "patient" to understand his or her feelings and attitudes. Dr Anthony Storr writes, as a Jungian psycho-therapist (in *The Art of Psychotherapy*) "Making interpreta-tions is part of the therapist's task; some would say his most important task". He stresses that this does not necessarily require initiation "into the esoteric mysteries of the Uncon-scious" nor familiarity with the "incomprehensible jargon" which is "often misused to lead a spurious air of profundity to utterances which are nothing of the kind". What then is involved in the technique of interpretation?

Foremost, Storr states, its aim is "to make the incompre-hensible comprehensible". Often, a sensitive listener, by reflecting back a person's words and the feelings behind them, can throw light onto the basic problem. An all-pervading dread or regret is all the more threatening if the reason for it is not understood: it looms menacingly large because it does not make sense. Interpretation, by clarifying the interaction between inner feelings and life circumstances, can help to explain what is happening. To make the incom-prehensible comprehensible does not abolish the problem, but can cut it down to size and thus bring significant relief from anxiety.

A further element in this process of interpretation may be "tracing connections" between events, symptoms and person-ality characteristics which are not immediately obvious. Each of us responds to life-crises in different ways: a development which can reduce one person to impotent panic or desolation, may well leave someone else comparatively unperturbed. The difference is often explicable in terms of personality-forming events in a person's past: perhaps bad childhood experiences have pre-disposed us to reactions of heightened insecurity in certain circumstances later in life, which echo them: painful memories may be triggered by alarming developments in the present, and buried vulnerabilities are thus brought to the surface, with attendant feelings of distress.

Sometimes there will be a discrepancy between the way a person presents and expresses their problem verbally and their actual state of mind — a discrepancy which may be betrayed by body-language. For example, what may come across is a suspiciously over-confident attitude which is masking inner feelings of inadequacy.

Conversely, words conveying low self-esteem and self-reproach may in fact be invalid because the person's actual strength of character and upright behaviour indicate the inappropriateness of such feelings. We are all apt to deceive ourselves, in one or other of these directions — perhaps both, at different times — over-estimating either our good qualities or our bad qualities.

A wise counsellor can help us to see our state of mind and our circumstances in true perspective and to make sense of them; by owning the truth (rather than being driven by distorted perceptions) we will be better equipped to move forward away from anxiety and/or depression with positive realism.

The counselling approach described has resonances with the principles of the *Cognitive Behaviour Therapy* which is currently popular, and which bypasses the old, convoluted and prolonged (and expensive) process associated with the couch. In fact Cognitive Therapy has, in the minds of many in the psychiatric profession, helpfully superseded Freudian psychoanalysis.

Cognitive Therapy

In Cognitive Therapy a person ("client") is encouraged to challenge and reject false self-perceptions and resultant inappropriate reactions (which may well have their roots in upbringing) and replace them with a realistic appraisal of circumstances, self-acceptance, and the embracing of new, hopeful possibilities. In particular, ANTS (!) are exposed (Automatic Negative Thoughts) and more rational thought-patterns identified, internalised, and then lived out — by positive reinforcement.

For example, it is characteristic of anxious people to exhibit what Albert Ellis calls "awfulizing" — they convince themselves that if some feared development took place (and they are pretty sure it will) they would be finished. Nothing could be more dreadful, more awful. Or, commonly, "my depressive state is uniquely terrible. No one but no one, has ever felt, could ever feel, so dreadful".

What is clearly at fault here is the mental attitude: fear or despair dominate. Arguably, the cure begins by "de-awfulizing" such thoughts and replacing them with a rational, realistic perception of the situation. This will not mean escapism, pretending that there is nothing to be worried about, nor ignoring the very real anguish of anxiety or the desolation of depression. But it will mean changing the way that we *think* about a problem.

A book which has sold in great quantities sums up the principle in its title: *Mind Over Matter — Changing How You Feel By Changing the Way You Think*. Essentially a practical work-book (by Dennis Greenberger and Christine A Podesky) it carries a commendatory foreword by Aaron T Beck (Professor of Psychiatry, University of Pennsylvania) who first began developing Cognitive Therapy in the late 1950s. The authors were among his students.

But the underlying principle of Cognitive Therapy has long been recognised. The Greek philosopher Epictetus wrote "It is not things in themselves which trouble us, but the opinions we have about things." More importantly, certain elements of Cognitive Therapy can find biblical support in such verses as *Proverbs 23:7*, "as a man thinks within himself, so is he"; and *Romans 12:2*, "be transformed by the renewing of your mind" — where the conforming of our thinking to the revealed will of God is the means of changing both our inner motivations *and* our outward behaviour. Perhaps we may say that *Psalms 42 and 43* (which probably form one unit) provide an example of Cognitive Therapy of the best kind, *because* it is theocentric. David addresses both God and his readers over the grief and despondency (a mix of depression and anxiety) which are afflicting him — misery exacerbated by a felt absence of God's comfort.

With extraordinary vividness he describes the almost un-bearable load which weighs him down so heavily and also causes wildly disturbed thoughts to sweep over him, like waves of a turbulent sea *(Psalm 42:3, 7, 9)*. But he then takes his thoughts in hand. He asks questions of himself. What is causing him to be so downcast and disturbed? Why does he feel as he does? That is a good start. However, relief comes, not from introspection: a desperate search for reasons can either be in vain, or induce self-pity and resentment. Better to look upward to God and re-order his thoughts in the light of the reality of his saving love. Three times the same refrain occurs:

"Why are you downcast, o my soul?
Why so disturbed within me?

Put your hope in God
　　For I will yet praise him,
My Saviour and my God"

Commenting on this, John Stott writes, "the cure for depression is neither to look in at our grief, nor back to our past, nor round at our problems, but away and up to the living God. He is our help and our God, and if we trust him now, we shall soon have cause to praise him again. Thus, as one writer sums up, 'faith rebukes despondency and hope triumphs over despair'" (from *Psalms... — John Stott*).

I am reminded of an old devotional volume by Amy Carmichael, which reflects this approach. The book, entitled *His Thoughts Said, The Father Said* demonstrates the spiritual wisdom and therapeutic effectiveness of bringing our thoughts into line with God's Word.

The root spiritual problem being addressed here by this "Christianised" Cognitive Therapy is usually *mis*belief rather than *un*belief: not so much distrust of God's Word, as its distortion — by wrong thinking. But this raises a poignant question: are negative thought-patterns which can lead us to mis-read Scripture, the cause of emotional unease, or a consequence?

Probably, the answer is likely to be along the lines of both/and rather than either/or.

Wrong, unbiblical thinking can exacerbate anxiety and depression; but conversely, these maladies can, for a time, close off our minds from "God-thoughts" and make the reading of Holy Scripture difficult — neither Cognitive Therapy, nor any other kind of counselling, in itself, gets through. But as the Christian waits patiently on God, the Holy Spirit *will* cause truth from his Word to bring about a re-ordering of our thoughts, *and*, in association, of our feelings.

The unfolding of his words will give light (*Psalm 119:130*) and encouragement, joy, peace, and hope (*Romans 15:4 and 13*) (these principles will be expanded in the following chapter).

One further factor relevant not only to psychoanalysis, but to every school of psychology, is the prevalent symptom of guilt-feelings.

Guilt — Real and Imaginary

Guilt looms large in psychology and is recognised by all psychotherapists as a commonly occurring cause of distress and inappropriate behaviour.

It is possible, for example, that some obsessional rituals are unsuccessful strategies to atone for the "guilt" which underlies much (though certainly not all) anxiety and depression. The classic example is Shakespeare's Lady Macbeth, consumed with blood-guiltiness, sleep-walking for long periods, making hand-washing motions and crying, "What, will these hands ne'er be clean? … here's the smell of blood still: all the perfumes of Arabia will not sweeten this little hand."

Clearly, Lady Macbeth is a one-off (fictional) case. However, as C T Hulme writes, representing many other psychologists: "Guilt is fundamental to almost every problem of the human personality: it begets anxiety, is manifested in the inferiority complex and follows resentment. Any counselling — whether it is religious or secular — that is going to succeed in helping people with their problems must know what to do with the problem of guilt."

The issue of guilt is particularly relevant to Depth Psychology, and Freud took very seriously its damaging and all-pervasive presence within the inter-actions of id, ego and super-ego; and he confronted the problems it raised openly and plainly.

But it is vitally important to recognise that his view of guilt differs radically from the Christian perspective: in fact, it turns it on its head. For Freud, "guilt" is a neurosis: an unnecessary psychological hang-up arising from the tension between the overbearing demands of the super-ego and the under-attainment of the id-threatened ego in response. Thus the moral sense of guilt is derived from inner conflicts and is part-and-parcel of anxiety; it does not necessarily relate to any infringement of some external ethical code.

"Guilt" is triggered by *impulses* disapproved by the super-ego, rather than actual misdeeds. Ironically though (it must immediately be stated) this internal discord, located for the most part in the Unconscious, can lead, if unresolved, to serious misconduct and/or masochistic (self-punishing) acts.

In other words, for Freud, the "guilt" *precedes* culpable, anti-social behaviour.

"Unconscious" guilt, if aggravated, can turn people into criminals: it is as if relief from the pain of (unnecessary) guilt *feelings* is found by fastening it upon *real* crimes. ("I feel bad: I'll prove I'm bad"). Or, as with masochism, some people may seek relief (or atonement) in the punishment of self-inflicted pain (mental and/or physical) or by regression into the "comfort" of illness and an obstinate resistance to a cure.

Thus distressing physical symptoms can sometimes disguise an underlying disquiet attaching to guilt.

"Guilt" is the bogey behind all these grim, pathetic "games" and pains.

Starting from this Freudian position, the solution to "guilt" lies in psychoanalysis by which the demands of the super-ego are unmasked and shown to be cruelly and punitively over-demanding, and the ego is strengthened to stand against these unreasonable "oughts" and "shoulds". In this way the personality (it is claimed) can be rid of the misery of inhibitions, and released into "guilt-free" self-expression, without resorting to the criminal or masochistic or regressive behaviour referred to above.

The danger of this approach is obvious, even on its own presuppositions: the primitive impulses of the id, no longer restrained or rebuked by the weakened super-ego, are now more likely to swamp the ego and find sexual and aggressive expression. This will probably cause damage to others and lead to the come-uppance of *real* guilt, incurring social disapproval, if not forensic punishment.

Moreover, Freud's "naturalistic" view of guilt diminishes the person by undermining his or her sense of responsibility for personal conduct. No human being should be considered as helplessly dominated by conflicting psychic energies or encouraged to find relief by giving way to these uninhibitedly.

This is not to deny that there is some truth in Freud's hypothesis concerning guilt. The Christian pastor will not wish to discount "false guilt-feelings" derived from an inner sense of moral shame, which *may* be invalid for the person concerned. Our conscience (super-ego) may indeed condemn us without good cause: we may have absorbed prohibitions from our childhood environment which are not actually required by biblically-based Christianity but which still govern our lifestyle. Conscience is not, in itself, infallible. Moreover, a spirituality dominated by unbiblical and grace-denying moralism and legalism will probably exacerbate the anxiety and depression attaching to the guilt-feelings common to us all. The "God will get you for that" mentality is hard to live with.

The fact is, however, guilt attaches to us if only because none of us does fulfil our potential for good — we all fail by not rising to our own expectations of ourselves, quite apart from the perceived expectations of others and, most importantly, the requirements of our Creator as revealed in Holy Scripture.

The last-named element can have no place in Freudian thought because there is no recognition of our accountability to a personal, holy God whose laws cannot be broken with impunity but only at the price of actual guilt — including guilt-feelings which are valid. Nor can Freud's position have any place for that divine mercy and love whereby the peace of pardon, achieved by Christ's atoning death, is communicated to the repentant heart, and a new, moral centre implanted by the indwelling Holy Spirit. From being in the wrong with God, and struggling unsuccessfully with warring motives and impulses, we can be "born again" into a new life, equipped now with new spiritual resources.

The super-ego (conscience) can be thus sorted out, freed from the tyranny of false demands and re-formed, re-educated by the Holy Spirit, strengthening what *is* consonant with moral requirements drawn from Holy Scripture. In this way conscience can be restored to its God-given function of hearing his voice and governing our behaviour by approving (or disapproving) thoughts and actions, in accordance with his Word.

The importance of the role of the Holy Spirit in this re-ordering of our inner life cannot be over-emphasised. Only he can expel wrong thinking, and correct moral confusion, by renewing the mind. Only he can instil true self-knowledge, in contrast to perceptions of self distorted by stress and sin. And, to this end, he can make the vital, healing *connection* between Holy Scripture and the human spirit.

Divinely imparted understanding of stress and its causes which is derived from God's revealed truth is one thing; actualisation of this in healed emotions, cleansed conscience and responsive obedience, is another. The Holy Spirit, as "The

Go-Between God" is the divine agent of "actualisation", for he enables us to "test and approve what God's will is — his good, pleasing and perfect will". And a mind renewed by the Spirit has its outcome, by the power of the same Spirit, in a process of *actual transformation* affecting the whole person. This truth is echoed in *2 Corinthians 3:18* where the same word is used: "we, who with unveiled face all contemplate the Lord's glory are *being transformed* into his likeness with ever-increasing glory, which comes from the Lord, who is the Spirit". But this is to anticipate the next chapter of this book.

It is right to acknowledge, with gratitude, Freud's greatness. He was an atheist, and his works will be read by the Christian with an awareness of the serious limitations which this position imposes. But the fact is that his concepts, theories, and descriptive expressions related to human problems have indeed passed into the common language. In fact, for most people "psychology" and "psychoanalysis" and its associated terms are virtually synonymous.

The psychologist G A Miller is among those who paid tribute to his ground-breaking realism: "Freud struggled to see man as he is, not as he ought to be or as Freud would have liked to imagine him"; and he concluded that "few men have influenced us so deeply" (*Psychology: The Science of Mental Life — G A Miller*).

Even H J Eysenck, who was strongly critical of Freudian psychology and questioned the value of psychoanalysis wrote "the brilliance of (Freud's) mind has opened doors which no one now would wish to close again, and his keen insight has given us a store-house of theories and hypotheses which will keep researchers busy for many years to come.

All this one can appreciate without accepting the totality of his views" *(Uses and Abuses of Psychology — H J Eysenck; quoted in Psychology and Christianity: the View Both Ways*

— *Malcolm A Jeeves).*

An obvious point, too often forgotten, is that Freud was motivated by great compassion, and he was not without humility! In a non-triumphalist assessment of his own methods he said with disarming realism that psychoanalysis can only offer the possibility of transforming neurotic misery into common unhappiness. There is no cure-all. Indeed there is not. But perhaps he regretted the spiritual bankruptcy of his atheistic approach.

In contradistinction to Jung, he said "I have not the courage to rise up before my fellow men as a prophet and I bow to the reproach that I can offer them no consolation". Nevertheless he did believe in a human ability, with skilled help, to change, to improve: he once defined the goal of psychoanalysis as giving "the patient's ego the freedom to choose one way or the other". Such a statement does beg some questions from a Christian standpoint. But all should salute the human sympathy and pity which lay behind his desire to alleviate the misery of life-cramping neuroses: he once wrote to Jung (in 1906) that psychoanalysis is "a cure through love".

Bruno Bettelheim has sought to rehabilitate Freud among antipathetic English psychiatrists by correcting the presentation of him as a cold, clinical practitioner whose approach is based on biology, physics and medical models. He blames those who have translated Freud's writing for these misconceptions: "the English renditions of Freud's writings distort much of the essential humanism that permeated the originals"; for example, "nearly all of Freud's many references to the soul and matters pertaining to the soul, have been excised in translation ... *dieseele* (soul) is substituted, in translation, by 'mind', and *seelisch* is translated as 'mental'.

The effect of this is to rob Freud's approach of warm, human concern. *Mutterleib* (mother-womb) becomes 'uterus'".

Bettelheim bitingly comments about the world of difference between wanting to get back to the womb and wanting to re-enter the uterus! Similarly the words *ego, id,* and *super-ego* used to translate *Das Ich, Das Es,* and *Das Über-ich* sound like scientific, clinical jargon-words. It is argued that French translators more accurately capture Freud's thought with *le moi, le ça, and le sur-moi.* "How different a sense we would have of Freud's work if we were to call the ego simply the 'me'".

(And, arguably this would have more resonances with Paul's teaching about the battle between "me" and the "deeper-than-me" (sin living in me) *(Romans 7:14-25)).*

Do these slanted translations reveal a discomfort with the deeply personal implications of Freud's thought by objectify-ing poignant issues, and applying them to others rather than to ourselves? Bettelheim argues that this distancing-by-translation does not fairly represent Freud's compassion.

After all, he believed that by psychoanalysis a person can be helped towards a greater degree of inner integration — this will never be complete but it can produce considerable release of tension, a more healthy integration of the different ener-gies within the psyche, and a more mature moving forward into the future.

This claim is, for the Christian, inadequate for it lacks the spiritual dimension which is essential for healing and whole-ness. Nevertheless, Freud should, arguably, command the kind of respect expressed so movingly by W H Auden. Here are some lines from his long poem "In Memory of Sigmund Freud" (D Sept. 1939).

He wasn't clever at all: he merely told
the unhappy Present to recite the Past
  like a poetry lesson till sooner
  or later it faltered at the line where

> long ago the accusations had begun,
> and suddenly knew by whom it had been judged,
>> how rich life had been and how silly,
>> and was life-forgiven and more humble,
>
> able to approach the Future as a friend
> without a wardrobe of excuses, without
>> A set mask of rectitude or an
>> embarrassing over-familiar gesture.

Shortly, in the following chapter, we must take further a brief appraisal of Depth Psychology, drawing on relevant themes of Holy Scripture. We shall seek to identify some biblical resonances with Freud's thought but also continue to challenge and discount much that is invalid, or plain wrong, according to God's revealed truth. By the same token, we shall attempt to draw out some Christian perspectives. But before this it is important to take note that Freud's conclusions came to be questioned even by certain of his contemporaries working in the comparatively new field of psychology — and as we have noted, Freud's views have also been modified by a number of respected post-Freudians. By far the most eminent of those contemporaries taking issue with him were Alfred Adler (1870 to 1937) and Carl Jung (1875 to 1961).

Alfred Adler

Adler's best-known idea is the "inferiority complex" and it does serve as a useful focus of his psychological views — especially in relation to his break with Freud (in 1912).

Like the subsequent "post-Freudians" referred to earlier, he held that it was not the libido's passionate energy, inhibited by the super-ego which was the primary source of neuroses. This was, rather, inner feelings of inferiority.

These feelings obviously stem from the helplessness of infancy, and lead to an urge to overcome them and gain acceptance and approval. Adler maintained that "to be a human being means the possession of a feeling of inferiority which is always pressing on to its own conquest". The key to attaining a compensating status and superiority is the manipulation of inter-personal relationships — primarily, of course, in the family — so as to win affirmation. The approval of others becomes the basis of the child's sense of self-worth. We all start with the basic life-position of "I'm not OK — You're OK": and this can persist into adulthood. If it does so, the position can lead, broadly, to two ways of dealing with its discomfort: one, is by over-compensating (trying too hard to please, or becoming bossy, pushy, arrogant); the other, involves under-compensating (attracting attention and sympathy by retreating into a feigned inadequacy, perhaps "explained" by "illness" or misfortune).

The first ploy carries with it a commitment to social climbing, the second is an apparently brave resignation to loneliness and dependence which in fact serves to draw out solicitude and admiration. But both strategies subserve, in different ways, the same urge to conquer feelings of inferiority by achieving status.

Adler summed up this basic motivation as the "will to power"; and he used the term "life-style" for the methods adopted to achieve such fulfilment.

The therapeutic aim of Adler's "Individual Psychology" (as his theory of personality was called) is to show that neurotic ways of compensating for inferiority-feelings will always be unhelpful: social climbing, and attention-seeking withdrawal, both undermine authenticity and integrity. The only emotionally healthy way forward is the way of self-acceptance and accepting others, based on rational thought.

To borrow the language of Transactional Analysis (de-rived from Adlerian psychology *via* Harry Stack Sullivan): not the life-position of "I'm not OK, you're OK" (poor old me); not "I'm not OK, you're not OK" (everyone, including me, is inferior); not "I'm OK, you're not OK" (I've made it, you haven't); but "I'm OK, you're OK" — for this attitude is based not on feelings but reason. (I am a unique human being of equal worth, no more no less, with every other human being. As an adult, I can accept myself as I am, teach myself to see feelings of inferiority as hangovers from a childish attitude, and relate, on the level, with other adults.) *(See I'm Ok – You're Ok — Thomas A Harris)*.

Perhaps, from a Christian stance, we could add, without irreverence, a fifth position: "I'm OK, God's OK". If we know ourselves accepted by God through faith in his Son, we really can accept ourselves, in him! And we can see other people true — as persons like ourselves, needing God's grace and able to experience that grace through the Holy Spirit's ministry communicating forgiveness and the life of Christ. We can love because God first loved us, and has put his love inside us — enabling us to relate to others as equals in God's sight.

Freud, Adler — and Jung

Carl Jung was intrigued by the differences between Freud and Adler. How was it that the two psychologists, both coming from the same position inherent in Depth Psychology, could put forward different interpretations of what goes on in the mind, and of how our behaviour is motivated and actualised? Since both views seem to be true to observable facts and have equal psychotherapeutic value, perhaps the contrast in their conclusions indicates a difference between *them*, as person-alities.

Jung coined two expressions to describe this apparent difference in their temperaments: Freud's attitude was *extraverted*; Adler's was *introverted*.

As we have seen, Freud saw the subject's inner tensions as being produced mostly by the inhibiting and punitive pressures from outside influences channelled through the super-ego in the form of *oughts* and *shoulds*. Resolution of conflict meant weakening the super-ego by unmasking these controlling, externally derived dictatorial powers, breaking their hold, and relating to them in a new, undominated way. This attitude Jung described as extraverted, because it is directed outwards to those socially-determined, forbidding factors, with the aim of release into unrestricted self-expression.

Adler, by contrast, (in Jung's view) was introverted in his psychoanalytical attitude because his starting point was the individual's inner feelings of inferiority as being determinative; therefore, inwardly-directed comfort, and affirmation, is the primary felt need. Relief would come from *introjecting* these from outside sources. In particular, relationships, where possible, will be used to boost inner self-esteem, and thus lead to the acquiring of some kind of independent life-style. The primary direction of this attitude is thus *introjection*: hence introverted.

It is not hard to see that extraversion and introversion, in psychoanalytical terms, although divergent, are not really opposites, for they are derived from the same underlying psychoanalytical cause i.e.: inner conflict, though differently interpreted.

But the terms have taken on a much broader connotation, and are commonly used to describe predominant temperamental traits. Thus it is said that people who are mainly extraverted tend to move outward to other people, are interested in events and stimulated by busyness and relationships; at their best, they are communicative, sociable, practical, and take the initiative; a possible danger lies in losing contact with their real self and a dread of solitude (which is not the same as loneliness).

Introverted people, it is averred, tend to withdraw into themselves and reflect upon inner feelings, experiences and ideas, and these become their main source of energy; clearly, their strength lies in a thoughtful, considered response to the needs of others, swift understanding of issues, and depth of concern; extreme introversion, however, can lead to an excessively enclosed personality, cut off from the outside world and life as it really is in day-to-day terms.

Just as each of us possesses elements of both features in varying degree, ideally both should come into play in a manner appropriate to different relationships and circumstances. And we should seek to cultivate and strengthen the less prominent temperament of the two so as to become a more balanced personality. As Christians, we should surely recognise differences of temperament within the Church and be grateful for the distinctive contributions both can make. Yet it remains true that in our spiritual journey as individual Christians, we need, ideally, to be both introvert and extravert — concerned, for example, both for our inner communion with God and our outward demonstration of his grace and truth. Perhaps the promise of *Psalm 121:8* may bear this added nuance of interpretation?: "The Lord will watch over your coming (in) and your going (out) both now and forever more".

Jung expanded his categorisation of personality types into more sub-divisions — they are all about how we handle our conscious lives — but we will not pursue them here. (Those who have encountered the Myers-Briggs Personality

Indicator Process will be familiar with these.) The main thrust of his advice is that we should seek to bring out into the open, if only for the benefit of others, those "opposite" aspects of our temperaments which are in the background. He called this process of self-development and growth towards wholeness, *individuation* — which will be considered a little later.

Jung's stance, *apropos*, Freud may, like Adler's, be described as introverted since he delved deeply into the inner world. He parted company from Freud (in 1913) over several aspects of psychoanalysis and, as a corrective, coined the phrase Analytic Psychology which became the basis of his psychotherapy. Like Adler, he questioned Freud's exclusive emphasis upon the inhibited libido as being the sole cause of painful, debilitating conflict within the Unconscious. Jung did not discount drives associated with sex and aggression; his own term for this primitive, wild, "animal" factor in the Unconscious was the "*shadow*" — but this also incorporated dark and destructive "spiritual" elements, foreign to Freud's thought.

He also recognised that the power of the *shadow* is affected by the individual's social environment: the more prohibitive this is, the larger will be the *shadow*. But for Jung, a deeper reality was indicated: just as, in the natural world, there is no shadow without the sun, so behind the *shadow* (psychologically speaking) and permeating it, there is a "light". This light is, in fact, a creative force within urging growth towards wholeness and integration.

And just as, physiologically, the body possesses in-built healing processes which come into play following infection or injury, it was Jung's view that this is also true in a psychological sense. We possess innate impulses towards emotional and spiritual health, and it makes sense, with skilled help through counselling, to cooperate with these in the relief of mental distress. Thus the pain of neuroses is to be understood and relieved not only by a Freudian psychoanalytical approach, for to delve into causes of the trouble *can* have a debilitating rather than a healing effect: it is better to complement this approach by identifying positive aspects of the condition which may well be inherent in the neurosis itself. Often, inner pain has a future-orientation pointing ahead to a new direction, away from an attitude, a life, that has become distressingly empty and meaningless.

"In Jung's view, every neurosis has an end: it is an attempt to compensate for a one-sided attitude to life; it is a voice, as it were, drawing attention to a side of personality that has been neglected or repressed.... The symptoms of a neurosis are not simply the effects of long past causes, whether infantile sexuality or the infantile urge to power, they are also attempts at a new synthesis of life — unsuccessful attempts let it be added — yet attempts nevertheless, with a core of value and meaning" (*An Introduction to Jung's Psychology — Frieda Fordham*).

Through therapy that core can be identified, strengthened and developed. (I once heard a thought-provoking address on the subject of "nervous breakdown" by a Jungian psychologist along these lines. The speaker's thesis was that many, *not all,* such illnesses had within them the seeds of recovery and stronger health which could be recognised, watered and nurtured. The title of the talk was "Breakdown or Breakout?").

Consonant with this, Jungian psychologists encourage patients to interpret dreams primarily in terms of what they may be suggesting about a way-out from a negative present and a way-ahead into a positive future — rather than the Freudian emphasis upon their revelation of dark *causes* of inner conflict. (Jung's view has resonances with words of T S

Eliot: "We take it for granted that our dreams spring from below; possibly, the quality of our dreams suffers in consequence".) Certainly, in the Old Testament, dreams were understood as a means of divine revelation and communication (*Genesis 28:12ff; 1 Kings 3:4-15; Job 33:14-18*). Joel celebrates the fact that in the last days dreams, in association with prophecy and visions, will be a means by which God's will is intimately made known.

However, it is recognised that dreams can also be misleading and misused (*Jeremiah 23:32; 27:9; Zechariah 10:2*), and insubstantial (*Psalm 73:20, Ecclesiastes 5:3*). *Numbers 12:6-8* emphasises that revelation through dreams is inferior to first hand messages from the Lord. In the New Testament, particularly in Matthew's Gospel, God's guidance continues to be given in dreams occasionally. The Holy Spirit speaking in Holy Scripture has replaced dreams as a medium by which divine truth is conveyed but may also help us to interpret dreams correctly. (Can true pre-cognition and guidance be conveyed through dreams checked out by Scripture? Some Christians say Yes. Discuss!)

According to Jung, the release and strengthening of the in-built principle of healing and growth can then lead to outward expression in the form of creative enjoyment — of music, art, literature, sport, whatever … and this outward expression can, by a reverse process, flow back into the self with further positive energising power. Thus Jung encouraged his patients to practise "active imagination" in order to engage with inner promptings towards the previously unrealised and unexercised experiences of fulfilment, and seek to actualise these. In this way we can *become* so much more than the person we *are*. He also describes the four highest achievements we can strive for in our quest for wholeness as faith, hope, love, and insight, which are forged through experience but are ultimately "gifts of grace".

Indeed, in this process of self-development towards wholeness ("individuation") we are aided, he claimed, by an inner spiritual reality, the God-image within — not only in a personal sense but connecting with a universal divine Archetype in the recesses of the *Collective* Unconscious i.e. of the whole human race. Indeed, he seems to equate this "God-within" with the principle of wholeness itself.

Reflecting on his clinical experiences he avers that many mature people (usually those in the second half of life) continued with analysis, though "cured", because they "were unconsciously but unswervingly seeking a goal, which eventually defined itself as the quest of wholeness — that mysterious entity 'the whole man' — and which necessitated the forging of a link between the conscious and unconscious aspects of the psyche. *The experience could also be formulated as the finding of the God within." (My italics). (An Introduction to Jung's Psychology — Frieda Fordham).*

This "psychologized theology" clearly has resonances with the position represented by Tillich and John Robinson, where "God" is to be found in the depths of our psyche as the source and ground of our being.

It also presents similar problems for orthodox Christians. Logically, from this premise, salvation does become synonymous with personality-integration, self-fulfilment or whatever (wholeness); or, at a deeper level, it represents a kind of oceanic one-ness with the divine Archetype underlying and permeating the whole human race. So, by extension, theology becomes psychology or sociology, and all pastoral ministry becomes psychotherapy.

On the other hand, it is possible to interpret Jung's meaning of "the Self" as simply the place where God makes his presence known. It is not easy to sort out his views.

Significantly, Jung had rejected, early in his life, the Protestant faith of his father who had been a pastor of the Swiss Reformed Church — probably because he found it over-cerebral, lacking emotional content. That he retained a strong religious sense is obvious but this was to find formulation and expression conditioned by his psychological views in the ways indicated above.

The famous quotation, reproduced earlier, about the need of people to find "a religious outlook on life" in order to experience healing, is followed by the words "this, of course, has nothing whatever to do with a particular creed or membership of a Church". Above Jung's front door was a plaque bearing the words "Bidden or unbidden, God is present" and he constantly reminded his patients and himself that "the awe of the Lord is the beginning of wisdom" *(Psalm 111:10).* But, for Jung, what content does the word "God" and even the Psalmist's "the Lord", have?

James Houston *(Founding Principal of Regent College, Vancouver)* affirms that it was the lack of emotional content in the faith as he was taught it by his pastor-father that "caused Jung to turn his attention to myth and intuition. Without any historic content to his religious enquiries, he reverted to paganism". In support of this view, Houston quotes a revealing letter Jung wrote to Freud in the early days of their friendship:

I think, dear Dr Freud, we must give psychoanalysis time to infiltrate into people from many centres, to revivify among intellectuals a feeling for symbol and myth. Ever so gently we want to transform the Christ back into the soothsaying god of the vine, which he was and in this way absorb those ecstatic instinctual forces of Christianity for the one purpose of making the cult and the sacred myth what they were — a drunken feast of joy where man regains the ethics and the holiness of an animal. That is the beauty and the purpose of classical religion.

Houston continues: "In other words, Jung was advocating the take-over of Christianity by the classical paganism that it had once conquered" (*The Heart's Desire — A Guide to Personal Fulfilment — James Houston*).

So, much as we may respect and value this great man's recognition of a spiritual dimension to human life and his deeply compassionate commitment to helping people to be open to "God", many of his religious convictions clearly conflict with biblical teaching. The Jungian "God-within" can in no way be identified with the "God and Father of our Lord Jesus Christ" revealed in Holy Scripture.

Christians will acknowledge that there is a sense in which God is indeed partially present deep down within us — for the Logos-light in human beings, though dimmed, has not been extinguished by sin nor has his image in us, though defaced, been obliterated; *but he is also over us and above us.* And in both his immanence and his transcendence he is not an impersonal principle-of-wholeness or ground-of-our-being but can be known, loved, trusted and obeyed in personal relationship as a holy Creator, Sustainer — and Father, through Jesus Christ (*Colossians 1:9-14*).

And *individuation* while resembling some aspects of Christian conversion and sanctification, cannot possibly be equated with that essential work of grace which alone can effect deliverance from the *"shadow's"* death-grip and bring forgiveness, cleansing and new life to believers in Christ.

The Shadow

At this point, a further note about the *"shadow"* is needed. Jung — in contrast it must be said to some psychologists and, to their shame, to some theologians — does not underestimate its dark energy which, in his view, can break out with devastatingly damaging results. He also suggested that the individuals' *"shadows"* in a group, tribe or nation can, so to speak, coalesce and lead to such ugly manifestations as mob violence, the blood-lust of "tribal" conflict, and the savagery of "ethnic cleansing" — the Nazi Holocaust being a terrible example of this.

It is possible, from a Jungian perspective, to see such dreadful phenomena as bastardized "religion": for he acknowledged that it was not only the divinely perfect Archetype which would be encountered in the Collective Unconscious. Based on his personal experience of traumatic encounter resulting from a "journey inwards", Jung described the fearful, destructive presence of evil which was also there.

Consequently, "individuation", he taught, must involve not only the integrating into conscious life of the wholesome and creative aspects of the collective and personal Unconscious (derived from the God-within) but also screening out shadow-contents which were irredeemably evil.

But here, Jung admitted, he approached an area fraught with great difficulty (how to distinguish what *can* be "reabsorbed" and "positivised") and great danger (the evil can drag us down and produce disintegration).

In such a sea, stormy and swept by deep powerful currents, an anchor would be essential but surely that anchor cannot be found within the psyche itself. Here is a serious weakness in Jung's psycho-theology. The "God-within", the divinized "principle-of-wholeness" as an anchor substitute is, bluntly, a hopelessly inadequate, unbiblical concept. Christians do have an anchor of hope but it is attached by an unbreakable chain to the throne of God, fixed there by Christ on our behalf. He, alone, on the cross combated the total power of evil, seemed to be defeated by it, but in fact endured it without breaking, and then exclaimed in triumph "*It is finished*". His resurrection gloriously demonstrated that victory; his ascension to the place of supreme honour and authority establishes him as king; his sending of the Holy Spirit to indwell believers ensures their possession of his life and eternity; his promised return presages the creation of a new heaven and earth where there will be no darkness and nothing that defiles or harms.

No wonder that *this* anchor, this hope (unlike Jung's) is both "firm and secure" (*Hebrews 6:19-20*).

To be fair to Jung, perhaps a distinction should be made (if possible?) between his views of God expressed as an investigative psychologist ("God-within us") and his personal belief. Writing privately of this, he said "How on earth did you get the idea that I could replace God — and with a concept at that? I can establish the existence of psychological wholeness to which our consciousness is subordinate and which is, in itself, beyond precise description. But this 'self' can never take the place of God, although it may, perhaps, be a receptacle for divine grace" (from *Preface by J Stafford Wright* to *Man In His Right Mind — Harold W Darling*).

Morton Kelsey, Episcopalian priest and prolific, erudite writer in the area of religious experience and psychological phenomena has made a strong case for integrating such Jungian thinking with aspects of traditional Christianity (particularly in his books *Encounter With God* and *Christo-Psychology*) but he also makes clear from his writings that, as Roger Hurding puts it in *Roots and Shoots*, "Jung's position with regard to orthodox Christianity is an elusive one." And not without problems.

But even with its bewildering less-than-Christian content it can be seen that Jung's stance as a psychologist is refreshingly different to that of Freud, which was dismissive of all religion as a damaging illusion. Inevitably, the split between them led to a frequently made distinction in terms of Jung's "numinous" concerns and Freud's atheistic biologism. To orthodox Freudians Jung is embarrassingly obscurantist.

But countering charges of an unscientific, mystical approach, Jung protested that his conclusions about human beings possessing "a natural religious function" which was of vital importance for moving towards wholeness, were formed and verified by his clinical experience — no less than Freud claimed for his conclusions.

"It would certainly have never occurred to me to depart from Freud's path if I had not stumbled upon facts which forced me to modify his theory."

Depth Psychology and Human "Botany"

For Freud, the roots are pulsating with powerful biological energy but, being seriously constricted, can develop grotesque malformations and stunted growth; in Adler's view the roots are weak and desperately striving for growth; Jung sees our roots as going down deep into the Collective Unconscious where they are vulnerable to evil forces which can strengthen their primitive dark vigour but also able to engage healingly with the divine Archetype, the God-within, and produce ordered beauty and fruitfulness.

So this chapter has been a survey of Depth Psychology using the broadest of brush-strokes. Many aspects have been omitted (particularly those related to more recent developments) but in outlining the approaches of the three "founding fathers", Freud, Adler, and Jung, my purpose has been to show its main shape and thrust.

At the beginning of his book (about as far as I got!), *A Brief History of Time*, Steven Hawking warns us "a theory is just a model of the Universe, or a restricted part of it — It exists only in our minds and does not have any other reality". This does not render such models useless. But the usefulness of a theory depends, states Hawking, upon two factors: "it must accurately describe a large class of observations — and it must make definite predictions about the results of any future observations."

In relation to psychology the issue is complicated by the fact that the subject of all psychological theories and models is the "universe" of the mind itself. Can the mind devise a model of itself? Can it describe, or prognosticate about, its own functions? Is objectivity possible?

Sir Peter Medawar dismissed the theory of psychoanalysis as "a stupendous intellectual confidence trick" (quoted in *The Times 20/3/2001*). Arguably, that opinion is too dismissive. But we certainly need light and truth from outside ourselves in order truly to evaluate all psychological theories.

For these reasons we now attempt a broad but radical critique in the light of biblical teaching. The aim will be to open up some channels between this whole area of Depth Psychology and the cleansing, living water of God's Word: channels through which, hopefully, the rain can reach the roots.

CHAPTER 4

REGENERATION

"You must be born again" John 3: 7.

Born again. Favourite buzzword among hot-gospelling fundamentalist freaks? Jokey put-down describing a quaint brand of yesterday evangelical Christian? New Age code-word for a person's rejuvenated inner divinity? Quasi-poetic cliché for any kind of sentimental/romantic turn-on ("Woman, give me your softness: with you I am born again" sang Johnny Matthis some years back). Catch-phrase introducing any new image projected by a person, product, corporation, or political party (new Labour equals born again Labour)?

Great pity about the trivialisations. Originating, of course, with the Founder of Christianity, the expression contains a world of hope — especially against the gloomy background of Depth Psychology. It signifies, not a simplistic psychological panacea, but certainly a new inner centre of healing and wholeness; in fact, new life, stemming from a new relation-ship with God. "If anyone is in Christ, he is a new creation: the old has gone, the new has come!" (*2 Corinthians 5:17*).

"You must be born again". Christ's statement is all-inclusive and emphatic. Even Nicodemus is included. This scholarly and pious religious teacher, respected member of the Sanhedrin, may well have anticipated prominence in the coming Kingdom of God, which he genuinely longed to see. But Jesus cut short his compliments with their "touch of complacency." As the poet Blake put it:

> When the rich learnèd Pharisee
> came to consult him secretly
> upon his heart with iron pen
> He wrote, Ye must be born again.

The same truth applies to us all, for "Ye" is plural. Why? What is it that makes spiritual new birth emphatically essential in order both to "see" and "enter", the Kingdom of God? Jesus' own answer to that question is summed up in one telling word "*flesh*": "flesh gives birth to flesh, but the Spirit gives birth to spirit. You should not be surprised at my saying, 'you must be born again'".

"Flesh" means, quite simply, the "earthly" part of human nature which we are all born with: it signifies human existence apart from God, motivated by desires and thoughts opposed to him (*Ephesians 2:3*). It is New Testament shorthand for the innate sorry mess that psychoanalysis reveals, and more — although it also, perhaps unexpectedly, modifies Freud's extreme negativism concerning the contents of the "Unconscious".

Usually paraphrased in translation as "the sinful nature" the word "flesh" (*sarx*) sums up the inherited moral and spiritual rottenness at the core of human nature which is the seed-bed of degrading and destructive behaviour (*Galatians 5:19-21*). The mindset controlled by the flesh, being inevitably hostile to God and repugnant to him, is therefore synonymous with spiritual death — that is, an existence cut off from God, the Source of life.

This does not mean that, governed by the flesh, we are "dead" to moral issues, (accountability persists) but that we are fatally disequipped to rid ourselves of accrued guilt and to live a life of pure moral goodness approved by God. Worse, ruled by "fleshly" self-centredness and self-gratification rather than love for God, we become increasingly hardened by sin which leads us deeper into rebellion against him and separation from him, compounding the "death" syndrome (*Ephesians 2:1-3*).

The theological formulation of this grim flesh-principle is encapsulated in the Doctrine of Original Sin. Most statements, having been put together in a previous age, inevitably come across as literarily pretty heavy. As an example, Article 9 of the Church of England states: "Original sin ... is the fault and corruption of the Nature of every man, that naturally is engendered of the offspring of Adam; whereby man is very far gone from original righteousness, and is of his own nature inclined to evil, so that the flesh lusteth always contrary to the spirit; and therefore in every person born into this world, it deserveth God's wrath and damnation".

Strong stuff! Interestingly, there are significant resonances here with the Freudian view of the Unconscious as the engine-room of virulent drives which produce pain and damage — a view which, arguably, is irrefutably supported by history, great literature, our own experience of life, and contemporary media headlines. As we have seen, Freud also posited a Death Instinct (*Thanatos*) thought of as a dark, destructive force directed inwards but mostly exteriorised aggressively onto others — a view which echoes aspects of biblical teaching about "death".

As an atheist, however, Freud could only interpret such personality malfunction in terms of an in-built psychological pathology; God is not in the frame. As far as it goes, there is truth in Freud's analysis: theologically, the flesh (the sinful nature) can certainly be described in pathological terms. Article 9 speaks of a "corruption" and an "infection" of the Nature of every man (*cf Isaiah 1:6; Jeremiah 30, 12-13*). Also, it is indeed endemic — i.e. "naturally engendered": original sin is "birth-sin" (*Psalm 51:5*). In fact, the Bible goes deeper, in a way which darkens Freud's negativism (as we shall see) but which also *lightens* it.

"Original Righteousness"

The Article refers to a beginning-time for the human race characterised by innocence, pure pleasure, and positive moral goodness — a state of affairs depicted in the Garden of Eden before the Fall. Adam and Eve, as perfect human beings in unclouded fellowship with God would both have demonstrated complete physical and moral excellence.

And the relationship between them was also without any imperfection: they enjoyed mutual sexual delight, complementary companionship, and effective cooperation in managing the created order. How can this perfection be expressed in terms of the physical and psychological constitution of human beings?

The key is the "Image of God". This is never defined in Scripture, but its meaning may be inferred. Clearly, the expression implies similarity, correspondence. God's nature is incomparable; his glory is beyond the power of words to describe. Nevertheless, human beings, as the unique crown of God's creation, do have very special worth, and even a "glory" which partially reflects his own (*Psalm 8:4-6*). They bear his image. In what ways?

Commenting on *Genesis 1:26-27* Alec Motyer writes "We can feel the 'scandal' of the idea the words convey by translating 'Let us make man in our form and shape' as 'Let us make a "look-a-like"'.... There is a visible 'form' which is specially and exactly appropriate to the invisible glory of God. In this 'form' man was created. The physical is as much 'the image of God' as are those aspects of human nature which (with our

'Greek' background) we might more readily think of as our 'higher nature'" (*Look To The Rock — Alec Motyer*).

But obviously the aspects of our 'higher nature', our distinctive human attributes, do also reflect the image of God. Just as God is presented to us in Scripture as speaking, feeling, acting and re-acting in accordance with his own nature, so we also relate to him and to each other in these ways, reflecting our humanness. The *Imago Dei* prompts the *Imitatio Dei*.

At this point it is important to dissociate biblical psychology from a further aspect of the Greek-derived model. The latter speaks of human faculties as separate entities e.g. intellect, emotions, will, conscience. "Faculty Psychology" is rooted in this concept (though originally it was also associated with phrenology, which supposed that an individual's various faculties were related to the size of bumps seen or felt in the skull!).

Clearly, the "faculties" are useful concepts, and they have entered common speech: for example, we talk about thinking, feeling, determining, as functions of the "head", and "heart" and "will" respectively. But these categorisations are not always accurate or helpful. What, precisely, is conveyed by the statement "I knew in my heart what I had to do"? What faculty is engaged in the deep appreciation of beautiful, moving art (a symphony, a poem, a picture, a novel, a drama)? Is it the intellect that is stimulated, the emotions moved, the will challenged, the memory stirred, the conscience pricked (or cleansed)? Is it possible, or desirable to separate out these strands?

Psychological "departmentalisation" finds little support in Scripture. True, words like mind, heart, will and conscience do occur, but they are often used interchangeably and they are not perceived as isolated entities. By the "mind", for example, is meant *the whole person thinking* i.e. not some separate part of our make-up which specialises in mental processes. The biblical word which is much larger than "mind" and which incorporates all other personality-functions is "heart".

C Ryder Smith suggests that: "The First great Commandment probably means 'Thou shalt love the Lord thy God with all thy heart — *that is*, with all thy soul and with all thy mind and with all thy strength' (e.g. *Mark 12:30 and 33*)." This interpretation is supported by the fact that in the Old Testament "heart" is used for intellectual activities (204 times), in addition to emotional states of consciousness (166 times), and volition or purpose (195 times); and in the New Testament it is the seat of the intellect (e.g. *Mark 2:6 and 8*); of feeling (e.g. *Luke 24:32*) and of the will (e.g. *Mark 3:5*). "All this means that 'heart' comes the nearest of the New Testament terms to mean 'person'" — or, we could say, "soul" — *psyche* — (the essence of personhood).

Throughout the Bible a human being is not depicted as a conglomerate of psychological functions but simply as an "embodied soul" and an "ensouled body". Theologians use the expression "dualist" to describe this view of human beings. Clearly, this corrects not only the Greek-derived concepts of Faculty Psychology but other models including Depth Psychology's *id, ego, and super-ego*. While it is possible to adduce resonances with these Freudian terms from Holy Scripture, in fact an analytical approach such as this is absent.

As body-soul creations bearing the image of God we were made for relationship with our Creator and with other human beings in order to fulfil a *purpose*. "The real point (of the 'Image of God') lies in the purpose for which the image is given to man". Biblical theologians emphasise that this purpose has its focus in a governmental role: human beings are to employ all their attributes in representing God's presence, authority and dominion in the world. This relates both to the world of nature and to human society. They are to be his vice-regents, maintaining Order in the total creation.

And that's how it was before things went horribly wrong. The total situation at first in the Garden of Eden was proto-typical for the human race and the whole of creation as the Creator intended it to be. In other words, "original sin" does not refer to the original constitution of human nature, which in its beautiful perfection mirrored God's likeness in human form and human relationships. I have been at pains to underline this important truth because it is easily overlooked. It can happen that Christians with a grim orthodoxy about the ghastliness of human sinfulness can bypass the wonder of humanity's Original Righteousness, *which is not completely lost.*

Common Grace (page 35) ensures that the outworking of sin's corruption is restrained, and goodness furthered. Human beings, notwithstanding their fallenness, may act with justice, kindness and decency, engage in the beneficial advancement of science and the promoting of civil order, become instruments of healing, and produce works of brilliance and beauty. True, even the good done is inevitably defective and will have been stimulated by mixed motives, and may even discount God. Nevertheless, ironically, the good works which truly benefit human society are, literally, godsends. Moreover, they are a consequence of the atone-ment: "many blessings flow to mankind at large from the death of Christ, collaterally and incidentally, in consequence of the relation in which men, viewed collectively, stand to each other" (quoted in *Systematic Theology — L Berkhof).* It follows that the good which men and women do can deserve the sincere approbation and gratitude of others and, at least to some extent, be pleasing to God. Arguably, this is particularly true of God's "sourcing" of, and delight in, artistic expression:

> Yes, we know your heart rejoices
>> In each work divine;
> Using minds and hands and voices
>> In your great design;
> Craftsmen's art and music's measure
>> For your pleasure all combine.

Thus the biblical view of human nature, expressed in psychological/moral terms, is "both-and": it is both "determined" and "free"; both "disequipped" and "able"; sinfully self-centred yet capable of altruism and self-sacrificing heroism; spawning ugliness which degrades but also creating beauty which elevates; corrupt, yet retaining vestiges of the image of God. On the one hand, as J I Packer puts it, "no-one is as bad as he or she might be", while on the other "no action of ours is as good as it should be". Figuratively, the Unconscious contains seeds both of evil and of good. It is, of course, the culpable infection of the latter by the former which puts all human beings in the wrong with God; and to the guilt and defilement of that evil and its hideous strength we must shortly turn.

However, it is appropriate first, within the context of the present chapter, to register this doctrine of Original Righteousness, and the reality of the image of God in us which, to a degree, we retain, as a corrective to Freud's reductionism. One biographer (Frank Sulloway) has entitled his book *Freud, Biologist of the Mind*. Interpretation of human behaviour in terms of biology (and physics) must inevitably detract from human ideals and achievements. For example, the creative imagination which produces works of art appears to be reduced by Freud to a kind of escapist fantasising which is, actually, a mark of immaturity i.e.: an inability to come to terms intellectually with reality and enjoy the world as it really is. In a paper "Creative Writers and Day-Dreaming" he wrote: "we may lay it down that a happy person never fantasises, only an unsatisfied one. The motive forces of fantasies are unsatisfied wishes, and every single fantasy is the fulfilment of a wish, a correction of an unsatisfactory reality" (quoted in *Solitude — Anthony Storr.*) A mature person would not need to take refuge in imagination nor find pleasure in the artistic products of imagination but should adapt to reality with rational thought.

Such cynical principles of psychological determinism applied to human inspiration and creativity are even applied to philosophies, which Freud dismissed as "intellectual forms of fantasy life". But surely this stance undermines any search for truth and wisdom, and makes impossible any discussion of meaning and values — even in relation to psychotherapy. Views dismissive of such concerns as aspects of "fantasy life" must, on the same premise, be themselves dismissed in the same way — for they, too, are merely the product of interacting psychic energies, intellectual fantasising. Clearly, this position is a non-starter.

In a logical extension of his position, Freud often expressed the view that cures for mental illness (which indicate, at root, dysfunction in the mind leading to psychic disequilibrium) may result, in time, from the application of the natural sciences. "The future may teach us to exercise a direct influence, by means of particular chemical substances, on the amounts of energy and their distribution in the mental apparatus ... but for the moment we have nothing better at our disposal than the technique of psychoanalysis." Some would say that there has been a partial fulfilment of that prophecy in the growing use of (and *over*-dependence upon?) psycho-pharmacology. And Freud's view is not unrelated to a current tendency to locate causes of mental and emotional illness in the brain-cells, or nervous system, or a person's DNA

Against the Freudian background of thought, belief in God as our Creator dignifies us because it reminds us that we are rational creatures and moral agents answerable to him for our responses to his laws — laws which are made known to us by the interacting testimony of his voice in our "hearts", and, primarily, written revelation.

Similarly, as stated earlier, our ability to communicate (verbalise) but also to love, to make moral choices, to create, to appreciate beauty, to establish and enhance Order, are, to the Theist, evidence of the image of God in us, however marred. Humanity, even with its signs of depravity, retains a dignity and potential which must never be discounted or despised.

No human being must be regarded as anything less than a child of God by creation, bearing his image. The Bible teaches us that every person, child or adult, is of infinite worth and possessed of unique possibilities, however disfigured by disease, hunger or neglect, or degraded by vice, or maimed by violence or abuse, or impeded by neuroses or psychoses.

All individuals bear God's image; they are loved by him: Christ himself came to share their humanity, died for the salvation of all who will believe in him, and lives to be their Redeemer and Friend. Though sinners, their "original righteousness" is not demolished.

But things did go disastrously wrong in Eden, and the continuing effects are all too obviously still with us.

The Tragic Riddle

Born but to die, and reas'ning but to err;
   Alike in ignorance, his reason such,
Whether he thinks too little or too much;
   Chaos of thought and passion, all confused;
Still by himself abused, or disabused;
   Created half to rise, and half to fall;
Great lord of all things, yet a prey to all;
   Sole judge of truth, in endless error hurled;
The glory, jest, and riddle of the world!

(Pope)

What did happen in Eden? The third chapter of Genesis narrates a tragic failure of belief, love, and obedience which breached the relationship between human beings and their Creator, caused the first pair each to become a "divided self" (crippled by inner dissociation), and skewed their relationship with each other. Thus "death" invaded life. Humanity, focused in Adam and Eve, is now cut off by guilt from the Source of true life; spiritual alienation with its baneful moral and physical consequences is exacerbated by a giving-way to self-gratification and self-justification.

Here, biblically, is the origin of the Freudian sex/aggression incubus, evidenced, initially, by those pathetic fig leaves and, a little later, by the blood of Abel.... The sick games of mutual shame and blame spread and led, with a terrible inevitability, to deceit and violence and accelerating moral chaos.

What started as a guilty pair hiding from God "among the trees of the garden" escalated into wholesale defiant wickedness (*Genesis 6:5*) in a now disordered natural world, itself the consequence of the sin of humankind, the crown of creation. Here, too, in the Fall and its aftermath, we can discern the beginning of the depression/anxiety syndrome rooted, as it is, in an awareness of past loss and fear of the future. Adler's inferiority complex and compensating "will-to-power" can also be seen to have its origin here. And Jung's "*shadow*" looms large....

As a person-focused statement of this sad situation there are no words in the Bible more striking than those used by king David in the confession and prayer following his sins of adultery and murder:

> "Have mercy on me, O God
> > According to your unfailing love;
> According to your great compassion
> > Blot out my transgressions.
> Wash away all my iniquity
> > And cleanse me from my sin.
> For I know my transgressions,
> > And my sin is always before me.
> Against you, you only, have I sinned
> > And done what is evil in your sight,
> So that you are proved right when you speak
> > And justified when you judge.
> Surely I was sinful at birth,
> > Sinful from the time my mother conceived me.
> Surely you desire truth in the inner parts;
> > You teach me wisdom in the inmost place."
>
> *(Psalm 51)*

Three words are used about sin. To quote A J Motyer again: *(Look to the Rock)* "in measure the whole Bible vocabulary of sin is here. '*Sin*' expresses the basic reality of mistake or failing. It is a 'failure to hit the target/a missing of the mark/a short-coming' whether in thought, word or deed. It is the specific thing that has to be confessed. The word translated 'iniquity' goes deeper. M Tate approves of John Goldingay's translation 'waywardness' with its suggestion of a fault of character lying behind the fault of conduct. This is agreeable to the root meaning of 'distortion', a twisting out of shape, misdirecting, perverting. The picture which these two words have begun to build up is completed by 'transgressions'. Its meaning is 'wilful rebellion' as of a subordinate against the known will of his overlord."

This sin-factor, states David, can be traced back to the very beginning of his life: "it is the child, indeed the embryo at the very split-second of conception that carries the infection of sin.... Sin is undeniably a (culpable) fact of life and experience, but it is also a fact of inheritance and of personality."

So the problem of fundamental personality disorder is more intractable and convoluted than even Freud taught. The Bible's picture is darker: real guilt permeates the pathology. David acknowledges before God the objective, as well as the subjective, aspects of wickedness: "Against you, you only, have I sinned and done what is evil in your sight" and "I was sinful at birth ... surely you desire truth in the inner parts...."

Only through confession, cleansing, reconciliation to God, and the indwelling Holy Spirit can he be restored to joy and moral consistency, and become a convincing witness to others of divine grace (verses 7-12).

Such radical biblical realism about the human condition suggests certain caveats in relation to psychoanalysis. First, delving into the depths of the Unconscious, under the tutelage of an analyst, will always prove to be an interminable exercise. It would be impossible to uncover and map all the past's entwined memories and early influences, mistakes and misdemeanours, and their continuing effect.

There is also a questionable value in bringing into conscious awareness those profane basic instincts which are also buried deep down. The extirpated contents of the "heart" will be found to include what they always have included since the Fall — evil thoughts and the seeds of "murder, adultery, sexual immorality, theft, false testimony, slander" (*Matthew 15:19*). Jesus' grim catalogue is echoed by Paul's description of "the sinful nature" and its acts (*Galatians 5:19-21*). Jeremiah had stated, centuries before: "The heart is deceitful above all things and beyond cure. Who can understand it?"

Peeling an onion usually produces tears; so does removing layers of the Unconscious — tears all the more discomfiting because completely unprofitable. The persistent probing of those darkly potent forces within serves only to foment them and entrap the mind; and an endless ransacking of the past can become a depressing downward spiral which may hit bottom in the form of a sullen, or bitter, hostility towards God — or aimed at significant human beings deemed to be blameworthy. Moreover, Jung's *"shadow"* is a reality and does indeed connect with the Evil which has infected the whole human race and which emanates from the devil: (*1 John 3:8; Hebrews 2:14-15*). The journey inward and downward can indeed be a perilous one: a descent too far?

It would be foolish to discount completely the value of psychoanalytical insights into the hidden origins of present distress, for many of these have biblical support. We have acknowledged that compassionate, skilled counselling can uncover, and help us to interpret, the deeply-buried reasons for debilitating emotions, and suggest more healthy attitudes. But many psychologists themselves are sounding caveats about "negative rumination": dwelling on past miserable memories "serves only to increase the pains they cause us", so backward looks should be brief lesson-learning glances rather than dominant pre-occupations. Martin Seligman at the University of Pennsylvania who, it is claimed, has been the world's leading researcher on depression over the past thirty years writes (in his popular book *Authentic Happiness*): "insufficient appreciation and savouring of the good events in your past, and *overemphasis* of the bad ones are the two culprits that undermine serenity, contentment and satisfaction."

That's all very well. But "positive thinking" is not always easy: sin is sin and guilt is guilt and both are grim realities. The root-trouble is that Depth Psychology has no lasting antidote for the alarming contents of its Pandora's Box. The Bible does. It is found in Jesus Christ himself and is made clear in his own words: "You must be born again".

Because of original sin our problems are, indeed, deeply-rooted. Nothing less than radical renewal will do. Jesus said, "You should not be surprised at my saying 'you must be born again'". Nor, therefore, should we be surprised that regeneration must be from outside ourselves, from above, of the Spirit: for we cannot "beget" ourselves anew: "flesh" can only give rise to "flesh" — fallen human nature cannot transform itself. But "the Spirit gives birth to spirit (a new, spiritual nature)".

In an early, seminal psychological approach to religious experience William James, the American Philosopher and Psychologist penned a well-known definition of this transforming spiritual experience from a psychological perspective: "To be converted, to be regenerated, to receive grace, to experience religion, to gain assurance, are so many phrases which denote the progress, gradual or sudden, by which a self hitherto divided and consciously wrong, inferior and unhappy, becomes unified and consciously right, superior and happy, in consequence of its firm hold upon religious realities".

Some ingredients of William James' definition fit Christianity but some points are questionable from a biblical point of view: the conflation of different spiritual experiences and of psychological effects is confusing.... In particular, it is time to be more theologically precise about "regeneration" and "new birth".

Strictly speaking, they are not synonymous. The latter is contingent upon the former. "Regeneration" describes the hidden work of the Holy Spirit instilling new spiritual life in the deepest recesses of personality — psychologically speaking, at the deepest level of the Unconscious. "New birth" speaks of the *signs* of this in conscious life — new understanding, new attitudes, new acts.

First consideration: how is regeneration effected? Christ himself stressed, as we have stated above, that we can never fully comprehend this because regeneration is indeed a work of the Holy Spirit which is secret and mysterious. He likens it to the wind, which cannot be directly perceived but is nevertheless known — by its effects. Regeneration is made manifest by new birth and its accompaniments.

However, the very metaphor of reproduction suggests an approach to understanding the *spiritual process* which is involved. Peter declares (*1 Peter 1:23*) "You have been born again, not of perishable seed, but of imperishable, through the living and enduring word of God ... the word that was preached to you". No analogy could be more radical — or startling. Just as, biologically, new life (birth) results from fertilisation, so new spiritual life from God is conceived in us by the fertilising power in the Word of God. Unlike biological life which, being derived from a "perishable" source (seed, or sperm) is subject to ultimate dissolution, the life of God in those who have been "born again" by the living and enduring seed of the Gospel (see verse 25) shares the same quality. The Word of God (the Gospel) not only bears the immortality of its author but this is communicated to the believer. James echoes this principle when he writes that God the Father "chose to give us birth through the word of truth" (*James 1:17-18*). And when he writes that this supreme gift is "from above" he may be echoing Christ's expression (*John 3:3 and 7*) which can be interpreted as "born from above" (i.e. communicated by the Holy Spirit) rather than "born again".

This teaching has important psychological/pastoral corollaries. First, the Holy Spirit touches and transforms deeper levels of the soul (the psyche) than any psychoanalysis can reach; in fact, the deepest level. When Jesus speaks (*John 7:37-39*) of the Spirit as "streams of living water flowing from within" the person who believes in him, the Greek phrase translated as "from within him" is "out of his womb". The word used here is usually considered by scholars to be a synonym of "heart", but arguably its translation as "womb" in several other places could indicate a graphic poetic metaphor for the *fons et origo*, the very spring, of personhood.

But secondly, though this seminal regeneration is a sovereign and secret work of the Holy Spirit in individuals, personal passivity, and non-involvement on the part of other people, is not implied. If God usually works by his Spirit and Word in *conjunction* (which Peter tells us is the case in regeneration) it follows that we may cooperate with the Spirit by being communicators of the Word. Thus the proclamation of the Gospel by a preacher becomes the means by which the Holy Spirit regenerates certain hearers. By the same token, the best psychotherapy and counselling will be consciously open to the Holy Spirit's power and influence, especially in the relevant sharing of Holy Scripture. The Word of life is the

Holy Spirit's agent in effecting regeneration; *and* in strengthening subsequently the results of new birth.

A healthy new-born baby immediately shows signs of being fully alive. Spiritual "new birth" is also signified by evident new life.

The first, conscious, results of regeneration are repentance and conversion, both the fruit of faith. The two chief words denoting them in the New Testament have significant psychological overtones, particularly *repentance*. Although the Greek word (*metanoia*) means, literally, a change of mind, the word "*nous*" cannot be limited to the intellect. Repentance involves a radical, *total* transformation of outlook, attitude, and moral direction, as well as of thought. Neither is this change without an emotional dimension; there is a "godly *sorrow*" which "brings repentance that leads to salvation and leaves no regret" i.e. it is an emotion which is a sign of the grace of God in operation, whereas "worldly sorrow" is merely remorse which is self-centred (*2 Corinthians 7:10-11*).

The twin word, *conversion* (Greek: *epistrepho*) means a turning, or returning, to God and Christ *from* sin, from the darkness of false religion, and from the rule of Satan (*Acts 14:15; 26; 18; 1 Thessalonians 1:9*). It is a decisive act of faith which, like repentance, involves the total personality as the whole life is set to move in a new direction which is in accordance with the revealed will of God, and empowered by the Holy Spirit.

Both repentance and conversion are signs of regeneration.

So what has happened to the "old nature"? Has it been completely replaced by the new? Has the "flesh" been eradicated? Christian Confessions of Faith, echoing the Bible's teaching, are realistic about a continuing presence of Original

Sin: though dealt a death blow, so to speak, by the new birth, it is not totally subdued. The Church of England's Article 9 states: "this infection of nature doth remain, yea even in them that are regenerated". In Freudian terms, the libido's destructive drives linked particularly to sex but also to aggression, for example, are not completely eradicated. Nor are other sinful motivations. In this life, regeneration is not *totally* effective in its outworking; the Christian lives with the reality of an interior civil war between a residual "old nature" and the new dominant (spiritual) nature.

This is not comfortable.

It also follows that the problems of right conduct due to inner moral, and intellectual, conflict, and undulating moods, will always plague believers. The fight against sin and Satan and the opposition of "the world" is endless this side of heaven. It would be pastorally irresponsible therefore, to imply that as a result of new birth Christians can anticipate a life of psychological equilibrium — or, spiritually speaking, day-to-day victory over sin, and unbroken peace. A life of satisfying self-fulfilment, free of inner dissonances, full of happy relationships unspoiled by disharmony, unclouded by the "*Shadow*", is not promised in Scripture. There is a sense in which repentance and conversion and other fruits of regeneration need to be continuously put into practice. So, we must not claim that the gateway of new birth leads to a rose-garden; it marks the beginning of the Pilgrim's Way.

But constant moral defeat is not inevitable along that way; neither are negative emotions or mental confusion. The indwelling Holy Spirit, now allied to the Christian's renewed human spirit, is a source of power, progressively producing practical holiness, emotional comfort, and clarity of thought, in accordance with God's revealed will. For this reason Paul exhorts us, as Christians, to "live by the Spirit" and "be led by the Spirit" so as not to "gratify the desires of the sinful nature". *This can be done.* Realism about Christianity as an arduous journey, a tough race, a testing fight, is good and necessary. But so is realism about the fact of the new birth — about new life strengthened by God's empowering presence within. This is not merely a doctrine; it is *experiential* truth.

Not in a euphoric sense: when Paul wrote "I can do everything through him who gives me strength" he was writing from the heart, *from prison*, recalling various ups and downs in his circumstances, which had included going hungry and thirsty, being clothed in rags, being brutally treated, and homeless, working hard to support himself, yet cursed, persecuted, slandered, and treated as scum (*1 Corinthians 4:11f*).

So no Christian can say "My circumstances are too tough. I haven't got it in me to live out the Christian life: the old nature with its fears and faults is too strong for me...." Believers *have* "got it in them": "if the Spirit of God lives in you ... the spirit of him who raised Jesus from the dead...." then you "are controlled not by the old sinful nature but by the Spirit." Things are different now — prove it!

God forbid, then, that we grieve or quench or resist the Holy Spirit by discounting, or disbelieving, or disobeying him. Nor should we leave everything to him in passive hopefulness. He who is the Agent of the new birth is also the strength of the new life. He it is who gives clarity of thought, comfort, and energy; who imparts spiritual gifts galore for the building up of his Church, and who releases in us his beautiful fruit: "love, joy, peace, patience, kindness, goodness, faithfulness, gentleness and self control". All to be actualised.

These ministries of the Holy Spirit clearly have very practical relevance to psychological problems which may have been obstacles to true well-being and which perhaps continue to weigh us down. New birth does not necessarily mean that such problems disappear, but it does mean that they can become, instead of obstacles, growth points, leading to gradual but steady personality-transformation to the glory of God.

Past failures can become stepping stones to peace of mind and greater spiritual maturity — usually because we re-learn our need of humble, trustful dependence upon God, and renewed gratitude for his grace.

The new birth has particular relevance to those dark, basic drives which, according to Freud, have their focus in sex and aggression....

The key factor for both areas is *love* — which is the focal centre of the born-again life. Charles Wesley, in a hymn celebrating the new nature which God gives, sums it all up in the last verse

> Thy nature, gracious Lord, impart,
>   Come quickly from above,
> Write Thy new name upon my heart,
>   Thy new, best name of love.

This resonates with *1 John 4:7* "Dear friends, let us love one another, for love comes from God. Everyone who loves has *been born of God* and knows God".

Love and Sex

Freud has little to say about love, but much to say about sex. In his view, *libido* is *the* fundamental driving force, deriving its energy from the *id*, and its aim is sensual gratification, compensating for feelings of emotional deprivation persisting from infancy, and socially-inhibited desire. It is as if the basic instinct of self-love is projected onto another person by sexual means. Such a narcissistic acting-out of libidinous desire can perhaps be accompanied by longings for intimacy, but these can hardly be labelled "love" — and can easily lead to the demeaning treatment of the other as a sex-object.

In contrast to this cynical, "biologised" view, the Bible teaches that men and women were created to be, within a marriage-covenant of love, a healing source of sensual delight to each other, and of sustaining, comforting companionship as well as partners in procreation.

The "love" which is restored by regeneration translates a Greek word *agape* which, in the New Testament, is invested with a much richer, deeper meaning than it had in secular use. In essence, *agape* is grounded in the love of God, flows from it, and reflects it (*John 13:34; 1 John 4:21*).

The relevance to sexual intimacy within marriage is this: new birth means that *agape-love* can permeate and enhance the spontaneity of sexual love (*eros*). The latter, when subsumed under the former, and kept firmly within the bounds of God's law, is reaffirmed as a beautiful, fulfilling part of our humanness — as evidenced by the sublime celebration of romantic, erotic love found in the Song of Solomon. Thus God's original intentions for marriage, recorded in the second chapter of Genesis (*verses 21-25*), are reinforced. A man and woman within a covenanted union, equal before God in their different sexuality but having complementary roles in the relationship, can mutually enjoy to the full the delights of self-giving, sexually expressed love as part of their companionship.

What about the unmarried? The principle of *agape-love* is no less relevant to wholesome cross-gender friendships.

"*Vive la difference*" is a phrase which does not necessarily carry a sexually suggestive innuendo. The enjoyable *frisson* of friendships and working relationships between men and women can be enriched by the respect, appreciation and kindness which are aspects of *agape*.

From a Christian point of view, the erosion within contemporary society of such honourable, pure sexual standards in relationships between men and women, the coarsening and cheapening of sexuality issues and the rationalizing of deviant sexual behaviour can be, must be, assessed in the light of the biblical guidelines about human love. Biblically, *agape* leads to individual fulfilment and social harmony. *Agape* and Order (conformity to God's plan for the human race) go together. "Love is the fulfilment of the law" (*Romans 13:10*): John Stott comments "love and law need each other. Love needs law for its direction whilst law needs love for its inspiration" (*The Message of Romans*). These principles are highly appropriate to relationships between the sexes, to all matters related to sexual conduct, and spell out regenerate living.

Love and Aggression

Agape can also undergird and pervade *philia* (the New Testament Greek word for friendship-love) which can be thought of as contrasting with aggression.

Freudian psychologists interpret aggression as a displacement phenomenon: negative emotions associated with anger are directed towards another person instead of being inwardly-directed. Adlerians see it (in a milder form) as a manifestation of the will-to-power — other people, usually perceived as threateningly superior, are dominated or manipulated by the aggressor (or, rather, "manipulator") in order to appear as top dog.

Biblically, the antidote to aggression, whatever form it takes (verbal put-downs or abuse, emotional pressure, physical violence) is not merely theoretical but involves the actual expression of the opposite spirit: love. In *1 Peter 1:22-*

24 the apostle appeals to his readers to be rid of aggressive attitudes and instead, having "sincere love for your brothers, love one another deeply, from the heart" in obedience to the truth. How is that possible? Because of regeneration: "you have been born again".

The new birth is indeed a radical, experiential reality: Christians do have it in them to love "deeply, from the heart" — perhaps we may say, from the Unconscious: love springing from that deep well of living water, and flowing out to others (*John 7:37*).

This is all very well, but the truth needs to be actualised, expressed, put into practice. Regeneration must be visibly evidenced. The New Testament is very down-to-earth about love being shown by a changed attitude and by kind actions — especially towards those who previously were the subject of our aggressiveness in thought, word or deed. For example: "you must rid yourselves of all such things as these: anger, rage, malice, slander and filthy language from your lips.... Therefore, as God's chosen people, holy and dearly loved, clothe yourselves with compassion, kindness, humility, gentleness and patience.... And over all these virtues put on love, which binds them all together in perfect unity" (*Colossians 3:8-14).*

Not that all "aggression" is wrong. Its dangers, for the Christian, are obvious. Paul writes "in your anger do not sin: do not let the sun go down while you are still angry, and do not give the devil a foothold" (*Ephesians 4:26-27*). His words, addressed to born again believers, emphasise the duty, and therefore the ability, to control aggressive attitudes. This is because they can be contaminated by ingredients inappropriate in a Christian (e.g. injured pride, a vengeful spirit). There is a possibility, too, that anger which is nursed will simmer and boil over in rage; the devil can exploit and ferment anger causing it to hurt others. A further caveat is mentioned three verses later (*verse 30*): a believer must avoid grieving God's indwelling Holy Spirit, his seal of ownership and guarantee of redemption. Therefore Christians should indeed "get rid of all bitterness, rage and anger, brawling and slander, along with every form of malice"; instead, they should "be kind and compassionate to one another forgiving each other just as in Christ God forgave you".

However, Paul's words also teach us that members of this new community of love, the family of God, may well feel and express an anger which is entirely appropriate, and honouring to God. The expression "in your anger do not sin" clearly implies that a righteous anger is possible, indeed desirable. In one sense, anger is the reverse side of love: David wrote that "those who love the Lord, hate evil" (*Psalm 97:10*). Jesus, more than once, expressed anger — for example, against the greed-driven defiling of the temple and the prohibitive exploitation of would-be worshippers (*Mark 11:15-17*); against those who prevent little children from being brought to him (*Mark 10, 13 − 16*); and against anyone who may spiritually harm vulnerable persons by causing them to sin: it would be preferable for that person, he said, to be thrown into the sea with a millstone tied round his neck (*Luke 17:1 − 13*).

Clearly, in each case, his anger was an expression of outraged love — for his Father's house and honour, for children, for the weak and vulnerable in society. Surely, we may extrapolate this principle of righteous anger, and question whether a professing Christian is truly born again if he or she is not angered by the evil and wickedness which defies God and, for example, results in lives destroyed by drugs, or the abuse of children. But so much else that is wrong in society should be aggressively denounced and opposed. And if justice is seen as the social expression of neighbour love, then anger at injustice, which negates this, is, surely, appropriate. As John Stott comments: "there is a great need in the contemporary world for more Christian anger.... In the face of blatant evil we should be indignant not tolerant, angry not apathetic. If God hates sin, his people should hate it too. If evil arouses his anger, it should arouse ours also...." *(The Message of Ephesians)*.

How can regeneration, love, and aggression, combine? "Be slow to become angry, for *man's* anger does not bring about the righteous life that God desires, therefore, get rid of all moral filth and the evil that is so prevalent, and humbly accept the word planted in you which can save you" *(James 1:19-21)*. Motivated and guided by that Word, and by the love of God poured into our hearts by the Holy Spirit, a born again child of God is equipped, if needs be, to feel and express, not "man's anger" but a righteous anger which reflects the character of God and is derived from him. This is far removed from the darkly aggressive drives erupting from the Freudian Unconscious....

Regeneration, Depression and Anxiety

Christians are not immune to either depression or anxiety. Far from it. So, does regeneration have any real significance? What help is it to be born again when assailed by either or both of these afflictions? What about the apparent credibility gap between doctrine and experience?

That gap *can* be bridged — by the Holy Spirit applying Holy Scripture to our hearts. The key of divine "Promise" can release us from the dungeon in Doubting Castle and the frightening mien of Giant Despair; and the sword of the Spirit in our hand can drive off Apollyon. "Though I have fallen, I will rise. Though I sit in darkness, the Lord will be my light" *(Micah 7: 8)*.

In psychological terms, this will not necessarily mean complete cure, total release from mental pain, or permanent emotional healing; our problems, especially those of psychological origin, are not always eradicated. But many such problems may well be alleviated by a thought-through and experiential appropriating, of what it actually means to be born again. By the same token emotional distress *may* be made worse by a woeful ignorance, or wilful discounting, of regeneration — as a doctrine, yes, but also as an experience communicated by the Holy Spirit.

Self-absorbed isolationism, which tends to shut out God and close off his life within us, will have negative emotional repercussions. There is a thin line between depression as a dreadful affliction deserving deep sympathy and skilled attention, and depression resulting from what, in past ages, was called *accidie* — that is, sloth, torpor, apathy.

Sometimes moody dejection and anxious fear are brought on by self-pity. A Cognitive Therapist may point out that we need to re-order reality-distorting thought-processes (*cf Romans 12:2*).

Regeneration counters the downward drag of self-centred inertia: it secures a renewed personality-centre which is now energised by the Holy Spirit. And by God's grace we can, so to speak, *cooperate* with our regenerate self. As Spurgeon reminded us (and many others) the depressed Christian will not find this easy: the understanding companionship of a fellow Christian, perhaps a counsellor, will be needed. Practical strategies for combating the power of anxiety and/or depression can be identified and, with God-given courage, put into practice.

No, this may not always work out; sometimes it's a matter of holding on — trusting, believing.... But the time will come, in God's providence, when the mind is able to reaffirm the *truth* that "I am a child of God by new birth, dear to him, protected by him". And in confirmation of this the Holy Spirit will again release in us the cry, "Abba, Father" (*Romans 8:15-17; Galatians 4:6-7*). God's peace and comfort *will* strengthen us.

Downcast? — Put Your Hope in God

When depressed, these experienced truths flowing from regeneration can kindle hope, for they have their focus in Christ and his risen life. Remember Peter. He knew abject depression. When the cock-crow sounded, shrill and mocking, and the Lord turned and looked straight at him, Peter went outside and wept bitterly. Mingled with his tears was, surely, an emotion deeper than remorse: despair. Then, at Calvary, he saw the Light of the world extinguished. Truth on the scaffold. With the other disciples he was overwhelmed by a terrible futurelessness; worse: the rule of evil seemed irresistible and irreversible. All hope seemed lost; in addition, personal guilt weighed them down. This was the deepest pit of depression.

Then came Easter morning. Peter met the risen Christ. And he was to be tenderly but firmly restored and re-commissioned by the Lord himself. Here are Peter's words of humble, exultant gratitude "Praise be to the God and Father of our Lord Jesus Christ! In his great mercy he has given us *new birth* into a living hope through the resurrection of Jesus Christ from the dead, and into an inheritance that can never perish, spoil or fade — kept in heaven for you, who through faith are shielded by God's power until the coming of the salvation that is ready to be revealed in the last time" (*1 Peter 1:3-5*).

Clearly no experience of depression in our lives could be so momentously traumatic as was Peter's. But the symptoms are replicated, at a lower level: despondency, desolation associated with feelings of irretrievable loss, and failure, which may (or may not) be linked to a guilty conscience, to remorse and to regret.

And we, like Peter, can be "be born again into a living hope" by an encounter with the risen Christ. This will not be a once-for-all event: for Peter, this was obviously a life-transforming personal meeting having continuing significance — it is a *living* hope (i.e. an undying hope) which displaced his despair, because it is linked to the living Christ, who "cannot die again". This continuing personal *renaissance* is necessary because depressing circumstances also continue. Peter is realistic about this (*1 Peter 1:6f*).

When this transforming spiritual experience becomes ours through obedience to the truth of the Gospel, it does not mean that depression will necessarily be completely dissolved but it does mean that it is very strongly countered by the expulsive power within of Christ's resurrection. And as he also keeps company with us day-by-day, we will be reminded that he, too, endured (in the Garden of Gethsemane) a "depression" far, far more crushing than anything we could ever know. But triumphed. And by his atoning death, and resurrection, he has robbed sin and Satan of their malign power. Now, having been tempted in every way, just as we are (yet without sin) he is able with complete sympathy to help us through our weaknesses (*Hebrews 4:15; 2:18*).

It would be facile to claim that reminders of revealed truth concerning a grace-given new nature will dispense with any discerned need for complementary, psychologically-informed counselling, and/or medication, to treat depression. But if and when we are depressed, it is our wisdom, almost certainly with the sensitive help of a compassionate Christian friend, to "tap in" to these spiritual realities by faith and prayer — and then, by God's grace, to live them out. Or, until we *can* live them out, allow ourselves to be sustained by them, to be calm and still in the presence of the risen Lord, believing that the heaviness, the suffering, is *"for a while"*: it *will* be lifted. Christ *will* "easter in us" (*Romans 8:9-11; Colossians 3:1*). And he will beckon us forward, in his company, into the future.

> "Lo! Jesus meets us, risen from the tomb;
> Lovingly he greets us, scatters fear and gloom".

Do Not Worry...

No-one understood more clearly and compassionately than Jesus the human proneness to anxiety, the grip it can have upon the heart, and the corrosive effect of it upon faith in God.

His repeated exhortations to trust and not be afraid reveal sensitive insight; but they are also firm instructions: his command "be not anxious" is a present-imperative. A significant clue to the damaging dynamics of anxiety lies in the word itself. The verb "to be anxious" in the Greek of the New Testament (*merimnao*) means to have a *distracted mind*. Jesus is putting his finger on a mental state which is torn in two, divided. In the Christian, "anxiety" describes a polarised tension between faith and fear, belief and doubt, trust and worry. David the Psalmist identifies the solution to this distressing discord when he prays (*Psalm 86:11*) "Teach me your way, O Lord, and I will walk in your truth: *give me an undivided heart,* that I may fear your name".

Regeneration provides for the answer to David's prayer: a mind and heart renewed, and centred on God. Jesus therefore enjoins us to exhibit this new nature by trusting God, and obeying him single-mindedly. Much anxiety is dispelled when we put first things first.

A primary allegiance to God will have an expulsive effect upon previous, demeaning, servitudes. When the old drivenness, derived from the unregenerate Unconscious is dethroned by the incoming Holy Spirit, he also washes us clean and renews us and motivates us to transform our conduct (*Titus 3:1- 8*). God helps us to "work out" what he is "working in" (*Philippians 2:12-13*).

In particular he helps us to discern and maintain the right priorities in life. Spiritual treasure accessed by prayer puts into true perspective the temporal acquisitions we get obsessed about, and which are likely to become moth-eaten and rusty anyway.

Materialism makes for perpetual spiritual insecurity. Self-gain and God are rival loyalties; the attempts to keep in with both reveals a divided mind, which is the essence of anxiety. A "single eye" (or "sound eye") is a metaphor for a life totally devoted to the service of God, thus seeing things true; it will lead to the whole person being spiritually and morally illuminated.

With typical down-to-earth bluntness, James raises the matter of our sincerity as Christians in this matter, and underscores the choices before us. To give way to double mindedness, he says, is pretty disastrous: a person who does so will have a hesitant prayer-life, miss out on God's generous gifts — especially that of wisdom — be plagued by inner turmoil, and show instability in outward life (*James 1:5-8*). Anxiety worse confounded!

But God honours those who honour him. He is ever ready to help us and lead us forward; when we sincerely approach him he will be there for us, holding nothing against us. The gifts he showers upon us are "good" and "perfect" — lovely, pleasant, beneficial and completely appropriate to our needs.

This is so because he is our Father whose love shines upon us with unvarying faithfulness (*James 1:17*).

Jesus himself asserts the same encouraging and reassuring truth. Seeking first God's kingdom and his righteousness is a consequence of new birth which signifies not only a new nature, but also a new status. To be born again is to become a child of God, to begin a new intimate relationship with him, to know him as Father. And because we are sons (and daughters) God sent the Spirit of his Son into our hearts, the Spirit who calls out "Abba, Father" (*Galatians 4:6*). This being the case, anxiety in a child of God is utterly inappropriate — and unnecessary and useless. Jesus says "your heavenly Father knows" your needs … and he will meet your needs. We are not to worry over present problems nor about possible troubles ahead — God our Father knows about those too. We are to live a day at a time, trusting him fully and single-mindedly (*Matthew 6:25-34*).

That's not always easy; but a little earlier, Jesus has talked about the wonderful provision of prayer, especially in the secret, personal place of intimate communion with God our Father "who knows what we need before we ask him". The Lord's prayer follows: essentially a prayer for God's children by regeneration for it is they alone who can call him "Father".

Paul also mentions prayer as the chief practical antidote to anxiety, and then reminds us of the promised peace which follows in its wake, communicated by God (*Philippians 4:6-7*). "Do not be anxious about anything, but in everything, by prayer and petition, with thanksgiving, present your requests to God. And the peace of God, which transcends all understanding, will guard your hearts and your minds in Christ Jesus".

Here are relevant words from St Francis de Sales, a godly man who combined spiritual and psychological insight: "Do not look forward to the changes and chances of this life in fear: rather look to them with full hope that as they arise, God Whose you are, will deliver you out of them. He has kept you hitherto, do you but hold fast to His dear hand, and He will lead you safely through all things, and when you cannot stand, He will bear you in His arms. What need you fear, my child, remembering that you are God's and that He has said 'All things work together for good to those that love Him'.

Do not look forward to what may happen tomorrow. The same everlasting Father who cares for you today will take care of you tomorrow and every day. Either he will shield you from suffering: or he will give you unfailing strength to bear it. Be at peace then, put aside all anxious thoughts and imaginations, and say continually, 'The Lord is my strength and my shield: my heart hath trusted in him and I am helped'. He is not only with me but in me and I in him. What can a child fear, surrounded by such a Father's arms?"

"*Our Father....*" All the first-person pronouns of the prayer are plural. New birth is a personal experience, but though born again as individuals we are immediately incorporated into the family of God. This experience fulfils what is, arguably, the deepest need and longing in the human heart: to belong. In a general sense we belong together by creation: a proverb familiar to Africans expresses their belief that community is the deepest truth about us — "I am because we are, and since we are, therefore I am".

"Lateral" psychology is rooted in similar convictions. The Christian religion is about being community in the truest, fullest sense....

CHAPTER 5

LATERAL PSYCHOLOGY

"I relate, therefore I am" Desmond Tutu.

As we move through the first decades and beyond of a new millennium the soil in which our lives are rooted is being defined as post modernist.

Post modernist? Professor Ernest Gellner (Professor of Social Anthropology at Cambridge) has written "post modernism is a contemporary movement. It is strong and fashionable. Over and above this, it is not clear what the devil it is." Is it possible to get a handle on it?

How about this as a succinct definition: "incredulity toward metanarratives"! *(J-F Lyotard).* Or, in other words, "there are no big stories anymore to give coherent meaning to anything". This leads (more simply put) to three dominant notions: relativism, secularism, and individualism (among other, less easily identifiable, factors).

These three terms should not be dismissed as pretentious buzz-words. They are in the air we breathe and can turn us into spiritual asthmatics. They are not merely ideological flavours of the month: they are poisons which can well-nigh destroy our religious taste buds. As trendy traits, they can both blind us to the glory of God and produce a deafness which cannot hear his truth, let alone respond to it. They can become obstructions between his rain and our roots.

Relativism, by definition, rules out any concept of objective truth and absolute moral standards. All current philosophies and ethical value-systems are equally valid. Moreover, they are essentially *secular*. Moral values and belief-systems, it is said, are derived from and reflect the society, the time, which is their context. Truth and morality are culturally determined and are therefore continually shifting. Within this populist "flow" *individualism* apparently flourishes, for every person feels encouraged to believe what they want to believe and to do what they want to do. Some may consider individualism to be an illusion: relativism and secularism surely rule out individualistic attitudes, for unwittingly we are all conditioned by prevailing world-views.

Referring to Jacques Derrida's and other post modernists' deconstruction of individual identity, N P Ricci writes "in current theory, identity — individuality, subject hood — is held to be a construct ... constituted by a web of forces of which consciousness is the effect rather than the point of origin." Does this imply that our sense of being distinct individuals is an illusion? That we are self-deluded in thinking that we are self-determining? Yes and no. On the one hand each of us is a part of the populace which shapes the very thoughts we have by the language society uses: we are products, *constructs*, of our culture.

On the other hand, the current relativistic, secular populism in fact *inculcates* hyper-individualism: it is part of "the flow" — its appeal is rooted in the insistence upon personal rights and uninhibited personal expression, and woe betide any authority which, in the name of religion or morality, rebuts those shibboleths. Despite appearances to the contrary, then, populism and hyper-individualism are not mutually exclusive.

Thus post modernism means that each society in becoming its own *milieu* becomes characterised, essentially, by openness — an openness to every individual's, or every group's, view and attitude. The only sin which cannot be tolerated is intolerance. This is, literally, a nonsense: the view that intolerance is intolerable is, logically, itself intolerable.

If openness means a willingness to assess all view points, it is clearly desirable. But if the implication is that nothing can be criticised, this much-vaunted openness becomes a stultifying closedness. "Everything is relative" becomes the final, unquestionable absolute. There is no way forward. Any person seeking a purpose and fulfilment ends up in a dreadful cul-de-sac of confusion.

If there are no moral rights or wrongs; if there is nothing that is, objectively, either true or false; if no absolute standards of honesty, purity, love or unselfishness exist — then life can have no meaning. In a society which becomes morally nihilistic, how do we bring up our children? How can we teach them what is just, what is beautiful, what is honourable, what is *true*, if such words are either contentless or have a thousand different meanings which are all valid? We are in danger of drowning in this sea of secular relativism.

In answer to the poignant question "What kind of 'self' are we faced with in post-modernity", Francis Bridger suggests four sad characteristics:

1. "It is highly *unstable*.... The instability of the post modern self has to do with its lack of assured identity and fixedness.... The self is left without hope or anchor. If there is no such thing as truth ... then the self can be sure of nothing."

2. "It is *lost*. The post modern self is directionless. It does not know what its goal should be, for reason and religion as final authorities have been removed from the scene.... The only thing it can do is carry on with purposes imposed upon it by the contingencies of survival or the force of others."

3. "It is *manipulable*. The denial of even the possibility of truth-claims results in the collapse of persuasion by

reasonable argument and leaves the individual subject merely to persuasion by pressure or even violence.. Terrorism is the ultimate outcome of post modernity".

4.   "It is *alone*. The breakdown of faith in shared values leaves individuals exposed and vulnerable. The loneliness of the post modern self is truly despairing." So many homeless minds *(Counselling In Context — David Atkinson and Francis Bridger)*.

Unstable, lost, manipulable, alone.... As Francis Schaeffer (influential evangelical writer of mid 20th century, founder of L'Abri Fellowship) might have said, anyone who can read the above analysis without feeling close to tears, is dead. For described in those words are multitudes of ordinary people "harassed and helpless like sheep without a shepherd". Such crowds evoked from Jesus Christ a deep, visceral pity and compassion which led him to move among them teaching truth, proclaiming good news of a different kingdom, and healing them.... If his Spirit is in us we will be motivated to emulate him and seek to be agents of his kingdom of light and love.

The soil itself, as well as the roots, desperately needs rain.

Only Connect....

Francis Bridger's analysis also exposes the bankruptcy of Freudianism to meet human need in a post modern society.

For, ironically, Freud's excessive individualism, an inevitable element of psychoanalysis, can have the effect of diminishing individuals. By treating persons as enclosed "psychological mechanisms" which function according to "scientific" laws akin to those of biology and physics, their humanness is reduced.

If the human psyche is an "apparatus" with three main interacting, and conflicting, energy systems (*id, ego and super-ego*) then such concepts as intrinsic dignity and moral responsibility must be deconstructed. With the best will in the world it is difficult to see how Freudianism can surmount this chilling reductionist view of personality, and its dehumanising tendency.

Notwithstanding a regard among post-Freudians for the importance of inter-personal relationships, the stated aim of psychoanalysis remains, primarily, to uncover *inner* causes of debilitating emotional disease, and to restore psychic equilibrium: does this amount to adjusting the mechanism and mending the apparatus? Such an approach will have little on offer to individuals caught up in a post modern society and feeling unstable, *lost*, manipulable and *alone*.

Every human being is a social being. Every person lives out their life within a life-context. An individualistic psychotherapy focused on intra-psychic conflict may well fail to perceive many social and circumstantial (let alone spiritual) causes of distress — or underestimate their significance. And it may fail to recognise the therapeutic value of outward-looking reorientation and positive behavioural adjustments, rather than endless interpretative analysis alone.

"Outside" factors will include relationships, prevailing social structures, current world-views, domestic environment, personal life-developments — and, above all, the claims of religion. An enlightened, realistic engagement with these factors can, in fact, lead to enhanced self-understanding, self-esteem and personality growth. Depth psychology needs to be complemented by "Lateral" psychology. Roots are greatly affected by the soil in which they are embedded, *and by surrounding plants*.

Inter-Personal Relationships

One of the first to modify the Freudian "biological" emphasis upon intra-psychic conflict was the Scottish psychoanalyst Ronald Fairbairn (1889 — 1964). He observed that human development basically takes the form of a desire to make connections with others; therapy should therefore major on "communicational" factors arising from the importance of growing away from infantile dependence into mature inter-personal relationships.

(Many other post-Freudians laid emphasis upon the significance of social interaction — see page 81 footnote).

But following Fairbairn, two particularly influential contributions in this area came from John Bowlby and Michael Argyle.

John Bowlby (1907–1990)

It will be agreed by all psychologists that the way we relate to others is very largely determined by the way we were treated in our early upbringing. Thus adult behaviour-patterns in relationships which are spoiled by aggressive traits often betray some kind of physical punishment, or even abuse, in childhood. A loving, caring manner is usually indicative of an upbringing reflecting security, affection, and moral guidance. These generalised conclusions may seem self-evident: dictated by common sense and borne out by observations from life. But we owe their convincingness, predominantly, to the psychiatrist John Bowlby.

Bowlby was commissioned by the World Health Organisation to produce a Report on the mental and emotional health of homeless children, and a summary of his findings was published in book-form in 1951 under the title *Child Care and the Growth of Love*. Extensive research, accompanied by observation of babies and young children, provided irrefutable evidence that early deprivation of intimate love and care leads to all kinds of retarded development — in both a physiological and a psychological sense.

What also became clear was that if a child, from infancy onwards, has supportive and rewarding "attachment-figures" he or she will generally grow up with feelings of security and inner confidence which, in turn, will lead to an ability to form mature relationships in adult life. Children deprived of such primary affection and for whom significant caring adults are absent will be disequipped in later years to trust and love others.

Bowlby developed these principles in three large volumes entitled *Attachment and Loss* which widened considerably the established psychoanalytic views, showing that primary human needs are much broader than those of sexual satisfaction. Fulfilment sexually is more likely to follow within a relationship of mature (i.e. not over-dependent) love and trust — (from a Christian point of view, when buttressed by mutual commitment within marriage).

The fundamental importance of inter-personal relationships persists through the whole of life. On the last page of the third volume of *Attachment and Loss*, Bowlby writes — "Intimate attachments to other human beings are the hub around which a person's life revolves, not only when he is an infant or a toddler or a school child but throughout his adolescence and his years of maturity as well, and on into old age. From these intimate attachments a person draws his strength and enjoyment of life and, through what he contributes, he gives strength and enjoyment to others. These are matters about which current science and traditional wisdom are at one."

Michael Argyle (1925—2002)

Argyle's ground-breaking book "The Psychology of Inter-personal Behaviour" was published in 1967 but was followed by a revised edition in 1972 and many reprints, and other, related, writings. His preface begins "Man is a social animal: he collaborates with others to pursue his goals and satisfy his needs. It is well-known that relationships with others can be the source of the deepest satisfactions and of the blackest misery."

He suggests that "previous psychological models of man were mistaken or incomplete, through not taking account of the inter-personal nature of man." Many psychological problems are too commonly attributed to some form of psychopathy: they are more usually caused by a felt inadequacy in the area of social interaction. But such failures in relating to others can be remedied by changes in behaviour brought about by the achievement of "social skills" — a term which has entered everyday vocabulary.

Such learned skills, sometimes springing from altered attitudes to others, sometimes leading to these, can be appropriate in both "formal" and "informal" encounters. Examples of the former would be interview-situations, committees, and public performances; the latter can encompass all those common daily meetings-with-people which *can* be the cause of anxiety and stress.

Relief from trouble and distress, and life-enhancing change in "self-presentational" behaviour does not depend upon professional help. "It has been found that much can be done by people who are untrained and unskilled in psychotherapy, provided they can establish a happy relationship. This involves an acceptance of the other, the sympathetic appreciation of his problems, and the provision of a warm and supporting relationship".

Humanistic Psychology
Those words may well call to mind the humanistic psychology

associated, particularly, with Carl Rogers and his "Person-Centred Therapy", and Abraham Maslow.

For humanism, also, may be seen as a reaction to Freudianism, especially in relation to the latter's negative view of human nature as dominated by dark, destructive drives. Humanists regarded all individuals as fundamentally good, born free, and naturally motivated to discover and live out a positive, meaningful existence *in association with others*. Such healthy self-actualisation can, in their view, be frustrated by the discouraging, life-cramping nature of many social influences. But, by the same token, can be furthered by relationships and circumstances which are liberating and encouraging. It was principles such as these which lay behind the development of a humanistic social psychology in America epitomised in comparatively recent times by Abraham Maslow and Carl Rogers in particular.

Abraham Maslow (1908–70)

Maslow stresses that the truly fulfilling life is about becoming rather than just being: it involves making growth choices. This will mean a conscious, optimistic embracing of all experiences which can engage an individual's innate will-to-health and draw out their personality-potential, especially through relationships with others.

The emphasis upon the formative significance of making choices attracted the description "existential psychology": the decisions an individual makes cumulatively determine self-identity and personal meaning to life. The following notes on some of the characteristics of such self-actualisation are taken from his book *The Farther Reaches of Human Nature*.... "Self-actualisation means experiencing fully, vividly, selflessly, with full concentration and total absorption.... Think of life as a process of choices, one after another. To make the growth choice instead of the fear choice a dozen times a day, is to move a dozen times a day towards self-actualisation.... It is 'listening to the impulse-voices', letting the self emerge.... It means, when in doubt, being honest rather than not. Each time one takes responsibility, this is an actualising of the self.... It means daring to be different, unpopular, non-conformist — being courageous rather than afraid".

Later in life Maslow acknowledged the value of "peak experiences" — transient, mystical moments of heightened emotional enjoyment or inspiration; these self-transcendent happenings can help to release us into "upward" growth. In other words, Maslow came to recognise that true self-actualisation requires an engagement with something "bigger" than we are — not necessarily divine (he remained an atheist) but certainly a "transcendent" dimension beyond a state of comfortable equilibrium.

Drawn by wonder and awe, we can rise up through a hierarchy of felt human needs, beginning with the most basic (food, shelter etc) and ascending through self awareness, spontaneity, creativity, an ability to love, an openness to peak experiences, leading on to higher quests involving goodness, truth and beauty — an in-touchness with cosmic harmony....

This double process of personality-fulfilment (self-actualisation) *and* self-transcendence (growth) is accelerated by the encouragement of others making the same journey — who are not necessarily therapists. Fellow travellers can assist each other to make those "growth choices instead of fear choices day by day".

Carl Rogers (1902—84)

Rogers was a contemporary of Maslow, sharing his optimistic view of human nature and its ability to progress towards self fulfilment, especially through relationships. In his very influential book *On Becoming A Person* he states his belief that, while people can possess "hostile and anti-social feelings" these are not innate, and every person at the core of their being is positive, forward-moving, constructive, loving. "There is no beast in man. There is only man in man....."; and man is fundamentally good. The unfolding of these in-born positive qualities into a harmonious whole, (becoming a person) requires favourable relational situations. The three particular conditions stipulated by Rogers, within a counselling context, are Acceptance, Empathy and Congruence.

Acceptance means unconditional positive regard for the other person, for we all have a need, and a right, to feel respected and valued unjudgementally; acceptance signifies recognition of the unique, infinite worth of every individual.

Empathy acknowledges a person's need to be understood; it implies the willingness to see and experience the world as the other person does, *in the present.*

Congruence — sometimes expressed as "an Experience of Genuineness", underlines the importance of sincerity, realness, authenticity in a relationship: it will involve the therapist and the other person being in touch with their own feelings and thoughts and attitudes as they flow between them, and a willingness for these to be spoken.

Counselling, within a relationship permeated by these core-conditions, must be non-directive, client-centred — better: *person-centred.*

Non-directive because a person must be given space and freedom to be in touch with their own inner feelings, allow these to be incorporated into present experience, and be guided by them. (Rogers wrote, "Experience is, for me, the highest authority"). In this way an individual can become increasingly self-directed.

Client-centred therefore, because self-esteem must be

genuinely boosted by the therapist's trust in the client, rather than in his or her own professional insight or psychotherapeutic technique.

Person-centred — because the therapy, the healing, comes by means of the *relationship* of mutual trust and understanding between two persons.

Rogers wrote, "Individuals have within themselves vast resources for self-understanding and for altering their self-concepts, basic attitudes and self-directed behaviour." Accessing these resources is not dependent on deep psychological knowledge but on two (or more) persons allowing themselves to be fully present to each other in terms of the above core conditions (acceptance, empathy, and experience of genuineness).

"The warm, subjective, human encounter of two persons is more effective in facilitating change than is the most precise set of techniques growing out of learning theory or operant conditioning" *(quote in Psychotherapy and Existentialism — Victor E Frankl).*

Such an approach does not imply a bland, undiscriminating acquiescence on the part of the counsellor to all that emerges from the counselee. In their book *Towards Effective Counselling and Psychotherapy,* Charles Truax (Rogers' colleague) and Robert Carkhuff add three "basic dimensions of effective counselling" to the core-conditions viz:

Concreteness — being real, definite, specific and particularly, avoiding vagueness.

Confrontation — drawing attention to inappropriate ambiguities and un-noticed resources.

Immediacy- awareness of the actual here-and-now, put into words.

(For the Christian person-centred therapist, in particular, sensitive confrontation over ethical issues will be an ingredient of the core-condition of genuineness (congruence) for this will mean being true to truths and moral values arising from Christian faith.)

In short, the essence of Rogerian psychology is an affirmation of *personhood* as fundamentally "whole", and capable of being actualised by means of affirmative interpersonal relationships. Basically, Rogers' view of life's loftiest aim is expressed in the words of Kierkegaard: "To be that self which one truly is".

Carl Rogers has written extensively about Encounter Groups for he sees them as the ideal context for the outworking of the principles outlined in the foregoing paragraphs. Writing back in 1970 he states "For more than thirty five years, individual counselling and psychotherapy were the main focus of my professional life. But nearly thirty five years ago I also experienced the potency of the changes in attitude and behaviour which could be achieved in a group. This has been an interest of mine ever since."

And it became a main focus of his work. Sometimes called T groups or IPGL's (Inter-Personal Growth Laboratories!), the following description of the aims of such a group makes plain the "lateral" dimension of the psychotherapy involved. "The over-riding goal of the Group is, of course, inter-personal growth. Inter-personal growth involves discovering new ways of being present to others. Personal growth, too, is a goal of the group, but it is assumed that all that is good in personal growth (e.g. reduction of anxiety, enhanced feelings of self-worth, a keen sense of self-identity), must be placed at the service of inter-personal relationships. Man is a relational being and the height of his growth lies in his relationship with others." (Taken from *Encounter Group Processes for Inter-Personal Growth — Gerard Egan, Loyola University of Chicago*).

Gestalt

Among other humanistic schools of psychology, all loosely classified under the human-potential movement, is Gestalt Psychology — considered here, though briefly, because it is probably the best known.

Gestalt is a German word (this psychological school was originated by Austrian and German psychologists) which has no precise equivalent in English. It speaks of the essential form or shape of an object seen as a "whole", and this "whole" is so much more than the sum of its parts. An example commonly cited is that of a melody, since its beauty and total impact cannot be described simply in terms of its particular notes.

Gestalt Therapy is mainly associated with Fritz Perls (1893 — 1970) and his wife, Laura.

In essence, it is maintained that personality is to be viewed holistically — that is, as a unified whole, rather than being analysed into psychic components.

Unfortunately, inner stresses and strains, and other people's expectations, can "induce" fragmentation. But rather than arrest, or avoid, or try to change elements of yourself which you do not like — perhaps because they are disapproved by others — it is much more healthy to become more aware of them and experience them fully. It is better to accept that everything in your past has become part of you, making you the unified whole that you now are.

Attempting to split off aspects of your personality deemed undesirable only damages the "Gestalt" — your wholeness or integrity; it is better to let it be expressed. "You cannot improve on your own functioning, you can only interfere with it, distort and disguise it." So Gestalt *Therapy* will be aimed at helping a person connect with their real self, owning that self, and expressing it. In short "be yourself — your whole self" for basically you *are* a Gestalt, a whole person with a unique shape or form having significance and meaning: be affirmed! Live it out! In this way, the individual is equipped more fully to enjoy inter-personal relationships and find them really satisfying.

To this end, often in a group setting, splits and divisions in the personality are clarified and got rid of. As with Rogers, group therapy is encouraged: "There are great advantages in working with a group; a great deal of individual development can be facilitated through doing collective experiments.... Chain reactions often occur.... The group soon learns to understand the contrast between helpfulness, however well meaning, and true support.... It is always a deeply moving experience for the group and for me, the therapist, to see previously robotized corpses begin to return to life, gain substance, begin the dance of abandonment and self-fulfilment. The paper people are turning into real people." (From *gestalt is* — ed. *John O Stevens.*)

Countering Behaviourism

The whole human-potential movement with its associated approaches to psychotherapy represents a reaction against, not only Freudianism but also against Behaviourism. As a parallel development with humanism but contrasting with it, behaviouristic psychology declared that all human behaviour is the result of conditioning. The concept of a person as autonomous, free to make character-forming choices, is an illusion. What people become is determined *completely* by their genes or their environment; they therefore have no real independence. Self-determination is an invalid principle.

B F Skinner, recognised as the main exponent of Behaviourism, has been called "The most influential of American psychologists — and the most controversial — of the last

Century". The title of his key book, published in 1971, sums up his view of human nature: *Beyond Freedom and Dignity*. Freedom and dignity are romantic notions which are in fact meaningless and need to be abolished, for human beings in every respect are the product of a causal chain of events. They possess no "ego" or personality-centre which is able to reason and choose; they can initiate nothing. The only way they can change is by conditioning, and only by recognising this fact and acting upon it can we improve society: there is the hope that the results of *past* conditioning can be altered by manipulative methods called by Skinner "Operant Conditioning".

Based on experiments with pigeons and rats, this technique, it is claimed, can reinforce positive, desirable kinds of behaviour by a system of punishments and rewards. Rats "learn" to avoid certain actions and to pursue others if, in the former case, they are always accompanied by "painful", and in the latter case by "pleasurable", consequences.

The first kind of "reinforcers" are termed negative because they have aversive effects; the second, which promote pleasurable results, are called positive reinforcers.

For example, if a particular action is always followed by the receipt of food, that action is likely to be repeated when the creature is hungry; this principle obviously derives from Pavlov's work with animals involving "conditioned reflexes". In relation to human beings also, it is believed that beneficial changes of attitude and conduct can be brought about by similar techniques. Examples of (negative) reinforcement — to combat and eradicate distressing phobias or damaging habits — are *aversion* and *desensitisation* therapy.

Aversion therapy involves undesirable behaviour being repeatedly coupled with a resultant unpleasant consequence. For example, if heavy smoking (or some other harmful habit which has become addictive) is linked to extreme nausea or to disturbing reminders of its damaging effects, it is more likely to be given up.

As an example of desensitisation technique, a cause of fear (or other distress) is cut down to size by facing up to it under controlled conditions, gradually and repeatedly, until its threatening power is eliminated.

But better than negative reinforcements in the battle against a whole variety of distressing neuroses, are the *positive* variety: "rewards" rather than "punishments" are more effective as inducements to change. Positive reinforcement techniques aim to demonstrate the benefits of healthily-altered modes of thought and action: in short, to show that the rewards of life-enhancing change are worth it. The pay-off works: it's good to be good. Animals can be conditioned to "get the message" on the level of their basic biological needs; humans can also be subjects of "operant" conditioning psychologically in order to improve their functioning in society — and to enhance their personal happiness.

Arthur Koestler levels a particularly damning charge against Behaviourism. He points out that just as the sentimental investing of animals with human faculties and emotions is a fallacy, the opposite fallacy inherent in the behaviourist approach, of reducing humanness to the level of lower animals is much more pathetic: "Behaviourism ... has substituted for the erstwhile anthropomorphic view of the rat, a ratomorphic view of man"!

Which is worse, some will ask: Freud's view of humans as biological machines driven by inner conflicting forces needing psychoanalysis, or Skinner's ratomorphism, which sees every individual as the product of crude deterministic factors needing operant conditioning?

In both cases similar crucial questions are raised: What

are the objective criteria for psychological well-being? What is "normal"? and "beneficial"? Who is to answer these questions? Who analyses the analysers and "repairs" them? Who conditions the conditioners?

To humanists, to Carl Rogers in particular, there was not much to choose between these two approaches (of Freud and Skinner): they are equally dehumanising. His own humanistic approach stands in sharp contrast to both. He abhors any thought of "professional" control or manipulation or conditioning as ingredients of psychotherapy. Ultimately, it is the individual who can and should determine their best way forward. As we have seen, the core conditions of unconditional positive regard, empathic understanding, and congruence — in other words, sincere recognition of each person's worth and potential — are at the heart of Rogerian psycho therapy.

Deeply human, compassionate, life-affirming. Here is an approach to human beings who are in emotional pain which surely should warm the heart of every Christian.

The Place of Christianity?

However, Carl Rogers was reacting not only against the doctrinaire "false scientism" of Freud's approach, and the controlling techniques of Behaviourism, but also against a Christianity which was experienced by him, during his upbringing, as grimly legalistic and *life-negating*.

Though the six Rogers children grew up in an atmosphere of family security and solidarity, their parents — particularly his mother — inculcated a strongly protestant faith of the "fortress" kind characterised by a separatist and somewhat joyless spirituality dominated by prohibitions.

Later, after graduating in history and marrying Helen, whom he had known since childhood, Carl Rogers did embark on an ordination training course. Significantly, he chose a college noted for its intellectually liberal approach to religious work, rather than the theologically conservative Princeton Seminary favoured by his parents.

Though grateful for the academic ethos of Union Theological Seminary, which he found mind expanding, (including psychological studies), he nevertheless drew back from the prospect of ordination, feeling he could not conscientiously commit himself to the obligatory beliefs and practices of institutional religion — let alone to proclaiming them. Released from the "chains of dogma" attaching, in his view, both to Freudianism and to the Church, he was free to develop an alternative approach to helping his fellow human beings. His humanistic/existential psychological emphasis — echoed by Abraham Maslow, and Rollo May — became focused in the person-centred psychotherapy associated with his name.

In his later years, Rogers was comfortable with concepts such as "spiritual" and "mystical". He could claim, for example, that in "the intense and transformational moments of the therapeutic encounter" ... "an altered state of consciousness gives access to a transcendent realm where 'something larger' enters in".

Within this shared experience "profound growth and healing energy are present". But he never lost his early distaste of institutional religion, expressed in "Becoming a Person": "Religion, especially the Protestant Christian tradition ... has permeated our culture with the concept that man is basically sinful, and only by something approaching a miracle can his sinful nature be negated." (From *Becoming A Person*).

Countering charges that his own view of human nature, in reaction, betrayed naïve optimism, he protested, as early as

1960 "I do not have a Pollyanna view of human nature. I am quite aware that out of defensiveness and inner fear individuals can and do behave in ways which are horribly destructive, immature, regressive, anti-social, hurtful. Yet, one of the most refreshing and invigorating parts of my experience is to work with such individuals and to discover the strongly positive directional tendencies which exist in them, as in all of us, at the deepest levels." *(Quoted in The Mystical Power of Person-Centred Therapy — Brian Thorne).*

His words are thought-provoking — not least because he writes, he says, out of his own experience as a person-centred therapist. The "strongly positive directional tendencies" at "the deepest levels" even in those who behave in dangerously anti-social ways are posited here, not as theory, but as *facts* — proved, he states, in his work with them.

All through his life he acknowledged that this stance was opposite to Christian teaching, which he regarded as on a par with the hated, baneful principles of Freudianism. In an article published a few months before his death he wrote "seeing the human organism as essentially positive in nature is profoundly radical. It flies in the face of traditional psychoanalysis, runs counter to the Christian tradition, and is opposed to the philosophy of most institutions, including our educational institutions. In psychoanalytic theory our core is seen as untamed, wild, destructive. In Christian theology we are 'conceived in sin', and 'evil by nature'".

Reflections and Correctives

The human-potential movement has made a profound impact upon psychology in recent decades. And few psychologists have been so influential as Carl Rogers, not least in Universities throughout the world, but especially in America and Britain. Today the global network of PCTs and Rogerian

Inter-personal Growth groups is very extensive, and numerous clients have been helped along their journey towards psychological healing and wholeness. Predictably, Rogerianism (with related forms of "lateral" humanistic psychology) has not been without Christian critics.

The sceptical dismissal of Christianity which underlines much Rogerianism triggers theological and pastoral concern. In particular, the up-beat assertions related to the three key areas of *human nature, human experience, and human relationality* as being, respectively, fundamentally "good", intrinsically reliable, and positively transformative, need to be questioned.

But it is all too easy for Christians reactively to decry these humanist notions as dangerously optimistic, and to go too far the other way in denigrating our humanness. Perhaps it is better to begin by agreeing with the humanist position where we can.

Human Nature

In Chapter 3 we concluded, on the biblical evidence, that human beings are a mix of bad and good. The Christian doctrine of original sin is to be interpreted in conjunction with those of original righteousness and common grace. For Christians, realistic recognition of the bad does not preclude genuine celebration of the good, in human nature.

One issue, among many others, where the non-religious humanist and the Christian part company is over who to thank. Both, alike, can appreciate the enriching contributions to our life together of many gifted individuals — in the fields of the arts, sciences and sport; public servants, thinkers, healers, teachers ... and countless ordinary people who have shown practical compassion in ordinary, and extraordinary ways — all these fellow human beings attract our gratitude.

But is that it? The secular humanist says, Yes: the idea of seeking a higher Source actually demeans human achievement. To posit God as our Creator and the Giver of wisdom, inspiration and artistic and practical skills, and who shares our enjoyment of their fruit, in fact subtracts from our humanness. The beauty and order in the natural world, in the universe, which artists and scientists "discover" and express, is simply *there*. God? "We have no need of that hypothesis".

I will not be alone in finding such an attitude depressing. It makes life grey and one-dimensional: and, ironically, it *diminishes* human beings. Whereas to thank God and give him the glory (Hopkins-wise) for all that brings us pure pleasure, including its human agencies, immeasurably deepens our enjoyment and elevates human giftedness.

This statement is not merely an expression of personal piety: it has pragmatic implications. As a Christian, I wonder whether truly fulfilled humanness is possible without true religion.... If God is our Creator, and if he is unacknowledged, ungratefully disregarded, can "goodness, truth and beauty" (which humanists, no less than Christians, admire and value) flourish within society?

Without God, their Fount, what content can those values have; what meaning attaches to them intellectually and ethically and aesthetically? Relativism rules. If we bear the image of God, which is the essence of humanness, can a thankless denial of this existential reality produce anything other than diminishment of human dignity and an impoverishing of relationships — for "love is of God".

In contrast, theism (not deism or meism) can lead to *true* humanism — an unfolding of the unique potential built into each one of us; a life truly fulfilling because it can be "something beautiful for God", lived out in creative relationships in harmony with his will for us revealed in his Word.

Hans Kung's central thesis in his *magnum opus On Being A Christian* is the claim that "Christianity cannot properly be understood except as radical humanism".

Human Experience

Similar points can be made about the Rogerian emphasis upon experience.

As we have seen, for him, "becoming a person" will mean identifying, owning, and living out our authentic self in relationship: becoming the person our experience indicates that we *are*. ("Experience" is used here meaning "a state of mind or feeling").

So, we need to be receptive to what our inner senses and intuitive reactions to life are telling us — rather than being driven by introjected mental concepts, taking instructions and swallowing prescriptions, from outside human sources. "When an activity *feels* as though it is valuable or worth doing, it is worth doing. Put another way, I have learned that my total organismic sensing of a situation is more trustworthy than my intellectual" (*On Becoming A Person)*.

Many of us will consider that this view makes claims for "experience" which go too far. In a Christian context, experience cannot be the arbiter of what is of God and therefore truly therapeutic: to elevate it in this way can be neither right nor helpful. The Bible affirms that we need to be radically, experientially, *transformed* if we are truly to fulfil our potential to the glory of God, and this can only be brought about by a *renewed* mind, able to desire and discern and obey God's will (*Romans 12:1-2; 1 Peter 1:22-25*).

However, this does not imply that a person's soul-experience should be disregarded totally; to stifle "the heart's voice" can be strangely disconfirming. Christians have, in recent years, recognised the need for the experiential dimension of the gospel to be re-habilitated.... I can look back to a time when (to generalise) evangelicals, in particular, were overly suspicious — dismissive, even — of *any* reliance on experience as a valid indicator of truth-about-God. Spirituality was to be bounded by the propositional and the intellectually-cognitive. Experience (associated with "feelings", a highly suspect phenomenon coming under the umbrella of the dreaded "emotionalism") was out of court as having any evidential value with regard to biblical Christianity, and definitely questionable as a way-in to it. Arguably, such an attitude is not biblical enough.

And actually this attitude was a temporary, and far from blanket, aberration. Within true evangelicalism there has been no dichotomy between doctrine and the believer's Spirit-given experiential relationship with God, enjoyed and lived out.

J I Packer summed up the essential inter-weaving of the two in a passage from his book *Knowing God* — "Knowing God is a matter of *personal involvement*, in mind, will and feeling. It would not, indeed, be a fully personal relationship otherwise.... We must not lose sight of the fact that knowing God is an emotional relationship, as well as an intellectual and volitional, and could not indeed be a deep relationship between persons were it not so. The believer is and must be emotionally involved in the victories and vicissitudes of God's cause in the world". The Renewal Movement, at its best, has led to a re-discovery and release of the experiential aspects of the Christian faith — especially in worship.

Evangelicals will, hopefully, always affirm that experience should never be used to interpret Scripture: the reverse is the case. To make room for spiritual experience as an intrinsic part of Christianity does not imply jumping the ship of propositional theology and clambering aboard the Liberal boat.

Most certainly, the "meistic" theology/spirituality of Liberalism, which majors on the "experiential-expressivist" interpretation of the gospel does need to be corrected by recourse to responsible biblical exegesis. But the baby should not be thrown out with the bath-water. God is truth, and he has made us: therefore all that remains true (authentically human, reflecting his image) in our inner experience will have its focus in him. God's self-revelation is not exclusively derived from Holy Scripture, nor will he engage only our *minds*.

Gerard Manley Hopkins reminds us of this; so can others, artists and musicians *etc* as well as poets. The Holy Spirit can make God known to us by connecting with (as well as our intellect) our imagination, intuitive discernment, memory, sensitiveness to beauty, creativity.... The Bible speaks poetically as well as in plain prose; in Scripture we find metaphor, parable, analogy, simile and synecdoche as well as factual accounts and linear teaching.

In all these ways connections are made with our total experience of life, our humanness. We are helped by the Holy Spirit to "make sense" of the gospel-message holistically. Cerebral understanding is not the only God-given faculty by which we can "know" him. Experience and reason *can* function together in harmony.

This is a far cry, however, from the Rogerian view of experience as infallibly authoritative and determinative in the matter of personality wholeness. There will be many occasions when the voice of experience (what our feelings are telling us) will contradict what God says in his Word. Which takes precedence? To be governed and guided by what we may "feel" about the value of various attitudes or actions may well mean entering a disastrous cul-de-sac of self-delusion and/or wishful thinking — or worse. "There is a way that seems right to a man, but in the end it leads to death" (*Proverbs 14:12*).

While acknowledging that the Holy Spirit can and does speak in and through our experience, it is essential that we honour as primary what he says in the biblical text. Only when the two voices *correlate* can we move forward towards true maturity with any confidence.

An even more important benefit of allowing the Word of God and the example of Jesus to have priority over experience rather than *vice versa* is that the Spirit uses Scripture both to illumine the mind and *to convey* authentic experience of the living God and of his Son Jesus Christ. That is the best kind of experience! John writes of his gospel-narrative, "These are written that you may believe that Jesus is the Christ, the Son of God, and that by believing you may have life in his name".

Human Relationality

For Rogers, interpersonal relations are the key to personality health, and growth. Therapy is therefore primarily concerned with a setting in which the core conditions of unconditional regard, empathy, and congruence can come into play. Essentially, it is the relationship itself rather than any therapeutic "technique" or approach which leads to growth. As two people, therapist and client, are committed to be fully present to one another, their innate positive, forward-moving, loving tendencies are released into actualisation: "profound growth and healing and energy are present".

This principle is also applicable to a group-situation. In fact, as we have seen, Rogers moved from a concentration upon individual counselling and psychotherapy to a growing interest in, and involvement with, Encounter Groups.

He writes that through the intimacy and trust which develops within such a group, negative feelings are exteriorised and meaningful concerns are shared; this can lead on, in turn, to self-acceptance and the beginning of change. As a result of being in the group a person "becomes deeply acquainted with the other members and with his own inner self, the self that otherwise tends to be hidden behind his façade. Hence he relates better to others, both in the group and later in the everyday situation" (*Encounter Groups*).

There are recognisable resonances in Rogers' principles with the New Testament emphasis upon community. The Church is, essentially, a community: a family, a flock, belonging to one Father and to one Shepherd. Individual Christians live in relationship with each other through the bond of the love of God which indwells them and enfolds them. Theirs is "the fellowship of the Holy Spirit".

This means that, strictly speaking, biblical theology is "communitarian": the Christian Church is the context in which believers grow in their understanding of the gospel which unites them, and by which they learn and practise its pastoral implications of mutual love and support. Clearly, this growth in understanding and compassion will be best furthered by meeting together so that relationships are deepened through communal praise, the Eucharist, attention to biblical teaching, prayer, shared meals and possessions, and providing for the needs of others (*Acts 2:42-47*).

These relationships will also involve in-depth openness, honest confrontation, practical empathy and humble affirmation of others (*Galatians 6:1-6*). Above all, relationality will be motivated and permeated by love (*1 Corinthians 13; 1 Peter 1:22-23; 1 John 4:7f*).

Between Encounter Groups and Christian fellowship-gatherings there are similarities and there are differences.

Rogerian style groups are prone to certain drawbacks,

which Rogers frankly faces in a section of his book (*Encounter Groups*) headed "Failures, Disadvantages, Risks". They include the frequent *temporary* nature of behaviour changes — that is, they are not carried over lastingly from the group into every day life; sometimes problems which begin to be revealed are not worked through; tensions within marriage can arise if only one partner becomes closely involved in a group — especially if causes of marital tension emerge into the open; closeness between two people, even in a group situation, can come to have a sexual component; and a certain know-how can be assumed by practised group-attenders which can have a stultifying effect, cramping spontaneity.

Common sense strategies can lead to the avoidance of such undesirable developments; among Christians, this will include spiritual common sense. For Christians, too, need to be aware of certain, perhaps similar, pitfalls in relation to fellowship groups: hopefully these will be countered by an objective focus upon the presence of Christ-in-the-midst, a concentration upon the Bible's revealed truth, and an openness to the Holy Spirit.

These latter factors throw up an essential difference between secular and Christian groups. The Rogerian therapy-through-relationship emphasis presents a serious weakness about Encounter Groups which is problematic for Christians. By definition, Person-Centred Therapy — one-to-one or in a group — is essentially non-directive and open-ended in the sense that it encourages the recognition and owning and expression of experience-based feelings as a means of growth towards personality wholeness.

Summing up the value of relationships within a Group, Rogers writes "This type of Group as it develops in the future should help us to sharpen and clarify the values we hold for man himself. What is our model of the human being? What is the goal of personality development? What are the character-istics of the optimum human being? I am sure it is evident from the thrust of this book that in a climate of freedom and facilitation group members move towards becoming more spontaneous, flexible, closely related to their feelings, open to their experience, and closer and more expressively intimate in their interpersonal relationships. This is the kind of human being who seems to emerge from an Encounter Group type of experience." He then adds "Yet such a model goes directly contrary to many religious … points of view" (!).

Perhaps this is because some "religious" people will be concerned about the *apparent* danger of moral indifferentism within such a *milieu*. Arguably, a group needs an agreed moral point of reference by which, and from which, all can get their bearings, *evaluate* their individual contributions, plot their course, and help and support one another in this exercise.

From a Christian perspective this need is met, as we have said, by an acknowledgement of the Lordship of Christ, respect for the Bible as a final authority "in matters of faith and conduct", and an awareness of "the fellowship of the Holy Spirit". Within that fellowship, relationships should ideally be characterised by a carrying of each other's burdens which fulfils the law of Christ (*Galatians 6:2*).

Sadly, there is often a snag: Christians commonly fight shy of admitting to personal burdens and seeking help from fellow believers. Sometimes deep-buried feelings of disturb-ing intensity which seriously undermine a sense of self worth are repressed thus exacerbating feelings of miserable self-rejection and isolation.

Why are such things covered up? Perhaps it is thought that to share them openly would be a denial and betrayal of the gospel, and lead to an undermining of the Christian assurance of others.... The New Testament does register a caveat about the open exteriorising of dark, sordid impulses — associated, for example, with "sexual immorality or any kind of impurity, or of greed … or obscenity"; such subjects form "unwholesome talk" which (among other ugly character-traits) grieve "the Holy Spirit of God, with whom you were sealed for the day of redemption" (*Ephesians 4:29-5:7*) This does not imply repression in the Freudian sense, nor the denial of deep-lying ugly motivations — a common failing among insecure Christians.

But it does mean being circumspect: expressing them (or not expressing them) in a manner dictated by the twin requirements of holiness of life, and love, focused in the Lordship of Christ. Rather than being "owned" and actualised they need to be repented of and "put to death" and banished from the Christian community (*Colossians 3:5-11*).

The Roman Catholic Church makes provision for the relieving of guilt feelings and a tormenting conscience by its practice of penance and priestly absolution. But the Church of England also recognises a need for confession and the assurance of forgiveness: the Book of Common Prayer in its quaint 17th Century English makes this clear: "And because it is requisite, that no man should come to the Holy Communion, but with a full trust in God's mercy, and with a quiet conscience; therefore if there be any of you, who by this means cannot quiet his own conscience herein, but requireth further comfort or counsel, let him come to me, or to some other discreet and learned Minister of God's Word, and open his griefs; that by the ministry of God's holy Word he may receive the benefit of absolution, together with (spiritual) counsel and advice, to the quieting of his conscience, and avoiding of all scruple and doubtfulness."

Today, Christian counselling and prayer ministry directed

and controlled by the Holy Spirit can bring personal release and the healing and deepening of relationships.

What these reflections and correctives add up to is an assertion that in the areas of *human nature, human experience and human relationships* there is a need for theological truth, moral absolutes, derived from the Bible. Yes, we are essentially, "social animals". We have much to learn from the African emphasis upon community illustrated by a proverbial saying: "I am because we are, and since we are, therefore I am". This contrasts with the more individualistic culture of the West. But as Desmond Tutu's great Initiative in South Africa emphasised, Reconciliation is not possible without Truth. And theologically, relationships must be undergirded and permeated by gospel-truth if they are to be authentic — the real thing. The claims made for Person-Centred Therapy, for all their positive aspects, do require closer examination.

In particular, biblical realism about human nature itself is essential. In a sense, this is a deeper need than even of objective moral absolutes (God's revealed requirements) for these can be neither recognised nor honoured by a nature which is basically antipathetic towards them: "The sinful mind is hostile to God. It does not submit to God's law, nor can it do so. Those controlled by the sinful nature cannot please God" (*Romans 8:7-8*).

This "flesh-principle" (which we have considered in the preceding two chapters) will, surely, always be an intrinsic part of our fallen human experience, causing us to choose and to do things that are wrong and harmful rather than right and good (*Romans 7:18-19*). The practical result of this is pictured by Paul as a captivity (*Romans 7:23-24*). He, and we, are held prisoner by a power that prevents our freedom, so that we cannot live out what our better nature tells us is the good life.

Worse: we are *enslaved* by the dictates of the "bad life", which even come to have a terrible fascination for us by their very forbiddenness. The evil in our nature takes over, degenerating into rebellion against God — chafing still further the distress of bondage.

Not completely.

That's the pain of it: intuitions of the honourable life, dreams of a better way persist, buttressed by what our minds tell us when pervaded by right thinking. We catch glimpses of the good, and even yearn for it. But painful tension ensues: "I have the desire to do what is good, but I cannot carry it out. For what I do is not the good I want to do: no, the evil I do not want to do — this I keep on doing" (*Romans 7:18-19*). We are dragged down and chained by dishonourable impulses.

How can we be liberated from this miserable condition — set free to fulfil our humanness in life-affirming relationship with others?

We need redemption.

Above all, we need a Redeemer whom we can know and trust — this is the supreme relationship. Our hearts cry out for Someone who can restore us and reconstitute us as the people we were meant to be: the people of God.

CHAPTER 6

REDEMPTION

"A people belonging to God" 1 Peter 2:9

Among the biographies on my book shelves is an old, musty volume published in 1908 (seventh edition) entitled *Twenty-eight Years a Slave* by Thomas L Johnson. It was given to me in 1961 by a very elderly Christian lady shortly before her death: I had visited her regularly to pray with her and listen to her reminiscences; it was a privilege to officiate at her funeral and tell others of her shining faith in Christ. The lady's husband, the Rev R J Peden (considerably older than her) had been a journalist before training for Christian ministry at Spurgeon's College, and he had regularly accompanied the great Baptist preacher on his speaking engagements in order to take down his sermons in shorthand for their subsequent publication. He also helped the author of the book in my study, who had been a fellow student at the College, to put together his manuscript.

Later, after their marriage, and through the years, the Pedens often welcomed this man, Thomas L Johnson to their home; the memories of his story which he recounted to them and which she shared with me filled out in moving detail the substance of his earlier published biography.

He had indeed been born in slavery — in 1836 in the State of Virginia. He writes "From what I have heard my mother say about her father, it would appear that he came from Africa, and was of the Guinea tribe. Both my mother's parents died when she was quite young. Her brothers and sisters were sold when she was thirteen years old. She often spoke of them, and of the cruel treatment she received in her youth."

As a small child, with other children, Johnson was happy, "Not knowing that we were slaves." But one by one, as they grew a little older, they disappeared ... taken away by a "Georgia Trader", or slave dealer. "I did not know what to make of it. A vague fear came over me, but I did not know why.... What seemed worse than all was the discovery that our mothers, whom we looked upon as our only protectors, could not help us." His mother taught him the alphabet and how to count to a hundred — and the Lord's Prayer. Even this was hazardous. State Legislature decreed that "If a slave were known to teach another slave he would be liable to be sent to the whipping post....

"They were forbidden education.... And slaves were not allowed to be taught in Sabbath Schools.... In the city of Savannah, Georgia, an ordinance was made by which 'Every person of colour who shall teach reading or writing (is) to be imprisoned ten days and whipped thirty-nine lashes'". As an older child-slave Johnson experienced a mixture of kindness and cruelty. Later, in his book, he reflected on the condition of his fellow slaves at that time: "They were doomed to drag out a miserable existence in bondage, classed as goods and chattels. Their condition was that of dumb creatures; their time, talents, mind and body were all claimed by the slave-owner, whose power over the slaves was absolute. The slave had no legal rights. In no respect whatever was he protected; beyond his master he had no appeal.... Some masters were very cruel, but others were very kind."

Eventually Johnson secretly and painstakingly taught himself to read and write. At the age of twenty one he was led to faith in Jesus by another slave and "Soon after my conversion I felt a deep desire to preach the gospel. But two difficulties presented themselves: first, I was a slave, for though I had a free soul yet my body was in slavery; then, second, I could not read the Bible with much understanding." There was no escape from his circumstances. But finding an old Bible he persevered in trying to read it and make sense of it.

Eventually came Abolition. In the English parliament, "On January 2nd, 1807, Lord Grenville presented a Bill called an 'Act for the Abolition of the Slave Trade'; and on the 5th his Lordship opened the debate by a very luminous speech. Among others who supported him was the Duke of Gloucester, who said, 'This trade is contrary to the principles of the British Constitution. It is, besides, a cruel and criminal traffic in the blood of our fellow creatures; it is a foul stain on the national character. It is an offence to the Almighty. On every ground, therefore, on which a decision can be made, on the ground of policy, of Liberty, of Humanity, of Justice, but above all on the ground of Religion, I shall vote for its immediate extinction."

Thus the backbone of slavery was broken, though it was not until much later, after the Civil War in the USA, that the four and a half million slaves there were freed. Johnson had witnessed the fighting and was present in Richmond on April 3rd 1865 when it was overrun by General Grant.

"The joy and rejoicing when the United States army marched into Richmond defies description. For days the manifestations of delight were displayed in many ways. The places of worship were kept open, and hundreds met for prayer and praise.... I cannot now describe the joy of my soul at that time. This was indeed the third birthday to me:

Born August 7th, 1836 — a "Thing".

Born again (*John 3:7*) June, 1857 — a Child of God.

Born into human liberty April 3rd, 1865 — a Free Man.

No longer was I a mere chattel, but a man; free in body,

free in soul; praise the Lord. It is impossible to give an adequate idea of the abounding joy of the people — the great multitude of liberated slaves — after the long years of toil and suffering. Strong men and women were weeping and praising God at the same time.... That scene of years ago comes up vividly before me at this moment.... The cries and groans and prayers of millions of poor and defenceless slaves, with the prayers of their friends in America, England, Ireland, Scotland, Wales, and everywhere had reached the throne of God.... And he had answered that cry."

After a growingly successful evangelistic ministry in the States, Johnson eventually, through the generosity of Christian friends, came to England, to Spurgeon's College — in 1876; here he experienced great personal kindness from C H Spurgeon himself, and a great company of Christian brothers and sisters. Many years of his subsequent Christian service were spent in Africa, as well as in the United Kingdom. He died, in his seventies, about 1910.

Redemption

I have reproduced these biographical extracts because they form a graphic illustration from comparatively recent history of what it meant to be *freed from slavery* — the biblical salvation-metaphor which is, indeed, drawn primarily from the world of slavery in Bible times: *Redemption*.

As later, so then, release from a helpless, hopeless bondage imposed by a despot could only be secured through the intervention of a third party — usually by payment of a price: a ransom. The beneficiaries of this process of manumission became beholden to whoever had redeemed them in this way. Consider the salient features of Johnson's story. A whole people, each individual bearing the image of God, mostly shared the misery of harsh domination in degrading conditions. The change of status brought about by Emancipation is followed by altered circumstances for the whole enslaved race, with restored dignity and joy to each slave. Individual liberty which could previously be bought (though on a shakily secure basis) was now irreversibly guaranteed for all through the supreme influence of one man, Abraham Lincoln; but, from another point of view, through a supreme price: the death toll of the Civil War. Lincoln himself was later to lose his life, by assassination.

For Johnson, this national liberation had been preceded, eight years before, by a personal, spiritual experience of redemption leading to a profound change of status — from being a "nobody" to being a citizen of the kingdom of God; this, also, had been effected by an irreversible decree — of divine grace — following incomparable cost: "the precious blood of Christ".

The foundational biblical paradigm of redemption is the Exodus. Egypt is a place of cruel bondage; the Israelites' corporate sense of national pride — even identity — is crushed; individual Hebrews feel broken and worthless.

Enter Moses, God's deliverer. The Lord appears to him in awe-inspiring splendour and proclaims: "I have indeed *seen* the misery of my people in Egypt. I have *heard* them crying out because of their slave drivers, and I am *concerned* about their suffering. So I have *come down* to rescue them.... So now, go, I am *sending you* to Pharaoh to bring *my people* the Israelites out of Egypt."

On Passover night, the greatest occasion in Israel's history commemorated regularly with deep thanksgiving and joy, a substitutionary lamb was sacrificed for each household, some of its blood was daubed on the door-frames, the angel of death passed over them, and they set out as a ransomed people for a new land.

Understandably, in New Testament times, this never-to-be-forgotten experience of a shared divine deliverance and guarantee of a new future was seen by the first believers, who were Jewish, as a dramatic illustrative parallel to Christian salvation. But because slavery was common in those days the metaphor of redemption was immediately understood also by Gentile converts.

Clearly, the deliverance achieved by Christ is infinitely greater than that experienced under the leadership of Moses, but similar factors are evident. Among New Testament references to redemption, a passage from Paul's letter to the Colossians (1:12-14) makes this parallel particularly clear: "giving thanks to the Father, who has qualified you to share in the inheritance of the saints in the kingdom of light. For he has rescued us from the dominion of darkness and brought us into the kingdom of the Son he loves, in whom we have redemption, the forgiveness of sins."

The expression "brought us into" translates a verb (*metestasen*) which "refers to a removal or migration of a people"; it "conjures up the picture of a conqueror who has overcome the enemy and has set free the people previously enslaved by him (as, for example, at the Exodus)".

Christian redemption signifies a spiritual migration from the "dominion of darkness" to "the kingdom of the Son he loves". Before their deliverance, Christians were under the tyrannous authority (*exousia*) of dark forces opposed to the light; but they are now transferred to "the kingdom of light" where the "reign" of Jesus our Redeemer ensures and seals the reality of *redemption* and *forgiveness*. By the first we are released from the power of sin (which is the essence of darkness) and the second releases us from the chains of guilt.

This is both an individual and a corporate experience: ours is now a shared inheritance. Christians have experienced a transference *together* from slavery to freedom, from darkness to light, from alien soil to their true homeland. As a result, their relationship both to the King and to their fellow citizens is formed and permeated by his love.

Fellowship

The New Testament word which sums up this new dual relationship is *fellowship* (*koinonia*). It speaks of a unity unfound in any other kind of social conglomerate, for it is brought about by the Holy Spirit. This does not imply a kind of divinization of an existing loose-knit community of the like-minded — a concept found in the old Mystery Religions, but still encountered today among various New Age groupies. Fellowship is not a collection of persons united by a common idea or ideals or preternatural awareness; it is more than friendly companionship.

It is not grounded in some view of human beings as "social animals"; that concept has some validity, but fellowship goes much deeper. It signifies a completely new relationship between individuals who have, each one, been radically transformed (born again) by the Holy Spirit. It is the company of the redeemed and the forgiven, formed by the creative intervention of God. Its focus is therefore Christ — the Redeemer, Saviour and King of every member and of the whole Christian community.

"The 'right hand of fellowship' (*Galatians 2:9*) given to Paul and Barnabas by James, Peter and John was not just a handshake over a deal but mutual recognition of being in Christ" — co-recipients of his grace. The celebration of Holy Communion, described in *1 Corinthians 10, 16* as "*koinonia* in the blood and body of Christ" clearly speaks of intimate union with the exalted Christ *together*: "Because there is one loaf, we, who are many, are one body, for we all partake of the one loaf" (v17) (see *Dictionary of New Testament Theology Vol 1 "Fellowship". Editor: Colin Brown*).

The breaking of bread may have been the most poignant expression of Christ-centred fellowship, but closely associated with it was earnest attention to apostolic teaching (authenticated by many wonders and miraculous signs) and drawing near to God in prayer (*Acts 2:42-43*). Thus the Holy Spirit, following Pentecost in Jerusalem, welded together through word, sacrament and prayer a company of Jesus' followers sharing the life of God the Father. Within this Trinitarian fellowship the individual is loved and supported by Christian brothers and sisters (*Acts 2:44f and 4:32*).

This mutual caring and sharing was necessary for very practical reasons: the first Christians were from Galilee (as was Jesus himself) and these fishermen, farmers and peasants who had migrated to the capital from the north would not have found life easy.... Galileans were despised in Jerusalem by Sadducees and Pharisees alike as unsophisticated and religiously ignorant. "How can the Christ come from Galilee?.... This mob that knows nothing of the law — there is a curse on them" was their contemptuous verdict. "Are you from Galilee, too?" was a smear, and "look into it, you will find that the prophet does not come out of Galilee" was an infuriated taunt (*John 7:41, 49, 52*).

As Jesus had been seen as a threat to the Temple establishment so now also was the infant Church. The communal sharing of goods was indeed necessary, as was the financial support sent to the Jerusalem Christians (and later to Paul) during a time of famine and unrest, by other Churches — a tangible expression of heart-felt fellowship-love (see *Romans 15:26* and *2 Corinthians 9:12-15*) where "your generosity in *sharing* with them" translates *koinonia* (See also *Philippians 4:14-18*).

These early Church circumstances were unique. But the principles of mutual love and practical care continued to characterise true fellowship. As John was to write later "If we have material possessions and see a brother or sister in need but do not share what we have with him or her, how can we claim that God's love dwells in us" (*1 John 3:17*).

"Christian fellowship is Christian caring, and Christian caring is Christian sharing. Chrysostom gave a beautiful description of it: 'This was an angelic commonwealth, not to call anything of theirs their own. Forthwith the root of evils was cut out.... None reproached, none envied, none grudged; no pride, no contempt was there.

The poor man knew no shame, the rich no haughtiness; so we must not evade the challenge of these verses. That we have hundreds of thousands of destitute brothers and sisters is a standing rebuke to us who are more affluent. It is part of the responsibility of Spirit-filled believers to alleviate need and abolish destitution in the new community of Jesus." — *(The Message of Acts — John R W Stott).*

The redeemed are to have a redemptive role in society — a role which will often begin with compassionate service in the name of Christ and lead on to evangelism: through the witness of those first Christians as they praised God and enjoyed the favour of all the people, "the Lord added to their number daily those who were being saved" (*Acts 2:47*).

So why doesn't it always work out like this?

Legalism and Associated Blocks

In the deserts of the heart
Let the healing fountain start
In the prison of his days
Teach the freeman how to praise.

(W H Auden)

I have read somewhere that after the Proclamation of Emancipation many slaves were unable to rid themselves of a slave-mentality. Deeply instilled fears of punishment and feelings of inferior humanness had been reinforced over generations by their owners' maltreatment of them. Many continued, after entering liberty, to exhibit a cowed and frightened servility. Downtrodden for many decades, they could not walk tall nor relate to each other with mutual respect. Legislation could taken human beings out of slavery; it was more problematic to take slavery out of human beings.

Christians will recognise biblical parallels.

Following deliverance from Egypt, for example, the Israelites lived through a whole series of peak experiences after the dividing of the Red Sea — miraculous demonstrations of God's presence and power. Nevertheless, they gave way to negative emotions of doubt and fear, even hankering after a return to Pharaoh's bondage. They gave way to a grumbling discontent and hardening of heart against God and against his servant Moses.

In New Testament times believers needed constant exhortation to enjoy and to *live out* their freedom-in-Christ and press ahead on the pilgrim-way with faith and perseverance. Their main, disastrous blunder was to re-impose upon themselves the old "yoke of slavery" which, in religious terms, stood for a required perfect compliance with the demands of the divine law.

When allowing themselves to be still burdened by the chafing heaviness of the law's demands their gospel-derived peace and joy were negated — a slave-mentality reasserted itself and weighed them down. In *Colossians*, (and other places) Paul mentions associated features which were shackling hangovers from the old Judaism: man-made taboos, the scrupulous observance of "sacred" days, outworn religious prohibitions, rites and regulations and ceremonies (*2:16, 20-22*). Such high-sounding, pseudo-humble religious attitudes and practices are, he says, ineffectual spiritually: far from combating the sinful nature, this kind of religious ascetism boosts it because, being self imposed, it panders to pride (*2:22-23*).

The next phase, all too commonly, is division caused by a judgmental arrogance which looks down on others considered less religiously assiduous: ultimately the spirit of resentful antipathy towards God ensues.

At the bottom of this regression to the bondage of "justification by works" and its required rituals, is *legalism*: the enslaving conviction that only by entire perfect conformity to God's law can peace with God be secured — a crippling impossibility.

In this way the divine law, in itself holy and good, given to God's people (including New Testament Christians) as a unifying privilege and as Rules for a fulfilling and happy life in harmony with him, becomes the means by which grace is cancelled out.

Gospel liberty is reinvented as a revived slavery; inner Spirit-given motivation is exchanged for external effort; and God's love in Christ is re-cast as *conditional* upon faultless conformity to his laws.

Sadly, legalism is a constantly recurring heresy among Christians, putting the dampers on the Church's worship and witness in a way which can have damaging and repellent results — as Carl Rogers found. From his wide knowledge of the Christian Mission Field, Bishop John Taylor wrote: "In the life and growth of every young Church, it seems, there is one perennial disappointment which more than any other grieves and bewilders both the missionary and the student of Church history. Before the first generation of converts has passed away gospel is turned into law. The first fine careless rapture of a new discovery deteriorates into a sorry story of rules of conduct, backsliding, and Church discipline. And in the eyes of the non-Christian neighbours the Church comes to be known not as a community with a new quality of life but a sect with a lot of unreasonable prohibitions." — *(The Go-Between God — John V Taylor).*

John Taylor, acknowledges, of course, that early enthusiasm resulting from an overwhelming personal experience of God in Christ may be accompanied by a thin knowledge of Christian teaching. "The second generation hears far more of the gospel, and understands more of its implications and demands." But why does this deeper understanding so easily produce guilt-trips which in turn lead to a stultification of spiritual growth by inducing the acceptance-through-perfect-obedience syndrome? "Is there, therefore, something inherent in human nature or in the nature of religion itself, which impels us towards legalism even when our starting point is a liberation from the law?"

Pace Rogers and others, this phenomenon cannot be attributed to the Christian religion itself properly understood: by grace, we are sons and daughters, not slaves.

But Taylor hints earlier at familiar semi-psychological causes of spiritual regression into legalism. "Natural man seems to grow up with the desperate need to be approved of. Whatever may be said to the contrary, he feels, 'in his bones' that he has to be a good child to keep his parents' love, and long before he has learned that love is not dependent on his goodness or badness he has created the great shadowy arbiter, his pitiless super-Ego.

'Let me be such' he cries 'that ... the law ... will approve. Let me be such that I need no longer be afraid of being found out. Let me be such that I can bear to live with myself'. So

guilt, shame and conscience are built into an iron cage" *(The
Go-Between God — John V Taylor)*.

Clearly, this aspect of human nature fights against the
gospel of forgiveness and acceptance through Christ who by
his atonement "ends the law that there may be righteousness
for everyone who believes" *(Romans 10, 4)*.

It *can* seem that Christians in their desire to be good "put
their faith in Christ only as a more successful way of enabling
them at last to keep the law".

This is to revert to a slave-mindset, inevitably prone to
anxiety and depression, and utterly inappropriate to the
children of God, to citizens of the kingdom of God, to *free
men and women*. Our Redeemer has paid the price, in full,
for our liberty. *He* has perfectly fulfilled the law's requirements on *our* behalf, as our representative, and borne the
total consequences of our guilty disobedience when he died
on the cross.

"Therefore, there is now no condemnation for those who
are in Christ Jesus, because through Christ Jesus the law of
the Spirit of life set me free from the law of sin and death."
Through faith-identification with Jesus we *are*, no longer
slaves, but sons and daughters of God. No longer chained by
legalistic religion we are free to live out our redemption — to
exteriorise with joy the love poured into our hearts by the
Holy Spirit, in the worship and witness and service of true
fellowship. This is the freedom of a new, dignifying "slavery":
for our new Master, our Redeemer, is the risen Christ, Lord of
love, Lord of glory.

Insider Know-how?

Colossians also reminds us that redemption's out-working
can be hindered by another kind of block quite different to
moribund religious traditionalism. A brand of false teaching

related to Greek concepts was invading the Church and endangering its faith and fellowship; most seriously (like legalism) it was undermining the pre-eminence of Christ. It was governed by two key words: "fullness" and "knowledge". "Fullness" was an abstract term for "God", in his utterly transcendent, impersonal, unapproachable perfection.

"Knowledge" was the know-how about approaching "him" and experiencing his fullness in this life. This was a complicated business because between "God" (- the Fullness) and "us" there was of necessity, it was stated, a lot of intermediaries — angels? — or cosmic powers or astrological forces. The false teachers claimed to be familiar with these, to have power over them, and to know the secrets of getting through them to "God". They had the "knowledge" which was needed to get round, to circumvent, the obstacles and to tap into the Fullness.

Later on, this teaching was to become known as *Gnosticism* — a complex, many-headed body of "knowledge" by which the soul can be brought into union with "God".

Is any of this relevant today? Very much so, for here was a current hotchpotch of pop-philosophy, oriental religion, astrology and asceticism which was super-imposed onto "Christianity". Moreover, Gnosticism both incipient (as in *Colossians*) and full-blown (in the second Century) had its numerous gurus. Anybody at all familiar with contemporary New Age movements will see remarkable similarities. And the church is seldom unchallenged, in any era, by some form of pseudo-intellectual (puffed-up) super-spiritual elitism.

Paul will have none of it. The teaching is dangerous if taken seriously: soul-destroying, fellowship-decimating, gospel-denying nonsense. The false teachers are denounced as impostors (*2:8*). Significantly, he warns against them as "slave-traders" who carry off those duped by them, body and soul: "See that no-one takes you captive."

False teaching, especially a gospel which is distorted in the plausible interests of mysticism, can lead back through the wilderness to Egypt: to psychological and spiritual captivity. It will rubbish redemption. The fullness of God, states Paul unequivocally, is to be found in Christ and in Christ alone.

And, as Immanuel, he has *drawn near to us* in his incarnation. Moreover, that fullness of divine life in him has been given to all believers in the here and now. "In Christ all the fullness of the Deity lives in bodily form and you have been given fullness in Christ" (2:9). He also shares with us his victory over all other spiritual powers (alleged intermediaries and cosmic forces) (2:10).

Through him we are delivered from "the dominion of darkness"; we are now citizens of his kingdom of light and love. Therefore we need no longer live in fear or dread: all spiritual enemies in the unseen world have been disarmed, humiliated and utterly defeated by Christ, for all to see. Like our forgiven sin and cancelled guilt, their menace has been removed, taken away, nailed to his cross (2:13-15).

And we have been made alive with Christ. We are *redeemed*.

Christian Humanism?

Slavery could be likened to a living death. Countless numbers of slaves were "weary, and sick of trying; tired of living and scared of dying". Their days were an existence of misery and painful emptiness. There was no future to look forward to. For many people, twenty-first century resonances are strong. No less than the Israelites in Egypt, or the exiles in Babylon, or the Jews subjugated by the pagan powers of Rome and confused by the Greek mystery-religions and philosophies, and like the slaves of pre-emancipation America, *we too need redemption* — in our case, from the wasteland of our post modernist culture where it is increasingly common to feel insecure, lost, manipulated and alone.

Liberation, as ever, will not entail some kind of special-ised know-how: psychological, political, philosophical or whatever, which will help people feel good about themselves. Thinking people will see through this anyway.

Redemption is about the creation of "a people belonging to God" having a redemptive role in society, promoting true human freedom and fulfilment which glorifies him — through commitment to Christ.

On this basis, it seems to me that the *ideals* of humanism (not its premises) need to be affirmed in a Christian context: its compassion harnessed to the gospel. Yes, it is indeed very sad when people feel themselves undermined and devalued by an inappropriately wretched self-image, and perhaps oppressed by a fear of futurelessness. Or when they feel disconfirmed by others and in their vulnerability become hungry for recognition and approval. It is even more tragic if a guilt-ridden (true or false) dependence upon "conditional love" becomes part and parcel of their "Christianity".

We must affirm that faith in Christ not only ensures peace with God accompanied by experienced love, joy and hope, but it enhances our distinctive, unique humanness to the glory of God our Creator, and brings us into the fellowship of the forgiven, to enjoy fulfilling relationships of mutual encour-agement. In this sense the gospel represents a *stronger* humanism than the secular psychological varieties. *First*, it gives a firmer, credible basis for affirming the intrinsic dignity and glory (though marred) of human beings, for they bear the image of God. *Secondly*, redemption through Christ achieves freedom from degrading servitudes, and conveys inner healing through forgiveness. *Thirdly,* the Christian's future is alight with the promises of increasing self-fulfilment, an actualising of personality-potential, *which glorifies God.* *Fourthly,* the company of the redeemed forms a new, Spirit-filled fellowship united by allegiance to him whose truth sets us free to love and to be loved, to affirm and to be affirmed.

Person-Centred Therapy

What bearing do these reflections have upon Rogerian Person-Centred Therapy?

Certainly not all practitioners of PCT are anti-pathetic towards Christianity. One notable exception is Brian Thorne, Emeritus Professor at the University of East Anglia and Director of the Centre for Counselling Studies. As a widely respected authority on Carl Rogers whom he knew as a personal friend, and as a member of the Church of England, prominent in his (and my) home diocese, he has a foot in both camps. He argues strongly for a recognition of PCT as an essentially spiritual discipline in which transcendent realities may be present, enhancing the therapeutic process.

What Rogers, latterly, came to recognise and to describe in a generalised way as a mystical "something larger entering in", Thorne does not hesitate to describe in specifically theistic terms: "the experience of person-centred therapy" he writes "can become for the Christian the means whereby the second great commandment is vibrantly enacted; an access is afforded to the living God within both persons and, by extension, within all that is" (quotations are from *The Mystical Power of Person-Centred Therapy* — *Brian Thorne).*

For Thorne, the doctrine of the Holy Trinity is foundational to the basic principles of Rogerian therapy, for it is (among other things) a reminder that human beings are essentially *relational* beings. This is because our Creator God "is a relationship and cannot exist except as an inter-related Unity". This is not an original thought, of course: it echoes Barth, Torrance, Moltmann, Kung and other theologians, who wish to delineate a Christian anthropology. Thorne's own, psychological, inference is two-fold. *First*, that because togetherness (a plural existence) is one aspect of God our Creator, being made in his image we require relationship for the fulfilment of our humanness. It follows, he claims, that as we allow ourselves, in a counselling context, to be fully present to one another in our God-given humanness, God himself will be present, further deepening our openness to each other and to him.

But this fulfilment-through-relationship must begin with healing-through-relationship, because the intimacy for which we were made, and which we crave, is obstructed by damaged self-esteem.

Worse: when people feel "fearful, wounded and self-punitive" and are haunted by the terror of "inner loneliness" many will withdraw further into themselves, erecting defensive social barriers; some may even give way to perilous strategies of compensation involving injurious, anti-social behaviour. Thorne's *second* Christian inference, therefore, is that PCT, with its associated core-values is the way *par excellence* by which such poignantly necessary healing is facilitated and inappropriate conduct modified.

If painful, undermining emotions are countered by empathy, congruence, and unconditional regard, a person will evolve into self acceptance followed by acceptance of and love for other people. In this way, he claims, the power of "evil" in individuals is negated by a released recognition of self-worth leading to a growing ability to live out, themselves, the core-conditions in a widening circle of relationships.

This approach is exemplified, in Thorne's view, by Jesus Christ. "For me" he writes "it is in no way ridiculous or blasphemous to see in Jesus Christ the perfect person-centred therapist: this man whose compassion never wavered, whose empathetic responsiveness extended to all he encountered and whose congruence permitted him to weep in public and to give expression to a cleansing fury.... For Jesus, it will be remembered, *never lost the sense of connectedness to his Father*".

That last sentence (my italics) is a very significant comment, for it challenges the secular-humanist championing of autonomy (self-rule, self-governance) as an ultimate ideal — bluntly, a deeply un-Christian, indeed anti-Christian, idea. Thorne is, I think, making the point that even Jesus, as the perfect human being, is dependent upon his trusting, obedient relationship with the Father (*see John 5:19-20a*). So, the way forward into wholeness for *us* will be through a realised connectedness with others which is experienced first as an affirming connectedness with God and Christ.

Brian Thorne's years of counselling experience has made him movingly sensitive to the "enormous pools of pain with which, it seems, so many people must contend in almost every sphere of their lives." His compassionate insights have been shared with numerous students and others. But along with this he acknowledges with a deeper realism than Rogers, in my opinion, the presence of evil in human behaviour because, as a Christian, he can relate this to its supreme manifestation in the crucifixion of Christ. And he can register caveats, in his own way, about that "altered state of consciousness" in an intense counselling encounter which gives access to a spiritual world beyond: "it also gives access to a world where hostile spirits roam". He adds, "this, in turn, provides insight into the problem of evil which the person-centred approach is frequently accused of evading or trivialising." Elsewhere: "It is, I believe, irrefutable that highly destructive forces can take up residence in me as in all human beings, and I have little difficulty in believing that they can be equally active in other dimensions of the invisible world" (quotations are from *The Mystical Power of Person-Centred Therapy — Hope Beyond Despair — Brian Thorne).*

The question for him is not whether evil ... exists ... "by far the more important question is how, given that destructive forces are rampant, can they be overcome. The claim I am making ... is that person-centred therapy has at its core an answer to that question." His overall emphasis is that the evil in human beings and its concomitant hurt and damage can be negated, surmounted, by an experience of God within a relationship permeated by the core-conditions of PCT. Thorne does not hesitate to explain this process in a Christo-centric way: "When as a therapist I am fully present to my client and 'something larger' enters in, then we are both, in Christian terminology, living the life of Christ within us and our suffering is placed in a new perspective."

A Critique

I respect Brian Thorne as a fellow-Christian and honour his desire to "baptise" Person-Centred Therapy — and his courage in this, for not a few of his Rogerian associates are atheist or agnostic; some will have an antagonistic attitude towards the Church. And ironically, he has also been made to feel exiled, he writes, by the hurtful suspicion of some "co-religionists". Such an attitude is unworthy.

However, I do suggest that certain elements of the approach represented, derived as it is, from theological liberalism, does actually present problems — not to do with doctrinal hair-splitting, but problems related to the essential nature of the gospel (e.g. John 3:16-21) and thereby to questionable pastoral consequences.

It is important to recognise where Brian Thorne is coming from: he empathises strongly with Rogers in his late friend's aversion to the kind of Christianity experienced in his early days. Not that his personal spiritual history is parallel by any means. Brian's steady church allegiance and Christian witness through the years are grounded, he tells us, in enjoyed childhood church attendance and a particular, overwhelming, experience of the Love of God at the age of 9. But, for his part, he is outspoken in deploring what he perceives as evangelical-ism within the Church of England, and in denouncing certain associated attitudes which he has encountered.

The following extracts are taken from a printed interview with Alison Leonard (from an *Appendix to The Mystical Power of Person-Centred Therapy*). "There has always been in the Anglican Church a very powerful evangelical wing. Their theology I find extremely distasteful because it seems to disregard the saving grace of the crucifixion and resurrection and to treat people as if they're still grievously in a state of original sin. As if they still need to be shown how vile they are before they can be saved".

Whereas having himself experienced the reverse, the un-conditional love of God....? "Yes, I know we don't need to grovel. So that theology is so abhorrent to me, and in my life as a therapist I have so often had to relate to people who have been so badly damaged by it, that at times I feel unspeakably angry and I have to be very careful with that anger."

There are also many in the ranks of the person-centred community he claims, who, like Rogers himself, have suffered grievously at the hands of condemnatory and life-denying religious beliefs and practices. "Their hatred and legitimate fury at the savage wounds inflicted upon them by the representatives of such perverse religion make it difficult and, in some cases, well nigh impossible for them to believe that there are those in the ranks of the religious believers with whom they could converse as friends and fellow-seekers."

Strong words — which, clearly, do explain, to a significant extent, the admixture of liberal theology in Thorne's personal beliefs.

I have reproduced them for another reason: so that Christian readers — especially evangelicals! — may ponder them.... I am an evangelical, and as an evangelical I *know* that "we don't need to grovel" in order to secure God's free mercy — an oxymoron if ever there was one! Grace is grace is grace. Repentance — yes. A chastened returning home from the culpable shame and smell of the pig sty to a Father's welcoming embrace — could well be! But we should face up to the question: does that freedom for which Christ has set us free, that full assurance of faith, characterise us as Church members? Are we markedly different? What of the charge that our Christianity does have the effect of belittling our humanness, diminishing enjoyment of life, and putting a damper on relationships?

To the extent that Rogers', and Thorne's, indictment of certain legalistic *presentations* of Christianity is valid, regret and repentance may be in order. Yes, sin *is* an endemic, destructive part of human nature which puts us in the wrong with God: but against that tragic background the gospel of redemption is glorious good news, to be proclaimed with persuasive, confident joy. Yet, there has been in the past (still is? God forbid!) a type of Protestantism which comes across as Law rather than Gospel: its effect is depressing rather than life-giving. And, there may be hangovers of a presentation of "evangelical religion" which can chill the heart, chain the mind, and clamp the will rather than convey the wonder of divine peace, exciting mental illumination, and buoyant hope which are to be found in Christ.

To represent the God of all grace as primarily a punitive deity would be reprehensible. To imply that human beings, made in his image are scarcely worth saving now (being "sunk in sin") would be literally, soul-destroying. To promote self-rejection, or reinforce it, without pointing to Christ as the Saviour who loves us deeply, dying for us while still sinners, and with limitless kindness welcomes all who turn to him in repentance and trust, filling their hearts with peace, hope, and overflowing love, would be a dreadful travesty of evangelism.

And when professing Christians stand opposed, daggers drawn, they are less than attractive advertisements for their faith. Religion can be made to appear so *joyless*. Did a protestant Northern Ireland journalist really say (in a report I have read) that he can't laugh at a Bob Hope joke because of the comedian's alleged link with Catholicism? One can understand where the humanist writer, (Sean Kearney), is coming from when he comments: "Woe betide us if there is any basis to the Christian belief in immortality.... Can anyone contemplate such an existence — forever — alongside such poker faced, pious people — the saved, the sanctified, the ones in a constant state of Grace?" (Kearney includes, among these Gerry Adams *and* the Rev Ian Paisley and their followers). "Then the idea of sharing an eternity with them sends a shudder up my spine!" Unfair! But Carl Rogers would probably concur.

But hey, none of this is evangelical Christianity as I know it. It is far removed from the authentic, biblical version which through the years has been used by God to revive the Church, transform lives, cleanse and reform society, and release creativity in every sphere of human endeavour. We certainly have no divine monopoly in these matters! But to write us off, Rogers-style, as intellectually stifling or portray us as a grimly pietistic ghetto would be over the top.

Let's direct our feet to the sunnier side of the street....

To begin with, evangelical theology is currently vibrant, adventurous, relevant and in constant dialogue with differing doctrinal opinions. In the ranks of evangelical scholars are theologians of international renown who are at the leading edge of theological method, engaging with contemporary world-views, connecting doctrine with spirituality, and exploring imaginatively God's self-disclosure in human experience and creativity, yet remaining rooted and grounded in Scripture and holding to it as the essential frame of reference. Their aim is to present the gospel, not as a way back to yesterday, but as a way that points forward from today's world of post modernism, post foundationalism, "post-Christianity" and potent paganism, to a richer and more rational future for all who turn to Christ.

At grass roots level the Renewal Movement has brought new life to countless churches, large and small. And thousands flock to Christian Festivals like Spring Harvest, New Wine and Keswick etc etc, for inspirational worship and pertinent Bible-based teaching. Huge numbers of individuals have come to personal faith in Christ through evangelistic initiatives such as the Alpha Course and Christianity Explored, and many Churches attract large congregations both of committed worshippers, and seekers-after-truth.

Of more practical import than all this, Christian Churches are making a difference by demonstrating the love of God in places where that is most needed. Here is a letter, written by Sir Fred Catherwood, (a prominent evangelical leader who died in 2015), which appeared a few years back in *The Times:*

Sir, the reason why the evangelical Churches are growing is not, as the Reverend Dr Karl Ayad (letter, September 25) imagines, to find solace in a changing world. It is to give solace and practical help to those who are the underdogs in our selfish secular society. As president (from 1992 to 2001) of the Evangelical Alliance, which includes all the Protestant denominations, I made over seventy visits to forty cities or London Boroughs to promote and encourage the networking of their rapidly growing social work. They looked after the homeless, helped addicts to get off drugs, looked after prisoners' families, sheltered battered wives, befriended the kids from the sink estates, helped single mothers and those dying of Aids. In other words, they followed Christ's second great command, that we should love our neighbours as ourselves — as the Good Samaritan who healed the wounded Jew.

Is it any wonder that the neighbours flock to the Churches which care for them when no-one else does?

Such compassionate enterprises could be movingly updated. At the time of writing, our daughter Sarah, a nurse, was working on a Mercy Ship with four hundred other young Christians, all supported financially by Christian friends — a force which includes Senior Consultants and Surgeons. Docking in third-world ports, their motive is to bring healing and hope in the name of Christ, through medical care and proclamation of the gospel. The name of the ship was *Anastasis* — Resurrection.

Triumphalism on the part of evangelicals would be out of place. We have no monopoly of truth or of compassion. But maybe the ultra disenchanted detractors *should* look across the street....

"Liberal Christian Humanism"

The alternative, Liberal *modus operandi* may well manifest a matching practical expression, in general terms, of the second great commandment but it is in danger of diluting the gospel — in particular, the biblical teaching about Redemption. For this reason it is also in danger of proving, ultimately, pastorally inadequate.

Some may want to question that last sentence. I am bringing up doctrinal issues: are they not, possibly, chillingly irrelevant and stultifying when so many are crying out for a healing experience of genuine, empathic, unconditional love which can well reflect the love of God — and where so many compassionate therapists are getting on with the task?

And yet ... a pastoral corollary of the statement "truth is for people" is "people need truth" — *truth* about the deeply flawed nature of fundamental humanness (as well as its positive potential) and truth about the nature of radical healing. These are not abstract considerations with no practical, pastoral importance. A counsellor's assumptions and presuppositions about the basic human condition will inevitably filter through into his or her approach to therapy. Personal viewpoints are not just viewpoints: they determine the perceived *aim* of therapy. "Man's greatest need, it has been well said, is to know what *is* his greatest need".

Jesus Christ affirms that it is by knowing "the truth" inherent in his teaching that we will be set free (redeemed). "Truth is the objective apprehension of things as they are", including ourselves! — as distinguished from a vaunted inner illumination leading to self-sufficient self-governance — an illusion which is the essence of sin. "Sin is the assertion of our own will as opposed to the acceptance of God's will". It all began in the garden of Eden — the Adamic *antecedent* sin and guiltiness tragically transferred to us with its distressing effects (to take up Brian Thorne's line of thought) of "shame, inner fear and defensiveness". And yes, these miserable traits can produce a woundedness and self-punitiveness leading to grievously inappropriate attitudes and actions which can exacerbate self-diminishment, cause social disruption and damage other individuals.

Thus the truth about our flawed humanness goes deep and far (*cf chapter 4*) It's about the Adam in us. It's about a captivity, a thraldom from which we need liberation-redemption. It's about a fractured relationship with God in which we need reconciliation. Who can liberate us and bring us into an intimate relationship with our Creator/Father in a son/daughter bond? "Only one who has in His own being the status of sonship and who, having it, can impart it. *"If therefore the Son shall set you free, really free ye shall be"*. *(John 8:31-36.* Quotations are from *Readings in St John's Gospel — William Temple).*

In short, at the root of the human problem is a *principle* of evil endemic in personhood: "it lives in our nature". The evil which can invade us from an outside source — i.e. from the devil and from the "world" — *connects* with this and reinforces it. In his sinlessness Jesus could say, "The prince of this world is coming, he has no hold on me" (literally: "he has nothing in me") — *John 14:30.* With us it is not so.

On the cross Christ becomes, supremely, the substitutionary, sin-bearing Messiah of the Old Testament prophecies and psalms: the "suffering Servant" of *Isaiah 53* upon whom the Lord laid the iniquity of us all ... crushed ... his life a guilt offering, in order to bring us back to himself, healed by the Servant's wounds.

Various biblical metaphors (redemption, reconciliation —
along with justification and propitiation) illustrate aspects of
this *salvation;* significantly, the word itself *(soteria)* and its
cognates carries the meaning of "cure, remedy, health,
wellbeing-deliverance from peril". Therefore, these doctrinal
word-pictures clearly have profound psychological implications, as well as spiritual and moral. Importantly, the focus of
them all is our Lord Jesus Christ: his incarnation, life, death,
resurrection and exaltation are central. He himself becomes
pivotal to our personal *experience* of salvation — that is,
healing at its deepest level.

Justification is a *forensic* metaphor drawn from the law
court. Sin makes us guilty before the righteous Judge. The
death of Christ is one of penal substitution: the Innocent One
dying in place of the guilty many; the Righteous for the
unrighteous. Faith in him secures pardon and freedom from
condemnation.

Propitiation is a *religious* form of speech which takes us
into the Temple. Sin defiles us in God's sight, putting us
under his holy wrath — which is never to be thought of as
capricious, emotional or arbitrary (as human anger can be)
but as a pure, steady, uncompromising antagonism to evil in
all its forms and expressions *(Romans 1:18-32).* Christ's
death on the cross is sacrificial. Through "faith in his blood"
we come into peace with God and are "cleansed from every
sin".

Reconciliation is a *social* word-picture which reminds us
of friendship and family bonds: relationships, however
intimate and long-standing, can be impaired, or broken. The
most fundamental estrangement is between us and God; it is
this broken "vertical" relationship which leads to rifts (often
ugly and violent) on the 'lateral' plane between persons and
peoples. On the cross, cut off from the Father through bearing

the sin which separates *us* from him, Christ's death becomes an atoning death: through faith in him, crucified and risen, we are made "at one" again with God, and with each other, as the reconciled family of God. God becomes *Abba*.

Redemption (as we have illustrated) is an image of salvation drawn from the slave market. Sin is viewed as a bondage from which release is secured at tremendous cost. The price of our redemption is nothing less than "the precious blood of Christ". His death is "a ransom in place of and for the sake of many" *(Mark 10:45)*. "The death of Jesus means that there happens to him what would have had to happen to the many. Hence he takes their place" (F Büchsel) This truth is echoed in *1 Timothy 2:5-6*: "there is one God and one mediator between God and men, the man Christ Jesus, who gave himself as a ransom for all men."

There is a view of Calvary, which sees it as the place where human self-rejection and self-hatred are vindictively exteriorised and projected onto Christ — and he, by absorbing and exhausting it all, "neutralises" it. Thus he becomes the supreme example for us of goodness triumphing over evil and love countering the vengeful loneliness of self-despair. Surely, there is some truth in this: "Father, forgive them, for they do not know what they are doing" *(Luke 23:34* and *1 Peter 2:21-25)*. But this awesome, illimitable, deeply-moving love of Jesus is conveyed, supremely, in the above biblical word-pictures illustrating the profound significance of his atoning sacrifice and its enduring achievements.

These wonderful benefits clearly have a corporate aspect: they are features of a *shared* joy-filled Christ-centred experience of divine love which is to be lived out and commended persuasively to others, in relationship (fellowship) with other believers. For all four images are presented with *plural* pronouns: thus, "being justified by faith we have peace with

God"; "herein is love — not that we loved God, but that he loved us and sent his Son as an atoning sacrifice (*lit. the propitiation*) for our sins"; "..we rejoice in God through our Lord Jesus Christ, through whom we have now received reconciliation"; "..in (Christ) we have redemption through his blood, the forgiveness of sins, in accordance with the riches of God's grace that he lavished on us..." (*Romans 5:1-2; 1 John 4:10; Romans 5:11; Ephesians 1:7-8*).

Nowhere is this cross-centred, fellowship-creating truth and love more dramatically and efficaciously brought home to us than in the Eucharist, where broken bread and poured wine recall the tender mercy of our heavenly Father who gave his "only Son our Saviour Jesus Christ to suffer death upon the cross for our redemption; who made there (by his one oblation of himself once offered) a full, perfect, and sufficient sacrifice, oblation, and satisfaction, for the sins of the whole world...." In receiving this bread and wine, with all that they symbolise, we can experience deep cleansing and renewal, together.

Is it, then, possible that in rightly desiring to emphasise the love of God, "Liberal Christian Humanism" is, in fact, in danger of watering it down, by discounting or underestimating the presence of inborn evil and underrating the momentous vital centrality of the cross of Christ (understood in the light of the above four images of salvation)? What is the quintessential *content* of "the love of God"? Paul says that "God demonstrates his own love for us in this: While we were still sinners, Christ died for us" — here was suffering in our stead which secured our radical healing. See *Romans 5:8; Isaiah 53:4-6*. It cannot be affirmed too strongly that the Father and the Son were together in this all-surpassing act of redeeming love. God was reconciling us to himself *through* Christ and *in* Christ. See *2 Corinthians 5:18-19*.

"And he has committed to us the message of reconciliation" — and redemption. I do realise that psychotherapy is
not evangelism or proselytism! Through the wonder of
"common grace" God's healing power can be at work deep
within the human spirit in a way that "transcends and
encompasses all our knowing and all our skill". The core
conditions of unconditional positive regard, empathy and
congruence between counsellor and client may well reflect
divine love — with no conversion-strings attached! And many
people will need a lot of such loving, which can cast out fear *(1
John 4:18)* before they are able to receive the truth which can
set them free.

Nevertheless, I suggest that, from a biblical premise, Person-Centred Therapy and allied approaches at their deepest
and fullest level of healing will be a means by which God's
revealed truth — sensitively communicated explicitly or
implicitly — becomes a lamp illuminating the dark places of
the mind, present circumstances, and the path ahead, and,
above all, *shining onto the Person of the Redeemer*. Always,
as we move forward in this light towards the light of his actual
presence we will find that he is drawing near to *us* with
infinite compassion, to give — as only he can — true healing
and wholeness: salvation.

Through over forty years of pastoral ministry I have
known so many for whom this has become, not a desperate
pious hope, but a truth of experience. They are among that
great company, "a people belonging to God" who "declare the
praises of him who called (them) out of darkness into his
wonderful light". And as they face the future, their song, the
song of the redeemed, is one of realistic gladness:

I will sing the wondrous story
    of the Christ who died for me, —

how he left the realms of glory
    for the cross of Calvary.

Days of darkness still may meet me,
    sorrow's path I oft may tread;
But his presence still is with me,
    by his guiding hand I'm led.

                     (F H Rawley)

And there is more — so much more — to come. For re-demption has also an eschatological orientation. A great day is approaching when we shall know *full* redemption; when we shall be totally released from all sin, pain, futility and decay, and enjoy the indescribable glory of a redeemed cosmos — a new heaven and a new earth, where we shall be together forever with the Lord.

Meanwhile, the pull of that eternal glory draws us onward and upward in the here and now. "Lateral psychol-ogy/theology" is caught up in "Height psychology/theology"! The indwelling Spirit is the seal and guarantee and first fruits of that final, ultimate redemption: the future has begun!

CHAPTER 7

HEIGHT PSYCHOLOGY

"Ideals are the very stuff of survival" Lt Col John H Glen, Jr

"What is needed today is to complement, not to supplement or substitute, the so-called depth-psychology with what one might call height-psychology. Such a psychology would do justice to man's higher aspects and aspirations, including their frustrations." (It is clear that the writer would be happy to put "lateral" alongside "depth" psychology, as needing to be complemented in this way).

And who is the writer? The eminent Austrian psychiatrist Victor Frankl (1905-1997), who quotes John Glen (above) as "a 'height'-psychologist, indeed!" Among the psychologist-authors I have read — admittedly a less than exhaustive selection! — it is Frankl who has most stimulated my attention: and whose premises and methodologies have, in my view, the most resonances with biblical religion, in comparison with those of other schools — though not without certain dissonances too.

Frankl was a Professor of Neurology and Psychiatry at the University of Vienna Medical School; his approach came to be designated as the "Third Viennese School of Psychotherapy" (after those of Freud and Adler): the School of "*Logotherapy*". He was a visiting professor and guest lecturer at many other Universities in other countries; he held twenty-nine honorary doctorates and published over thirty books. He died on the 3rd September 1997 aged 92. His insight and compassion were globally respected, not least because they were forged in the furnace of human suffering.

Frankl modifies the contrasting extremes of Freudian pessimism and Rogerian optimism with a realism which combines elements of both but transcends them. Human nature, in his view, is a mix. The presence of evil and wickedness is undeniable; but so is an amazing propensity for practical goodness, even in the face of appalling suffering, often inflicted by other human beings motivated by depraved malice.

This is not armchair theorising or merely academic conjecture. Frankl endured three years as a prisoner in four concentration camps during the Nazi holocaust, the last being the extermination camp at Auschwitz where his wife was also taken. His life was saved when he unknowingly switched queues among those moving towards the gas chambers; he also survived Typhus. Returning to Vienna in 1945 he learned that his mother, father, brother and wife had all perished.

Observing the reactions of his fellow human beings in these horrendous conditions, and reflecting on his own suffering, he saw that the human spirit could rise above unspeakable anguish and the blackest despair. Endurance was determined by finding a purpose in living, even when immersed in terrible physical and mental pain, and facing death. People are not products of their circumstances, however crushing, nor of overwhelming desolation, but of conscious choices related to finding and fulfilling a sense of meaning — even when existence seems cruelly meaningless. The last ultimate freedom is the ability, which cannot be taken from us, to "choose one's attitude" to whatever life brings.

His book, *Man's Search for Meaning*, written in the year of his release has sold over nine million copies in twenty-six languages and has never been out of print. It is both a compelling narrative of his experience in the Death Camps, and his conclusions concerning the human capacity for hope by finding a reason for living. Frankl often quoted Nietzsche: "He who has a *why* to live can bear with almost any *how*" The *why* becomes the basis for choices, even with death imminent, rather than a defeated resignation to Fate. The essence of humanness is to search for, and find, Meaning — even in suffering — and to will to live in accordance with that Meaning.

Frankl frequently refers to the fact that for many people, probably most people, Meaning is synonymous with God, though he acknowledges that not everyone will construe Meaning in theistic terms. But certainly, the rare fellow-prisoners in the concentration camps who "committed themselves to the fundamental possibility of preserving their humanity" (and who, in doing so, gave an infectious example to others) "experienced a moral progression — moral and religious. For there broke out in many a prisoner in confinement, and because of confinement, what I have designated as a subconscious or a repressed relationship to God.

Let no one judge this religiosity disparagingly, or dispose of it as 'foxhole religion', as Anglo-Saxon countries term that religiosity which does not show until one is in danger. I would like to say that the religion which one does not have until things go badly is to me still preferable to that which one has only so long as things go well. I call that a 'bargainer's religion'" (*Psychotherapy and Existentialism (P and E)* — *Selected Papers on Logotherapy — Victor E Frankl*).

Frankl's view of God departs from the Jungian version. Jung located "God" in the personal and collective Unconscious as a principle of wholeness which needs to be accessed and "actualised". This process is aided by "a natural religious function" possessed by all human beings: "Man needs to experience the God-image within himself and to feel its correspondence with the God-forms that his religion gives to it".

In Frankl's thought, Meaning, having its focus in God, "Stems from a sphere beyond man and above man". Meanings and values must not be "subjectified", otherwise they lose their obligative quality, and they cannot summon us upwards, or call us forward. God is transcendent and we relate to him by exercising choice and acknowledging responsibility for the kind of life we live.

The final, moving sentences of his book sum up his drawn-from-experience philosophy: "In the concentration camps … in this living laboratory and on this testing ground we watched and witnessed some of our comrades behave like swine while others behaved like saints. Man has both potentialities within himself; which one is actualised depends on decisions but not on conditions. Our generation is realistic for we have come to know man as he really is. After all, man is that being who has invented the gas chambers of Auschwitz; however, he is also that being who has entered those gas chambers upright, with the Lord's Prayer or the *Shema Yisrael* on his lips."

The goal-directed nature of behaviour is an assumption shared by all psychologists. "It is clear that it is as legitimate to ask towards what end a process is directed, as to inquire from what cause it originated, and I believe that any Psychological description of human beings must attempt to answer both questions" *(The Integrity of the Personality — Anthony Storr)* This in-built purposiveness is interpreted in different ways, by depth psychologists and "lateral" psychologists, and Frankl critiques both approaches, and others.

Goal-Directedness

Frankl first met Freud when he was a student in Vienna; he always respected the famous Professor, who was then his hero; and he was briefly a disciple of Adler. But his psychological thinking later took a very different direction; he became increasingly critical of the Depth Psychology represented by both these men, though somewhat variant. At the same time he sought to retain elements of Psychoanalysis and Individual Psychology in his own system.

Freud, it seemed to him, belittled both humanness and the religious quest: the will-to-pleasure, rooted in the need to resolve inner conflict by satisfying urgent libidinal demands, was too primitively biological as a concept — and in fact self-defeating. "The more a man aims at pleasure by way of a direct intention, the more he misses his aim.... This is due to the fundamental fact that pleasure is a by-product, or side-effect, of the fulfilment of our strivings, but is destroyed or spoiled to the extent to which it is the main goal or target" *(P and E)*.

Frankl acknowledges the importance of the Unconscious but insists that there is a spiritual core to it which permeates the whole personality and which is drawn *towards* Meaning, to "God". Freud's claim that "Religion is the universal compulsive neurosis of mankind" is neatly countered by Frankl: "Compulsive neurosis may well be diseased religiousness." When the basic human quest for Meaning, for "God", is ignored or repressed it can become moribund and lead to psychological illness. *Height* psychology would "do justice to man's higher aspects and aspirations, including their frustrations."

Adler's "Will-to-power" is no less inadequate and self-defeating. Power has no satisfaction as an end in itself, it is only useful as a means of achieving or acquiring something else. "Thus we could say that while the will-to-pleasure mistakes the effect for the end, the will-to-power mistakes the means to an end, for the end itself".

In his later years Frankl became more outspokenly critical of Freud's and Adler's views, seeing them as largely responsible for the last century's alarming increase in sex-saturated hedonism and status-hungry materialism, and a corresponding devaluing of noble ideals and self-transcendence.

Behaviourism and its associated manipulation therapies also diminishes our humanness — some have said, by showing "contempt for people". Attributing neurosis to certain learning, or conditioning, processes, behaviour therapy accordingly prescribes re-learning or re-conditioning, to counteract it. But the "rat model", as Gordon Allport called it, viewing human beings as manipulable, denigrates their intrinsic dignity, their fundamental will-to-meaning and their urge to achieve true significance through self-transcendence.

These principles also formed the basis of Frankl's questioning of *Humanistic Psychology* with its insistence on the prime importance of self-actualisation through affirmative relationships.

Abraham Maslow is sometimes classed as an *existential psychologist* because he emphasises that fulfilment depends upon choices and decisions, as did Frankl. But because of his war-time experiences, Frankl was cautionary about Maslow's model of a "hierarchy of needs" whereby "lower" needs must be met before "higher" quests related to transcendent values can be exercised. Amidst the appalling humiliation and deprivation of the Death Camps, where human beings were reduced to nakedness, to nothing, they could still rise above basic needs and any kind of (impossible) self-actualisation, and engage with transcendent Meaning.

Frankl quoted Carl Rogers approvingly with regard to the therapeutic value of person-centred counselling rather than reliance on "professional" techniques. It is worth repeating his quotation from Rogers: "The warm, subjective, human encounter of two persons is more effective in facilitating change than is the most precise set of techniques growing out of learning theory or operant conditioning." But Frankl writes elsewhere: "A concept such as self-actualisation or self-realisation, is not a sufficient ground for motivation theory. It appears to me to be quite obvious that self-actualisation is an effect and cannot be the object of intention. Mirrored in this fact is the fundamental anthropological truth that self-transcendence is one of the basic features of human existence. Only as man withdraws from himself in the sense of releasing self-centred interest and attention will he gain an authentic mode of existence" *(P and E)*.

Moreover self-transcendence needs objective meaning and values to aim for: that which is inside us, components of the self, are not enough for true fulfilment. "Since self-actualisation refers to the fulfilment of the available possibilities, or potentialities, within the subject, we might well call it potentialism. The life-task of the individual is conceived of as the actualising of potentialities which will fulfil his personality to the greatest possible degree". But such "potentialism" has snags. "What would be the result if a man should merely actualise the potentials within himself?

An answer comes to mind in the case of Socrates. He confessed to the potentiality within him to become a criminal and, therefore, if he had succeeded in fully developing his potentialities, the great defender of law and justice would have been a common law breaker. *The potentialities of life are not indifferent possibilities: they must be seen in the light of meaning and values*" (my italics). "An adequate view of man can only be properly formulated when it goes beyond homeostasis, beyond self-actualisation, to the sphere of human existence in which man chooses what he will do and what he will be in the midst of an objective world of meanings and values" *(P and E plus following quotes)*.

For the Christian there are recognisable resonances here with the words of Jesus: (*Matthew 10, 39*) "Whoever finds his life will lose it, and whoever loses his life for my sake will find it." Augustine's famous words also have relevance: "Almighty God, in whom we live and move and have our being, who hast made us for thyself, so that our hearts are restless till they find their rest in thee."

The Will-to-Meaning is a higher quest than Freudian or Rogerian motivations for two reasons. First, "precisely because it is willed: it is not an instinctual drive or an inbuilt need demanding expression — if it were, a man would no longer really be concerned with Meaning itself but rather with his own equilibrium and thus, in the final analysis, with himself. But the Will-to-Meaning signifies that he is reaching out for meanings to fulfil. He is motivated by a pull as well as a drive".

Secondly, Frankl is somewhat scornful of the hidden motive behind the aims of self-realisation and self-fulfilment which is, he believes, "to lessen the tension aroused by the gap between what man is and what he ought to become.... There is not only a pathology of stress, but also a pathology of *absence* of tension.... I deem it a dangerous misconception of mental health that what man needs in the first place is homeostasis *a tout prix*. What a man really needs is a sound amount of tension aroused by the challenge of a Meaning he has to fulfil."

"It is false comfort to tell a man to forget *objective* ideals and values since they are nothing but expressions of the self, and therefore that he should concentrate on actualising his own potential: Man therefore need not reach out to the stars, to bring them down to earth, for the earth itself is a star!" Frankl writes, "It is my contention that ... a man finds identity to the extent to which he commits himself to something beyond himself, to a cause greater than himself. He must confront Meaning". He quotes Karl Jaspers: "What man is, he ultimately becomes through the cause he has made his own"; and Goethe: "If we take man as he is, we make him worse — if we take him as he ought to be, we can help him to become it."

Neuroses may validly be explained partially in classic psychoanalytical terms but, beyond psychogenic factors there are "higher" causes: a Will-to-Meaning which is *thwarted* — through being either unrecognised or denied. Frankl sees this diagnosis as being deeply and widely relevant: the main collective sickness at every level in society is a prevalent sense of meaninglessness, which he termed "existential vacuum". Generalising, he states, "Patients no longer complain of inferiority feelings or sexual frustration as they did in the age of Adler and Freud. Today they come to our clinics or offices because of feelings of futility." In his experience this is particularly true of students. He quotes Albert Camus: "There is but one truly serious problem, and that is ... judging whether life is or is not worth living" *(The Unheard Cry for Meaning)*.

Existentialism

Frankl's frequent use of the word *existential* and his quotations from Jaspers and Camus and others are reminders that he, too, is generally categorised as an "existential psychologist". But his quoting of leading figures in this movement does not imply a total identification with their stance.

Existentialism is a many-headed phenomenon. But in a psychological sense, as used by Frankl, for example, it refers to "the striving to find a concrete meaning in personal existence, that is to say, the will-to-meaning". This ties in with the general emphasis of the existentialist position that "each individual is constantly making choices, great and small, which cumulatively determine the kind of person he becomes." Plainly there *are* echoes here of Maslow and Rogers but the latter, as we have seen, lack Frankl's "height" dimension.

Atheistic versions of existentialism reflecting, for example the God-is-dead, life-is-meaningless position of Nietzsche stress that man must go-it-alone. If God does not exist, Sartre wrote, "Man is nothing else but that which he makes of himself. That is the first principle of existentialism." In practice this position leads to pessimism, even despair, for life without God signifies that meaning and purpose and moral values derived from belief in him are absent. Relativism rules.

Eventually, *Nihilism* takes over. Life can become a place of terrifying loneliness and dread. To picture this meaninglessness Nietzsche used the metaphor of a great abyss of infinite dark Nothingness which induces acute anxiety and "spiritual" nausea. Perhaps it was this terror which led to his final insanity.

Frankl was more aware than most of the "abyss": the horror which can confront us, especially with regard to man's depraved inhumanity to man.... But in facing up to the basic existential reality that life must still be lived, he affirmed, in contrast to afore-mentioned writers, that there *is* objective Meaning — with which the subjective Will-to-Meaning correlates. "The Meaning which a being has to fulfil is something beyond himself; it is never just himself." In combating "existential vacuum", self-transcendence is far superior to self-actualisation. "If meanings and values were just something emerging from the subject himself — that is to say, if they were not something that stems from a sphere beyond man and above man — they would instantly lose their demand quality ... their obligative quality". Frankl also emphasises that a person is responsible not only "for the fulfilment of the specific meaning of his personal life" (the essence of the existentialist position) — but is "also responsible *before* something, or *to* something, be it society, or humanity, or mankind, or his own conscience. However, there is a significant number of people who interpret their own existence not just in terms of being responsible to something but rather to some*one*, namely to God" *(P and E)*.

And behind conscience, to which we are responsible, many will acknowledge "that Being of whom this conscience is experienced to be the voice"; which gives it its obligative quality.

On a more everyday level, for most people — who are not too aware of Nietzsche's abyss or overwhelmed by a sense of Terror at life's futility — there is, nevertheless, a recurring feeling of meaninglessness attaching to our existence. We experience various hindrances to making sense of life. Our innate Will-to-Meaning can be thwarted by past experiences, present circumstances, personal temperament; it is sad if we take refuge in lesser motivations like the will-to-power or the will-to-pleasure — a life of getting and spending and status-seeking which shows that we have forgotten simply how to be.... These belittling compensations would be indicative of what Frankl calls "existential frustration".

In the interests of *true* fulfilment, that is, self-transcendence, this frustration must be faced and countered.... Man can exercise his neglected *noetic* powers — "the ability to take a stand not only towards the world but also towards himself … to reflect upon himself … to identify Meaning for himself, and to reach out to the fulfilment of it".

Logotherapy

To aid this exercise Frankl developed his *"logotherapy"*, which can be combined with other psychotherapeutic approaches but which is more effective because of its "height" dimension.

"Logos", for Frankl, has to do with the world of meaning and values. *"Logotherapy* is that psychotherapy which centres on life's meaning as well as man's search for this meaning. In fact, *logos* means 'Meaning'. However, it also means 'Spirit'. And logotherapy takes the spiritual or noological dimension fully into account" *(P and E)* In practice, logotherapists seek to help a person discover the Meaning to be fulfilled for him or her in their circumstances, to confront it, to feel responsible for reaching out for it and fulfilling it.

This is far from being impractically theoretical.

Frankl suggests that life can be seen as meaningful in three ways — a claim which is applicable to every person in any situation; he briefly designates these as the *creative*, the *experiential*, and the *attitudinal*. By the first, he means *through what we give* to life, especially by creative works: personal gifts of temperament, practical skills and talents and, above all, love and deeds of kindness, can enrich the lives of others and spread enjoyment and encouragement as well as leading (as a by-product) to self-fulfilment and self-transcendence. By *experiential* Frankl means *what we take from* the world: the enjoyment of Beauty in nature and art, the pleasure derived from so much that is good in our culture, and of love and kindness received; and from the appreciation of truth and humour....

Attitudinal relates especially to suffering: it means *"the stand we take* towards a fate we no longer can change (e.g. an incurable disease, such as an inoperable cancer … for what matters above all is the attitude we take towards suffering.)" This calls for humility and courage; "even a man who finds himself in the most dire distress — distress in which neither activity nor creativity can bring value to life, nor experience give meaning to it — such a man can still give his life meaning by the way and manner in which he faces his fate, in which he faces his suffering, in which he takes his suffering upon himself. Precisely in this way he has been given a last chance to realise values" (*P and E)* As new attitudes to suffering and grief take over they can be "turned into something positive and creative."

In no way can such views, especially those of meaning-in-suffering, be dismissed as unrealistic when expressed by a man with Frankl's profound personal experience of horror…. Christians will wish to superimpose upon all such reflections the deep significance of Calvary….

Height Sociology

Frankl's emphasis upon the *correlation* between a fundamental subjective Will-to-Meaning and an objective "world of Meaning and Values" (supra-Meaning) is of supreme significance for Logotherapy. Interesting corroboration of his "height" psychology is found in a book written by the sociologist Peter L Berger. In *A Rumour of Angels — Modern Society and the Rediscovery of the Supernatural* he breaks away from the dispassionate, "value-free" approach required in sociological studies and which informs his many other works, to address religious questions as a sociologist who is also a Christian.

Berger coins the phrase *"signals of transcendence"* to describe observable factors in human responses, attitudes and behaviour which indicate the existence of a supernatural reality beyond merely cause-and-effect reality. Here is "height sociology" with strong psychological overtones; but "the phenomena I am discussing are not 'unconscious' and do not have to be excavated from the 'depths' of the mind — they belong to ordinary everyday awareness". In the following paragraphs I reproduce Berger's five chosen "*signals of transcendence*" ("by no means an exhaustive or exclusive list") and add some personal comments.*

Propensity for Order

The first is man's "propensity for Order". Human beings crave Order and seek to create and preserve Order so that society becomes a "protective structure of meaning, created in the face of chaos". Within this Order the life of the group and individuals within it can make sense. "Deprived of such Order, both group and individual are threatened with the most fundamental terror, the terror of chaos that Emile Durkheim called '*anomie*'" (literally, a state of being "order-less" or, by extension, meaningless).

A legitimate inference is that this felt need for Order and its construction corresponds to an Order within the warp and woof of the universe, and a transcendent Reality character-ised by Order (or Meaning). The subjective propensity chimes with an objective state of Being.

Echoing this, Anthony Storr writes, "The human mind seems to be so constructed that the discovery, or perception,

---

* Berger predicted that people in the 21st Century will continue to be "religious" and asserts that "the religious impulse, the quest for meaning that transcends the restricted space of empirical exis-tence in this world, has been a perennial feature of humanity.... It would require something close to a mutation of the species to extinguish this impulse for good".

of order or unity in the external world is mirrored, transferred, and experienced as if it were a discovery of a new
order and balance in the inner world of the psyche". (Thus
Wordsworth can speak poetically of the felt immanence of
God in creation and, correspondingly, in "the mind of man").
"Similarly," continues Storr, "the process of reducing inner
discord and reaching a degree of unification within the psyche
has a positive effect upon the subject's perception of, and
relation with, the external world" (*Solitude — Anthony Storr*).

Clearly there are echoes here of Frankl's Will-to-Meaning
teaching, which Freud would dismiss as escapist wishful
thinking having no objective validity. It does seem undeniable
that the human desire to make sense of things, to recognise or
impose order, is common. Perhaps (as Alister McGrath
suggests) the wide appeal of Who Dunnits with their challenge to recognise clues and identify the solution indicates
this. We could add to this example the fascination of cross-
word puzzles and the satisfaction of completing them. But
arguably, most significant of all is the exercise of using words
to *express* meaning and *impose* meaning — in Schaeffer's
view, this is the most distinctively human thing about us,
reflecting the image of God who reveals himself to us in
words, and supremely in the Word incarnate and in *his*
words.

Thus Tennyson, representing many other poets and authors writes of the solace found in striving to clothe strong
emotions, in this case incoherent sorrow, in words which
help, however inadequately, to make it understandable:

> I sometimes hold it half a sin
>   To put in words the grief I feel;
> For words, like Nature, half reveal
>   And half conceal the Soul within.

But, for the unquiet heart and brain,
A use in measured language lies;
The sad mechanic exercise,
Like dull narcotics, numbing pain.

In words, like weeds, I'll wrap me o'er,
Like coarsest clothes against the cold:
But that large grief which these enfold
Is given in outline and no more.

(In Memoriam)

Graham Greene declared, "Writing is a form of therapy: sometimes I wonder how all those who do not write, compose or paint can manage to escape the madness, the melancholia, the panic fear which is inherent in the human situation". Robert Frost describes a poem as "a momentary stay against confusion"; it does not solve problems but clears a sufficient space to think about them.

T S Eliot writes that in poetry especially, words, like notes in music, derive their meaning from their relationship with other words. It is in their relation to the pattern, the Order of the whole, that meaning is conveyed echoing the Meaning and Order at the heart of all things. "After *The Waste Land* Mr Eliot's poetry becomes the attempt to find meaning in the whole of his experience to include all that he has known." The distinctive music and language of his poetry reveals his vision of life, which "finds its definition increasingly in the historic Christian terms. We can then say, finally, that mystically the subject of each poem (notably *Four Quartets*) and of the whole poem is Christ, Alpha and Omega, the Beginning and the End, Author and Finisher of our Faith" (*The Art of TS Eliot — Helen Gardner*).

Hopefully, also, the harnessing of words to express truth

lies at the heart of systematic theology: which, whilst submitting itself to biblical revelation seeks to express that revelation in a systematic order — beginning with Creeds and Confessions of Faith. Underlying this recognition of God's self-disclosure in his Word is the perceived reasonableness of a Personal Creator communicating with his created persons in verbalised form. Our urge as human beings to express our feelings and grope for meaning, *in words*, reflects the fact that we are created as language-communicating beings. Thus we are at our best when we attempt to use words to expound and to set in order and apply what God has said to us. This reveals a propensity-to-Order of the first order! (In connection with this theological line of thought, the "*logos*" (word) of Frankl's "*logotherapy*" is pregnant with meaning, biblically: this will be explored in the next chapter (8)).

On a more day-to-day level, Berger cites the example of a mother comforting a small child who has awoken in the night from a bad dream and is afraid of the dark. She will do everything — turn on a lamp, cradle the child, speak gentle comfort — everything to communicate "*don't be afraid — everything is all right, everything's in order*". All such reassurance, which is a fundamental craving of all human beings of whatever age and in whatever circumstances "implies a statement about reality as such". "Man's ordering propensity implies a transcendent Order, and each ordinary gesture is a signal of this transcendence".

The mother's role, the problem solver's aptitude, the strivings of poets, artists, and composers, the work of systematic theologians — and countless other human activities, all point to and are derived from an ultimate Order. "Religion then, is not only (from the point of view of empirical reason) a projection of human order, but (from the point of view of what might be called *inductive faith*) the ultimately true vindication of human order". This principle of Order is foundational to Berger's other *'signals of transcendence'*.

The Argument from Play

Pleasure derived from play, entertainment, skilled perform-ance, artistic expression, is a basic human experience. Time stands still. We are temporarily distant from life's immediate concerns. For a short time we are transported into another world, and our own world and its preoccupations is sus-pended. This is particularly poignant when the context, in the real world, is acute suffering and the presence of death — as in the Death Camps; or if danger threatens. Berger cites the example of the continuation of concerts in Vienna during a time of invasion: "just before the Soviet troops occupied Vienna in 1945 the Vienna Philharmonic gave one of its scheduled concerts.

There was fighting in the immediate proximity of the city, and the concert goers could hear the rumbling of the guns in the distance. The entry of the Soviet army interrupted the concert schedule — if I'm not mistaken, for about a week. Then the concerts resumed, as scheduled. In the universe of this particular play, the world-shattering events of the Soviet invasion, the overthrow of one empire and the cataclysmic appearance of another, meant a small interruption in the programme. Was this simply a case of callousness, of indiffer-ence to suffering? Perhaps in the case of some individuals, but, basically, I would say not. *It was rather an affirmation of the ultimate triumph of all human gestures of creative beauty over the gestures of destruction, and even over the ugliness of war and death"* (my italics).

Where does this experience of joyful "play", unhindered by the hardest circumstances, come from? Freud would probably explain it in terms of regression to childish magic along the lines, again, of escapist wishful fantasy. But arguably "it" points beyond itself and beyond man's nature to a 'supernatural' justification. It is a *signal of transcendence* because it signifies an engagement with something breaking in from above: an echo (from a Christian point of view) of the joy and pleasure in his creation, and in human creativity celebrating this, which resides in the heart of Christ (*Colossians 1:16*).

Even holed up in a miserable Philippian dungeon, Paul could sing and write from his heart of the joy and peace of Christ and exhort his fellow Christians "whatever is true, whatever is noble, whatever is right, whatever is pure, whatever is lovely, whatever is admirable — if anything is excellent or praiseworthy — think about such things" (*Philippians 4:8*).

Whenever we are "surprised by joy", especially in contrastingly dismal situations, it is logical to conclude that the surprise element is released in us and comes from a source outside ourselves. "Though the fig-tree does not bud and there are no grapes on the vines, though the olive crop fails and the fields produce no food, though there are no sheep in the pen and no cattle in the stalls, yet I will rejoice in the Lord, I will be joyful in God my Saviour. The sovereign Lord is my strength; he makes my feet like the feet of a deer, he enables me to go on the heights. *For the director of music. On my stringed instruments*" (my italics) (*Habakkuk 3:17-19*).

The Argument from Hope

The prominence of hope as an essential element of the human situation, and in the psychology of individuals has been emphasised in recent decades by the theologians Jurgen Moltmann and Wolfhart Pannenberg, along with the Christian existentialist Gabriel Marcel.

Berger writes, "human existence is always oriented towards the future. Man exists by constantly extending his being into the future, both in his consciousness and in his activity." An essential dimension of this 'futurity' of man is hope. It is through hope that men overcome the difficulties of any given here-and-now.

And it is through hope that men find meaning in the face of extreme suffering.

Where does this hope come from? From a Freudian perspective, hope, especially hope with religious overtones, is essentially "childish" and contrasts with "mature" acceptance of things as they are (including the "final reality" — of death) and a stoic attitude, which has been called the "ethic of honesty".

"It hardly needs to be said," states Berger "that this kind of stoicism merits the deepest respect and, in fact, constitutes one of the most impressive attitudes of which man is capable. Freud's calm courage in the face of Nazi barbarity and in his own final illness may be cited as a prime example of this human achievement." This stance does reflect Greek culture with its absence of hope and where "in the final analysis men had to stand without hope before the hostile forces of guilt and death", and any "religious" promises of immortality were pipe-dreams.

But it is difficult to dismiss hope by interpreting it in merely psychological terms. Hope really does seem to spring eternal in the human breast. It appears to be "an intrinsic constituent of our being"; it exists at the very core of our *humanitas*. And this persisting presence of hope in the human psyche, Berger suggests, *points towards a transcendent reality beyond present experience.*

Biblically, this intuitive *rapport* between "natural expectations" and "supernatural fulfilment" is supported by the revelation that God is both the origin and the object of hope: that is, hope as a personal attitude in his people is a gift of God, and he himself and his blessing is the fulfilment towards which hope is directed. The two aspects, subjective and objective, are frequently juxtaposed. The Psalmist writes "Find rest, O my soul, in God alone; my hope comes from him. He alone is my rock and my salvation; he is my fortress, I shall not be shaken" (*Psalm 62:5*) Similarly (*Jeremiah 29:11f*) "for I know the plans I have for you, declares the Lord, plans to prosper you and not to harm you, plans to give you hope and a future. Then you will call upon me and come and pray to me, and I will listen to you. You will seek me and find me when you seek me with all your heart. I will be found by you".

The classic New Testament expression of the combined meanings of hope as attitude and object is *Hebrews 11:1* where faith gives "substance" to our hope, that is, it is "the assurance of things hoped for". Present hope and that which is hoped for are conjoined by faith: "one cannot separate hope as a personal attitude from the objective content of hope".

Clearly this biblical perspective does not validate all forms of human hope: hope is not automatically authentic — the real thing. It may be wishful thinking. The Bible itself recognises that subjective hope may be futile and erroneous, lacking any valid basis: "the fool's hope" (i.e. that of the godless) "will come to nothing" (*Proverbs 11:7*). Nevertheless, Berger claims, hope, by its very existence in the human heart, however irrational and confused is, arguably, a "*signal of transcendence*" — in Frankl's terms, an indication of man's basic Will-to-Meaning.

From a Christian point of view this may well be true, but not the whole truth. God *has* "set eternity in the hearts of men". Human beings are not merely creatures of time; there is within them that which transcends time, intuitions of God's eternity (echoes of hope?). It is true that immersed in their history, in the time-process, they cannot discern the plan and pattern of the whole: "they cannot fathom what God has done from beginning to end".

They can, however, be grateful for his blessing and for the enjoyment of his gifts and perfect workmanship, and be drawn to revere him — thus glimpsing something of his Eternity in their Today (*Ecclesiastes 3:11f*). And this position, this attitude, can, by grace, lead to a reaching out and up towards a personal engagement with the eternal God — the God of all hope. The *link*, when, by the power of the Holy Spirit, this connection is truly made and experienced, is Christ. It is through him that God's salvation-fulfilment has broken into our "today". What was previously, in Old Testament times, future, has now, in him, become present to faith.

"Realised Eschatology" is focused in him and its blessings are communicated to us by the Holy Spirit: for this reason, (that is because it is Christ-centred), this hope does not disappoint us either with respect to the here and now, or to the future glory which is kept in heaven for us.

The Argument from Damnation

"This refers to experiences in which our sense of what is humanly permissible is so fundamentally outraged that the only adequate response to the offence as well as to the offender seems to be a curse of supernatural dimensions".

Commonly, monstrously evil crimes such as the murder of children trigger a reaction deeper than incredulity and abhorrence and condemnation: they provoke a demand for *damnation*: "may he rot in hell". Such moral and emotional outrage reveals a conviction that certain deeds not only offend a sense of justice: they cry out to heaven. And "deeds that cry out to heaven also cry out for hell". In other words, not only does a person guilty of such wickedness put himself outside the community of fellow human beings; "he also separates himself in a final way from a moral order that transcends the human community, and thus invokes a retribution that is more than human."

Bluntly, the capacity, in the human psyche, for such moral horror is validated as a *"signal of transcendence"* by the biblical revelation of divine revulsion and justice in relation to heinous deeds, and the existence of hell.

For the Christian it also points with overwhelming poignancy to the awe-inspiring relevance of Calvary, where wrath and mercy meet in atoning sacrifice … and eternal salvation, even for the worst sinner who truly repents and believes, is secured.

The Argument from Humour

Lots of earnest analyses of humour have been written. "Humour can be dissected, as a frog can, but the thing dies in the process and the innards are discouraging to any but the pure scientific mind" (E B White). In Freud's theory, humour is explained by the discrepancy between the demands of super-ego and libido! He may be onto something. As a generalisation, it is probably true that the comic *is* all about discrepancy — the incongruent juxtaposition of different elements. It is usually the *incongruous* that strikes us as funny.

The learned professor's trousers fall down in the middle of a lecture. "She had a penetrating sort of laugh. Rather like a train going into a tunnel" (P G Wodehouse) The final 'e' of a gravestone inscription is unfortunately omitted, so it reads "Lord she was thin". Journalist to Olympic athlete "Are you a pole-vaulter?" Puzzled reply, "No, I'm a German, but how do you know my name?". —

Vicar (me) to very elderly Norfolk village resident: "Have you lived here all your life?" Answer: "Not yet, sir".

Jewish humour is particularly funny in its tongue-in-cheek familiarity with the Almighty: Granny on beach with small grandson; freak wave sweeps the child out to sea; Granny looks up to heaven, "you gotta do something — quick". Next wave deposits drenched grandson, spluttering, at her feet. Again, she looks up: "he was wearing a hat. Where's his hat?". *Etc etc etc.*

Humour as a signal of transcendence? Berger's point is that we find the incongruous funny *because* it does not conform to the congruousness we expect — to Order, to the predictable, to life's serious purpose. The banana skin interrupts our assumed human dignity. (I love James Thurber's Wordsworthian definition: "humour is emotional chaos recollected in tranquillity.") Also, by laughing, we escape from various imprisonments of the human spirit. Humour releases us into an appreciation of the absurdity of human self-sufficiency: nuances of humour point to an awareness that human beings are not all-wise and omni-competent. It reassuringly cuts us down to size. Humour wrecks over-weaning seriousness, punctures pomposity, relativises the seemingly rock-like certainties of a current world-view. In doing so it signals the existence of true Congruity — the Order and coherence at the heart of things, conformity to which constitutes our true dignity: in a word, putting God first.

Humour in both Testaments of the Bible makes this claim: it is certainly present, and reveals spiritual truth; we laugh and learn. For example, the spontaneous laughter of Abraham and Sarah in response to the startling prognostication that at the age of one hundred, and ninety, respectively they are to have a child, is faithfully recorded. It would be a bit much heavily to construe this mirth as simply shameful disbelief — who *wouldn't* laugh in their situation? True, Sarah is reproached by the Lord for her laughter and her nervous denial — but only gently (dare we say good-humouredly?). Calvin uses the phrase "friendly reprehension" and "tender indulgence" in commenting on the incident. The serious point of the narrative is, surely, that God can make the laughable believable. Sarah's laughter of incredulity becomes the laughter of joy. Thus the child is to be called Isaac meaning "he laughs" and through him God's everlasting covenant with his descendants will be established (*Genesis 17:15-19; 18:10-15; 21:6-7*).

The laughter of pure joy derived from God's blessing is referred to in *Psalm 126* "when the Lord restored the fortunes of Zion we were like men restored to health. Our mouths were filled with laughter, our tongues with songs of joy".

Other examples of Old Testament humour-pointing-to-God could be cited. For example, David the shepherd-boy submerged and completely incapacitated under Saul's outsize body-armour resorts to his sling — and trust in God. The book of Proverbs frequently provokes a smile within its over-all aim of commending a way of life dictated by God's wisdom — see *Chapter 6:9-10; 19:24; 27:14-15* (e.g. "if a man loudly blesses his neighbour early in the morning, it will be taken as a curse"!).

Jesus himself uses humour in this way in certain parables and word-pictures: by making his hearers laugh at comical foibles and pathetic pretensions which they instantly recognised, he brought home to them in home-spun ways the wisdom of putting God first. There is the picture of a man rushing out of the Temple leaving his offering behind (*Matthew 5:23*). One writer says, "Matthew 24: 43 alludes to the idiotic attitude of a man who does not prepare against robbery unless he knows the thief is coming!" — a picture of lack of readiness for the coming of the Son of Man. There is surely humour in the account of Zacchaeus, the little man up a tree — who ends up finding salvation in his own home. There is humour in the lessons Peter learned through the Lord's teaching (*John 13*) and in the account of his personal experiences: his escape from prison (*Acts 5:17-32*), the unclean food from heaven offered to him (*Acts 10, 9-16*), being left knocking at the door (*Acts 12:12-16*), and the tribune's misunderstanding (*Acts 21:37-40*).

In all these droll narratives, God is in the background working out his purposes.

"Paradoxical Intention"

Back to Frankl: a particular therapeutic technique he promoted was that of "paradoxical intention" which utilises two human attributes — a spiritual dimension and a sense of humour. The approach addresses the phenomenon, well-known to psychiatrists, of anticipatory anxiety. "It is commonly observed that such anxiety often produces precisely that situation feared by the patient." It is self-fulfilling. Ironically, excessive *attention* to the problem (self-observation) and excessive *intention* (striving for a contrasting attitude) can increase the debilitating power of such neuroses *(P and E)*.

Detachment from, and rising above, the symptoms can be enabled by laughing at them. Frankl quotes Gordon Allport (from his book *The Individual and His Religion*) "the neurotic who learns to laugh at himself may be on the way to self-management, perhaps to cure". "Paradoxical intention represents a therapeutic application of Allport's statement: it makes use of humour to release a healing detachment, and self-transcendence. Practitioners claim to have proved its effectiveness 'in many cases of phobia, obsessions, impotency, and depression'" *(The Christian and the Couch — An Introduction to Christian Logotherapy — Donald F Tweedie).*

How does it work?

By encouraging a person who is afraid that something will happen to him, to intend or wish for, even if only for a second, precisely what he fears — rather than anxiety-increasing avoidance or desperate obsessive resistance. Laughable exaggeration of the threat can serve to diminish the symptoms of anxiety.

Imagine a person who fears a fit of panicky trembling in a dreaded social situation: applying the principles of paradoxical intention he determines, when the situation comes about, to out-tremble anyone who has ever trembled — to be the world's greatest trembler. Result: the more he tries, the less he can do so. The whole thing becomes a giggle, and the dread is dissolved because his attitude to his symptoms has been changed by humour.

A woman fears that she will collapse in the street following an onset of palpitations. Sure enough the palpitations do begin to happen. She is encouraged, when they next begin, to go into the street and *make* her heart beat faster, and try to collapse there and then. This endeavour is so comically unsuccessful that laughter gets the better of her. Soon, the symptoms fail to transpire, and the fear of them disappears. The fear of blushing, or stammering in confusion, in company becomes an anticipatory anxiety — so much so that it inevitably materialises. The principles of paradoxical intention suggest that, instead of trying *not* to blush, *try* to blush: this is so ridiculously impossible that the fear is cut down to size.

Similarly, to resolve, in a group, to excel at stammering and talking gibberish, like no-one has ever heard before, is such a hilarious picture, and so impossible to actualise without laughing, that the obsessive phobia related to the problem soon ceases to incapacitate social mixing, because of detachment from it. Numerous other, more poignant, examples are given. In all cases, humour is used to reveal what makes for true health and well-being which, in turn, has to do with self-transcendence: a *rapport*, and an in-touchness, with Meaning.

"Height psychology" and "Height sociology" direct our attention to the transcendent. But they are not *necessarily* theocentric — and certainly not Christo-centric as the Bible is. It is possible to construe Frankl's "Meaning (*Logos*)" as an abstract principle: Berger's *Signals of Transcendence* can be thought of as no more than that — "a rumour" of God. Neither require belief in an infinite-personal God as a source of truth and authentic religious experience.

They are encouraging us to look in the right direction — "upwards" — but that's all. Both need to be given content and truly healing relevance by the "Height Theology" of Holy Scripture, centred, as it is, on Jesus Christ: *Logos-incarnate*. "May the God of our Lord Jesus Christ, the glorious Father, give you the spirit of wisdom and *revelation*, so that you may know him better" (*Ephesians 1:17*).

CHAPTER 8

REVELATION

"Teach me your ways so I may know you" — Exodus 33: 13

The *doctrine* of *Revelation* is about God making himself known, revealing to us truths about himself and how they impinge upon us, of which we would otherwise stay ignorant. Without his self-revelation God would remain hidden and therefore inaccessible. But he has disclosed himself to us in order that we may know him, love him, worship him and serve him in a personal relationship.

In terms, then, of *systematic* theology, revelation is foremost: it comes first, *before* regeneration and redemption and every other doctrine, because these depend upon revealed truth for their accurate formulation and experiential verification. But revelation does have particular relevance to height psychology — and, more importantly, to "height theology" — and that is why it is considered in this chapter.

For God's self-disclosure is, of necessity, transcendent in origin: it comes to us from above. In this sense, all theology is "height theology": its source and its terminus is God. For the Christian, therefore, it follows that all talk of a height dimension to human existence linked to transcendent Meaning is contingent upon a correlation between our lives and God's revelation of himself.

Key question: how does God reveal himself? What form does revelation take? The answer demonstrates further theological relevance to Frankl's height psychology — and especially his *logotherapy* — because *Logos* may be seen as the key. Biblically, *Logos* (translated as "Word" in the Bible) denotes God revealing himself in creation, and in words, written and uttered; both signify God "speaking". He speaks things into being and into continued existence ("God said ... and it was so" — is the recurring *motif* of Genesis Chapter 1 and all things are sustained by his powerful Word, through Christ (*Hebrews 1:3*): his is a *creative* and *maintaining* Word). It is accompanied by its *verbal* form: God tells us about himself, explains his will and his acts, in *words* which can evoke the response of intelligent faith (*1 Thessalonians 2:13 cf Romans 10:14-15*). Both these revelational aspects of God-speaking (immanent power and verbal statements) are expressed by the doctrine of *Logos*.

Theologians distinguish between the two by using the terms General or Natural Revelation (because it is given in and through created things) and Special Revelation (because it is found only in the words of Holy Scripture). The first *can* make sense to all people, and *should* lead them towards an awareness of God — but not always is this so by any means (*Romans 1:18-20*).

The effectiveness of the second (Special Revelation) depends upon reading or hearing, and receiving and obeying God's Word, which in turn depends upon an inner illumination — what we might call *subjective revelation* — by the Holy Spirit.

In reflecting upon his conversion through the gospel, Paul draws an interesting parallel between God's *creative* Word and his *saving* Word (between his General and Special Revelation): "God who said, 'let light shine out of darkness', made his light shine in our hearts to give us the light of the knowledge of the glory of God in the face of Christ" (*2 Corinthians 4:6*). The Logos-light of creation becomes the Logos-light of the preached gospel (*v 4*), which is internalised as a saving knowledge of God's glory in Jesus Christ, Logos-incarnate.

In the interests of pursuing its psychological significance it is worth exploring a little more deeply the background, development and "Christianisation" of the term *Logos*.

Logos

The "Logos-idea" (adopted by Frankl) was in existence before the time of Christ. Heraclitus (some six centuries earlier) seems to have been the first to promulgate the concept of *Logos* — as *the Divine Reason Immanent in nature and in man*. "He seems to conceive it as a rational principle, power or being which *speaks* to man from without and from within — the Universal Word which, for those who have ears to hear, is both audible in nature and in their own hearts — the voice, in short, of the Divine" *(Christianity According To St John — W F Howard)*.

This divine Word gives the whole of creation, including human beings, unity, coherence and meaning; in human beings this principle was evidenced supremely by reason and speech. The term "Logos spermatikos" (seminal Word) came to be widely used in the centuries leading up to and following New Testament times — because, like seed, it gives form to unformed matter. "Regarded as the *Logos*, God is the omni-present Wisdom by which all things are steered" *(W F Howard)*.

It seems to be this thought-form which lies behind Victor Frankl's use of the term, and his *logotherapy* seeks to facilitate a connection between the Logos-principle within the human personality and the supreme Reason, Purpose and Power (which obviously reflect divine moral values) in the universe. So, through counselling, a person's will-to-meaning is assisted in identifying and responding to the "pull" of supra-Meaning in a manner appropriate to that individual's state of mind and personal circumstances. "In logotherapy the patient is … confronted with meaning and purpose and is challenged to fulfil them." Obviously, this presupposes an "objective correlate" to the subjective will-to-meaning and "this (outside) world of meaning and values may rightly be termed *Logos*".

It is the "objective quality" which gives them their obligative quality and thus their therapeutic effectiveness: "what man needs is not a tensionless state but the striving and struggling for something worth longing and groping for" — that is, a meaning beyond himself, higher than himself, never just himself (*Psychotherapy and Existentialist (P and E)* — *Victor E Frankl*).

Arguably, to a certain extent Paul would agree (*Philippians 3:12-14*). But *his* "logotherapy" goes both deeper and higher than Frankl's because it is derived from God's revealed will in Holy Scripture and centred in the exalted Christ. However, many scholars aver that echoes of contemporary usage of the term *Logos*, duly "Christianised", can also be detected in Paul and other New Testament writers.

Shortly before the New Testament was written an interesting man called Philo came onto the scene. His dates overlap with Paul (c 20BC—c 50AD); he was a Jew whose intellectual home was Athens and his important contribution was to enrich the Greek Logos-concept inherited from Heraclitus by infusing emphasis from Hebrew religion.

In the Greek translation of the Old Testament, made about this time (the Septuagint) *Logos* is used to translate the Hebrew word *dabhar* which means, basically, "that which lies behind", and can relate to both "word" and "thing" or "event". It is what makes them meaningful. *Dabhar* is God's self-revelation by word and deed.

In fact, the Bible makes no clear distinction between what

God says and what he does: "words and deeds are quite indifferent modes of divine energy. Words are also actions, and actions are a kind of words" (*St John — R V G Tasker*) Thus in relation to the origin of the natural world, *dabhar* can describe the *creative Word* of God. Thus the Psalmist writes, "let all the earth fear the Lord; let all the people of the world revere him. For *he spoke, and it came to be; he commanded and it stood firm" (Psalm 33:8 –9).*

Philo develops the Logos-concept in accordance with this Old Testament view, and *Logos (dabhar)* comes to be understood as an extension of God's personality signifying his self-revelation: his Word, both spoken and "done". *But never truly personalised.*

The Good News of the New Testament, represented by Paul's writings (*e.g. Colossians 1:15-20*) and stated with particular clarity in the opening verses of John's gospel is that the *Logos* becomes embodied in a mortal man.

Jesus Christ is Logos-incarnate.

"In the beginning was the Word, and the Word was with God, and the Word was God. He was with God in the beginning. Through him all things were made; without him nothing was made that has been made. In him was life, and that life was the light of men…. The Word became flesh and made his dwelling among us. We have seen his glory, the glory of the One and Only, who came from the Father, full of grace and truth" (*John 1:1-3 and 14*).

God presenced himself among us, on earth, *as a human being. The incarnation means that Jesus Christ himself is, truly, God-with-us. He who, as the second Person of the Holy Trinity, was with God, was God from the beginning, the agent of creation by whom all things came into being and in whom they hold together, has made the glorious fullness of God visible in human form. And God, who in the past revealed himself frequently through the *words* of the prophets and other chosen spokesmen, has now "spoken to us by his Son" — through whom he made the universe (*Hebrews 1:1-3*).

By extension, the total gospel-message (good news) is true *Logos* because its sum and substance is Jesus Christ. Thus it is described as "the Word (*Logos*) of reconciliation (2 Corinthians Chapter 5: 19) and "the Word (*Logos*) of life (Philippians Chapter 2: 16) because it, too, brings about what it proclaims: transformation in response to faith.

To quote Peter again, writing to new Christians: "You have purified yourselves by obeying the truth so that you have sincere love for your brothers ... for you have been born again, not of perishable seed, but of imperishable, through the living and enduring word (*Logos*) of God ... *and this is the word that was preached to you*" (*1 Peter 1:22-25 cf James 1:18 and 21:* "he chose to give us birth through the word (*Logos*) of truth ... therefore, get rid of all moral filth and the evil that is so prevalent, and humbly accept the word (*Logos*) planted in you, which can save you").

We have established that biblically *Logos* has a threefold meaning.

(1) It refers to God's *immanent* power and wisdom (*cf Proverbs 8:22-31)* in the creation: all things were made and are sustained in being by the divine *Logos* (*Psalm 147:15-18; Psalm 148:8*).

To those with eyes that see, otherwise invisible and unknowable qualities of God are disclosed in Nature. "The heavens declare the glory of God" and "the whole earth is full of his glory" (*cf Romans 1:20*).

Logos is, therefore, the agent both of creation in itself and of "creational revelation".

(2) *Logos* describes God *speaking*: that is, his self-

revelation in *words*; to use Francis Schaeffer's expression, "He is there and he is not silent". Holy Scripture is the verbal transcript of God's mind: he has told us truth about himself in the words of the Bible's speakers and writers; their words (*logoi*) are correlative with the Word (*Logos*). What Scripture says, God says.

(3) *Logos* finds its definitive expression in Jesus Christ, who is *Logos-incarnate*: the Word-made-flesh. "He is the image of the invisible God.... In Christ all the fullness of the Deity lives in bodily form" (*Colossians 1:15 and Chapter 2:9*). In him all creation coinheres and divine verbal communication finds its zenith.

Logos as God-immanent and as God-speaking, has its supreme focus in Jesus Christ. In him we both meet God and hear God. Moreover, through him, who was the agent of a creation now spoiled as the result of human sin, all things are/will be reconciled to God — by his blood, shed on the cross. This eternal cosmic glory will be enjoyed by a redeemed humanity; of this we are assured in the *word* of the gospel (*Colossians 1:19-23*) and our response of saving faith is evoked by Christ's own spoken promises and invitations.

From this three-fold meaning of *Logos* we may draw a *logotherapy* which is profoundly healing — infinitely more so than Frankl's, for his own theism is fuzzy, he does not set great store by the Bible as logos-written, nor give credence to the unique glory of Jesus Christ as Logos-incarnate. Nevertheless he does direct our attention to transcendent Meaning and posits a corresponding will-to-meaning as the most fundamental aspect of our humanness, the ignoring of which leads to anxiety and despair. St Augustine famously makes this point in a theocentric way: "Thou hast created us for thyself, and our heart cannot be quieted til it may find repose in Thee".

Christian Logotherapy

It will be remembered that Frankl's claim for *logotherapy* was that it could make life meaningful in three fundamental areas which apply to us all: he called these the *experiential* (enjoyment of what life offers us), the *creational* (fulfilment through what we give to life) and *attitudinal* (the stand we take towards a fate we no longer can change). (I have switched the order of the first two).

It can prove profitable to examine the Bible's three-fold Logos-revelation in relation to Frankl's three areas of relevance. The first two aspects of Logos-revelation (general and special) will be considered in the following paragraphs; reflections on Jesus Christ as Logos-incarnate are reserved for the final chapter.

Logos as God-Immanent — General Revelation
The Enjoyment of What Life Gives

"You should get out more — and get a life!"

Not bad logotherapy — for someone stressed out by the claustrophobic pressures of an all-consuming job or hectic life style. Workaholics and compulsive activists can get to feeling equally done in and dejected; worse: thoroughly depressed.

When *logos* is not immediately discernible, banished by "the madding crowd's ignoble strife" and swamped by low spirits, it can make sense to escape to the open air. A stiff cliff top walk in the face of a strong wind, a stroll through pine woods, the sight of flower-filled meadows and green hills, the sound of bird song, even a drenching from a down-pour, any of these can make a big difference.

It may not yield counsel to the psyche, but it will yield oxygen to the body and balm to the emotions, which is next best. Countryside and seascape, fresh air, sun, wind and rain, can provide the best medicine for the morose, the best

refreshment for the fatigued, the surest tonic for the discon-
solate.

What is this life if, full of care,
We have no time to stand and stare?

Do these apposite words of W H Davis echo those of Jesus Christ in the Sermon on the Mount, when he exhorted us
to calm down and consider the birds and the flowers? Yes and
no. Christ *was* addressing the distracting, life-cramping
effects of care — anxiety: "Do not *worry* about your life." And
the word "stare" could serve as a fairly accurate translation of
"*look*", "consider so as to learn from" (*compare Matthew
6:25 and 28; Luke 12:24 and 27*).

But Jesus, who himself clearly delighted in the wonders
of nature, would have us see *beyond* birds of the air and
flowers of the field, to the God who created them, sustains
them in being and provides for them with loving care. And to
draw lessons: "therefore, I tell you, do not worry.... Are you
not much more valuable than they? ... Your heavenly Father
knows" your needs.

Truly understood, here is the greatest antidote to the all-
too-common problem of anxiety.

Jesus does not *stop* at the injunction "don't be anxious" —
this can take the form of a "repressive self-suggestion" which
can make matters worse. It is also unrealistic — as surely, we
all know. But to combat worry by trust in a loving heavenly
Father who is utterly dependable and faithful, is a very
different response.

Similarly, relief from anxiety-produced tension and exhaustion will not come from the contemplation of nature as
such: this can only lead to a solace which is, at best, temporary, and end in disappointment. The poet, George Herbert,
reminds us how we can lose out by resting in complacent

"nature-worship", and not looking through and beyond the creation to the Creator:

> He would adore his gifts instead of me,
> And rest in Nature, not the God of Nature,
> So both should losers be

As Elizabeth Barrett Browning reminded us, we can get hung up on the blackberries!

> Earth's crammed with heaven
> And every common bush afire with God;
> But only he who sees takes off his shoes;
> The rest sit round it and pluck blackberries.

C S Lewis issues a sterner warning about stopping short at Nature "religiously", "When it sets itself up as a religion it is beginning to be a god — therefore a demon.... Nature dies to those who try to live for love of nature." And elsewhere: "If you take nature as a teacher she will teach you exactly the lesson you had already decided to learn; this is only another way of saying that nature does not teach.... The only imperative that nature utters is 'Look. Listen. Attend.'"

William Wordsworth, one of our greatest nature-poets was concerned to help us to look, listen and attend so as to perceive "the God of Nature", by sharing his awareness of *Logos* in the natural creation (though he probably wouldn't put it that way!). His poetry has been described by some English scholars — and dismissed by some Christians — as pantheistic. I would hesitate to identify with that conclusion. And I note that the eminent literary critic, the late W E Williams, in the Introduction to his Penguin *Selection of Wordsworth's Poetry* writes "he is moved by the sense of purpose which he discerns in nature; and in his contemplation of people, too, he is always looking for the meaning in their fate. In a word, and in the best meaning of the word, Wordsworth was a religious man, a believer to whom poetry was, above all, the gift of interpreting nature and man in language which was as near as the average man's understanding as he could make it" (lines written in particular reference to Wordsworth's longer works — "the Prelude" and "the Excursion"). Those opinions ring true to me.

Four years of my childhood were spent near the river Wye in Herefordshire. It was a period I remember with enormous pleasure: the enjoyment, with a young boy's energy, of the farming year of sowing and harvesting, of cattle and daily milking, and sheep-dips, of fishing for perch by Bredwardine bridge, of climbing trees, and making dens.... Yet, even as a child, somehow sensing that "one dear Presence" — an awareness which can, in later years, "fade into the light of common day", as Wordsworth found.

But like him, I have sometimes returned as an adult to those scenes of childhood, to the familiar fields and woods, to the river and lanes with banks covered, in spring, with primroses.... And the tranquil beauty of the area has communicated a deep peace contrasting with the clamour of daily news and political sound-bites — a solace which would have been irrelevant to a carefree boy.... And permeating the whole mix of wonder and gratitude and quiet joy has been the presence of God. So I can identify with William Wordsworth's lines:

> For I have learned
>> To look on nature, not as in the hour
> Of thoughtless youth; but hearing oftentimes
>> The still, sad music of humanity,

Nor harsh nor grating, though of ample power
    To chasten and subdue. And I have felt
A presence that disturbs me with the joy
    Of elevated thought; a sense sublime
Of something far more deeply interfused,
    Whose dwelling is the light of setting suns,
And the round ocean and the living air,
    And the blue sky, and in the mind of man

So much for Frankl's "experiential" benefit of *Logos*, though much more could be added, for the Creator, in whom is our true wealth, security and hope, "richly provides us with everything for our enjoyment" (*1 Timothy 6:17*).

This enjoyment can open the prison-door of self-concern and self-seeking: it helps us to "get a life". Concert halls, art galleries, theatres, libraries, dinner parties, and meeting up for coffee, and sports grounds, as well as walks in the Wye Valley — can also connect us with *Logos*.

Giving to Life

"Don't just sit there: *do* something." "Get up off your thistle and create something; spread some sunshine around."

Human existence *can* be made more meaningful (and happier) claimed Frankl, by *giving* to life — especially in terms of creative acts which benefit others. These can free us from "existential frustration" and restore purpose in living — purpose which is derived from "values" which have objective moral force.

In other words, creative acts can be thoroughly worth while and positively beneficial (as well as being personally fulfilling) because they reflect *Logos*.

Christians affirm that the Creator prompts such creativity in those who draw near to him. God-given discernment of the beauty, order, structure and meaning in creation, reflecting his character, engages a latent desire to celebrate and display these qualities, particularly through art. When human beings lose sight of the Creator in his creation, and thereby forfeit also an awareness of their own creatureliness, their artistic expression sinks into ugliness, disorder, formlessness, meaninglessness.

But, open to *Logos*, artistic creativity can lead to works which — whether religiously-focused or not — delight the senses with beauty and truth: creativity is cleansed and inspired.

The composer Haydn was recorded as saying, "When I think of God, my heart is so full of joy that notes leap and dance as they leave my pen; and since God has given me a cheerful spirit, I serve him with a cheerful spirit".

It has often been pointed out that religious faith has in-spired the world's greatest art; arguably, this creative re-sponse to *Logos* echoes the worship-response of the creation itself, (*Psalm 19:1-4; Psalm 148; see also Psalm 136:1-9*) but human beings can respond with a creativity which is personal, rational and grateful. They can give artistic expression to a Logos-relatedness within themselves.

The completion of creation's worship by human worship is celebrated, following the Psalmist, by many of our hymn writers (e.g. *How Great Thou Art; All Creatures of Our God and King; O Worship the King, All-glorious Above; Morning Has Broken; Jesus is Lord, Creation's Voice Proclaims it*).

The creative celebration of the divine in the context of our culture, the affirmation through the arts, of Beauty, Truth and Goodness as reflections of God, can be a truly therapeutic corrective to today's chillingly impersonal pragmatism and materialism. Being part of a society ruled by productivity, consumerism and an over-riding concern for economic growth can prove strangely dehumanising. Distanced from *Logos*, "wonder, love and praise" dry up.

> The world is too much with us; late and soon,
>> Getting and spending, we lay waste our powers:
> Little we see in Nature that is ours;
>> We have given our hearts away, a sordid boon!
>>>> *(William Wordsworth)*

More importantly "little we see in 'the God of Nature' that is ours.... We have no heart for him". It is not only poets, artists and musicians who may respond to *Logos* by "what they give to life". Frankl is quite right to remind his patients, and all of us, that every person has the potential to live a deeply meaningful life through enriching the lives of others — and thereby glorifying God; nothing is more creative than deeds motivated by kindness and, above all, love for him. This is life's true Elixir, as George Herbert makes plain:

> Teach me, my God and King,
>> In all things thee to see,
> And what I do in any thing,
>> To do it as for thee:

> A man that looks on glass,
>> On it may stay his eye;
> Or if he pleaseth, through it pass,
>> And then the heav'n espy.

> All may of thee partake:
>> Nothing can be so mean,
> Which with his tincture (for thy sake)
>> Will not grow bright and clean.

A servant with this clause
   Makes drudgery divine:
Who sweeps a room, as for thy laws,
   Makes that and th' action fine.

This is the famous stone
   That turneth all to gold:
For that which God doth touch and own
   Cannot for less be told.

Sweeping a room is one thing; another could be re-decorating it, or re-designing the garden, or taking piano lessons, learning to paint or model in clay or master calligraphy, or writing some cheering letters, or taking flowers round to a depressed friend and spending time with them, or having an *Alpha* course in your home, and inviting neighbours.

Taking a Stand in Life
What about those life-situations where it is difficult, if not impossible to "get out more" and derive enjoyment *from* the world, or from giving *to* life in terms of creative acts? What price, then, the nature-poetry of the Romantics?

Where is purpose to be found when life seems cruelly to extinguish *Logos*? — when your world is, for the most part, bounded by four walls. Where is hope when media headlines shout confirmation of Yeats' alarm —

Things fall apart; the centre cannot hold;
   Mere anarchy is loosed upon the world,
The blood-dimmed tide is loosed, and everywhere
   The ceremony of innocence is drowned;
The best lack all conviction, while the worst
   Are full of passionate intensity.

In Frankl's view, *it is the stand we take*, the positive attitude of mind and associated conduct, which redeems a sense of meaninglessness and invests even suffering with meaning. This signifies a resolute refusal to give way to pessimism, to despair: a courageous, humble determination to accept incomprehensible distress and unalterably hard circumstances.

Logos can be lived out by such attitudinal values: the affirmation, against all apparent evidence to the contrary, that life has meaning. Frankl quotes Goethe, "There is no condition which cannot be ennobled by a deed or by suffering"; and he adds, "But we should add that the right kind of suffering is in itself a deed, nay, the highest achievement which has been granted to man" (coming from a man with Frankl's experience those words are particularly poignant).

From a biblical standpoint there are many resonances with these principles — particularly in the books of Job (which shows a man experiencing "a right kind of suffering"), and Ecclesiastes; but supremely in the teaching and example of Jesus (considered in Chapter 9).

Job

Oswald Chambers entitled his profoundly perceptive commentary on *Job*, *Baffled to Fight Better*; that says it all. He writes: "The problem in connection with suffering arises from the fact that there is seemingly no explanation of it.... God never once makes his way clear to Job.... Without any warning, Job's life is suddenly turned into desperate havoc and God keeps out of sight and never gives any sign whatever to Job that he *is*".

When *Logos* seems nothing more than a platitudinous philosophical concept, the temptation is to give way to despair, to espouse nihilism or be overcome by a feeling of blame-worthiness. Job refused to take these ways out despite the uncomprehending religiousness of his three friends, which he found a complete turn-off.

Their "explanations" betrayed a desperate, simplistic clinging to the principle of cause-and-effect: Job's suffering must be the result of sin. But when experience teaches us that there is a baffling, painful "wildness about things"; when rocked by the paralysing trauma of sudden personal grief; when assailed by bewildered fear and faced by "invincible darkness", we identify with Job, and revolt against the people who explain everything on the basis of "sound principles".

"What is needed is a sound *relationship* at the basis of things. This does not make the bafflement any easier, but it does give a reason — the only reason" for hanging in there and maintaining faith, not in a principle, "but faith in *God*, that he is just and true and right" — in spite of all that contradicts it in my experience. "Job's attitude is — 'I cannot understand why God has allowed these things to happen; what he is doing hurts desperately, but I believe that he is honourable, a God of integrity, and I will stick to it that in the end it will be made absolutely clear that he is a God of love and justice and truth. 'Nothing is *taught* in the Book of Job, but there is a deep, measured sense of Someone understanding." Christianity does not consist in coming up with the right answers, or adhering to principles; "Christianity is something other than all that, it is adhering in absolute surrender to a Person, the Lord Jesus Christ". In other words, holding to him who is *Logos-incarnate*, especially when life seems meaningless.

Ecclesiastes
The same precepts emerge from *Ecclesiastes*. J Stafford Wright succinctly sums up the theme: "The theme of the book

is a search for the key to the meaning of life. The Preacher examines life from all angles to see where satisfaction can be found. He finds that God alone holds the key, and he must be trusted — even when God's hand is at times inscrutable. Meanwhile we are to take life day by day from His hand, and glorify Him in the ordinary things" (*The New Bible Dictionary — Ecclesiastes*).

James Houston adds the comment: "Life is a riddle of the Sphinx, without the Creator. It is unknowable without him. Death sets the limit to human existence. There is therefore much despair and hatred of life, in disillusionment, because of death. Man's efforts to master life are therefore misdirected and futile.... Live then within the limits of such creatureliness, is the theme of the book."

This is the way of humble trust — an *attitude* which maintains belief in *Logos* in the warp and woof of life, when structure and meaning do not seem apparent in our personal lives. For the fact is that *Logos is* discernible — in the ordered natural world: "he has made everything beautiful in its time" and, it is implied, this *creation-logos* finds an echo within human nature: "He has also set eternity in the hearts of men", therefore, although "they cannot fathom what God has done from beginning to end" nevertheless "I know that there is nothing better for men than to be happy and do good while they live" (*Ecclesiastes 3:12-14*).

In Christianity, "what God has done from beginning to end" is done through Christ. Now glorified in heaven as the divine *Logos-incarnate*, he affirms "Do not be afraid. I am the First and the Last. I am the Living One. I was dead, and behold I am alive for ever and ever! And *I* hold the keys of death and Hades" In him, meaninglessness loses its power and final terror (*Revelation 1:17 and 18; 3:7; cf Isaiah 22:22*). Living in a world where life can seem empty of meaning and purpose, and when our personal lives are darkened by suffering or grief which seem cruelly arbitrary, what is the conclusion of the matter, what is the "stance we should take"? "Now all has been heard; here is the conclusion of the matter: fear God and keep his commandments, for this is the whole duty of man. For God will bring every deed into judgement, including every hidden thing, whether it is good or evil" (*Ecclesiastes 12:13-14*).

"What price the nature-poetry of the Romantics?" Wordsworth was certainly not insensitive to the world's suffering and meaningless developments — "the still, sad music of humanity". Neither was he blandly euphoric about Nature. He was realistic about the ugliness which spoils its beauty and order, and our own perceptions — the clouding, which experience of life brings, of childhood's 'innocent' joy — the fading of the visionary gleam, the glory and the dream.

> The rainbow comes and goes,
>> And lovely is the rose,
> The moon doth with delight
>> Look round her when the heavens are bare,
> Waters on a starry night
>> Are beautiful and fair;
> The sunshine is a glorious birth:
>> *But yet I know, where'er I go,*
> *That there hath passed away a glory from the earth.*

Nevertheless, rainbows persist. And, for the Christian, they convey not only pleasure at their breath-taking beauty but *hope*; for they are the God-given assurance of divine covenant love — and of an eschatological cosmic redemption (a truth which does not readily spring to the mind of a young boy!). But to boy or adult, the glorious bow in the sky against the threatening background of dark clouds, conveys a kind of surprised-by-joy reverence.

> My heart leaps up when I behold
> > A rainbow in the sky:
> So was it when my life began;
> > So is it now I am a man;
> So be it when I shall grow old,
> > Or let me die!
> The Child is father of the Man;
> > And I could wish my days to be
> Bound each to each by natural piety.

Gerard Manley Hopkins, an overtly Christian poet, celebrates the glory of the Creator in his creation, *notwithstanding* the deeply defiling effects of human exploitation and environmental abuse: the glory remains, uncrushed; dearest freshness will spring up from below; and the Holy Spirit will yet spread light and love and joy and hope.

> The world is charged with the grandeur of God.
> > It will flame out, like shining from shook foil;
> > It gathers to a greatness, like the ooze of oil
> Crushed. Why do men then now reck his rod?
> Generations have trod, have trod, have trod;
> > And all is seared with trade; bleared, smeared with toil;
> > And wears man's smudge and shares man's smell: the soil
> Is bare now, nor can foot feel, being shod.
> And for all this, nature is never spent;
> > There lives the dearest freshness deep down things;
> And though the last lights off the black West went

Oh, morning, at the brown brink eastward, springs –
Because the Holy Ghost over the bent
World broods with warm breast and with ah!
bright wings.

(Poem: *God's Grandeur)*

Logos as God-Speaking — Special Revelation

There is a branch of theology called epistemology. It is about knowledge — more particularly, the method and grounds of knowledge: it addresses the question, how do we know that we know? Especially, how do we know that we know about God?

Clearly, if we are to know truly anything about God we are dependent upon his personal self-disclosure in *words.* We need God to speak. *Logos* as God-immanent is not enough. We may well intuit God's existence and glean something of his presence, power and divine nature from creation. But our intuitive faculties are unreliable, skewed by sin. Moreover, the Creation is impersonal; we are persons.

If we are to *relate* to God as person to Person — rather than cling to an abstract theological principle on the basis of a religious presentiment — we must know who he is and what he is like. Indeed, we need to comprehend what the word "God" means, what content it has.

How can we know him, know how he wants us to relate to him, and how he wants us to live? We do need God to talk to us; words are an epistemological necessity.

This line of thought is not so highfaluting as it may sound. Words are a necessity at an everyday level. We get to know other people by conversing with them. We communicate with each other with words: we express our thoughts, feelings and intentions in speech. Within society, words are necessary for Order and social cohesion.

That is why the mis-use and distortion of words is such a serious threat; when they are emptied of their authentic meaning, when facts, truth and reality are misrepresented by spin, hype or lies, individuals are disorientated and communal life is undermined. "Just as Babel was destroyed in its own confusion, so too we live without any coherent worldview, in the babel of pluralism. When man no longer heard the Word of God, then he no longer heard his neighbour, for his words were for himself, to himself about himself."

This latter point, made by James Houston, points up the crucial importance of the complementary doctrines of Revelation and Inspiration in relation to the "inscripturation" of God's self-disclosure. Those theologians who question the whole notion of Scripture as revealed truth are prompting doubts which are very grave and potentially disastrous.

Arguably, "verbalisation" *is* the most distinctively human thing about us (cf Schaeffer): God has created us as beings who communicate with words. It is therefore logically to be expected that he will disclose himself to us in words.

If, ironically, certain theological writers use words to express their views questioning verbal revelation, how come it is thought incredible that God, in whose image we are created, should open his mind to us in words? To put the matter a little irreverently, isn't it the obvious thing for him to do? (This is not the place to enter into the theological area of Inspiration and how Holy Scripture came to be the reliable transcript of what God wanted written. Suffice it to say that Holy Scripture, as inspired words, is of supreme importance for the knowledge of God and the substance of the Christian life — *2 Timothy 3:14-17*).

It is to be acknowledged that the use of language presents well-known problems, not least in relation to the world of ideas and, especially, to supernatural Reality. Also, words themselves can prove flexible: they can change their precise meaning; their impact varies with different periods of history, cultures, and individual readers. In the elucidation of what the Bible is saying, linguistic analysis and hermeneutics are invaluable disciplines.

However, if at the end of the day there can be no intelligible correlation between Word and words (*Logos* and *logoi*), all theology (and Height Psychology with its *logotherapy*) must end either in silence or impractical mysticism. Four relevant points need to be made about biblical revelation.

One. It is not claimed that it is exhaustive! We cannot "possess" all that there is to be known about God and his ways with us: his truth is absolute, the depth of his wisdom and knowledge unsearchable (*Isaiah 55:8f and Romans 11:33f*).

Clearly, much about God remains secret, hidden from our finite minds; but the things that *have* been revealed are ours to appropriate, enjoy and obey and benefit from (*Deuteronomy 29:29*).

Two. In contradistinction to the gods (idols) of false religion, who have no voice nor creative power, God *speaks*, and his words achieve the purpose for which he sends them (*Isaiah 44:12-27; 55:10-11*).

Three. The purpose of God's self-revelation in words is not that we have our heads filled with theological information (the sort of knowledge that can "puff up" i.e. lead to pride and arrogance — *1 Corinthians 4:6, 18, 19*) but so that we may be led into a personal relationship with him permeated by love (*1 Corinthians 8:1-3*). Truth is not so much a precept as a person to be known, loved, followed, worshipped and served (*John 14:6*).

Four. The power of biblical words is not in themselves but in their Source: "He spoke, and it came to be; he commanded, and it stood forth" (*Psalm 33:9*). The Spirit of God empowers the Word of God; the Word of God is "the sword of the Spirit".

The relevance to Height Psychology of *Logos* as God-speaking is immediately discernible. The *logotherapy* by which, according to Frankl, life can be made meaningful in a three-fold way (the experiential, the creational, and the attitudinal) is greatly enriched when *Logos* is acknowledged and welcomed as God-speaking.... The written and pro-claimed Word of God.

God's Word and Our Experience
In illustration of the Word of God's healing meaningfulness in experience, I cannot do better than to quote a modern version of an old hymn

Lord your word shall guide us
    and with truth provide us:
teach us to receive it
    and with joy believe it.

When our foes are near us,
    then your word shall cheer us –
word of consolation,
    message of salvation.

When the storms distress us
    and dark clouds oppress us,
then your word protects us
    and its light directs us.

Who can tell the pleasure,
    who recount the treasure
by your word imparted
    to the simple-hearted?

Word of mercy, giving
  courage to the living;
word of life, supplying
  comfort to the dying.

(H W Baker)

Those words resonate in the heart and mind of every Christian to whom the Bible is precious as God-speaking.

Through all the changing scenes of life there is no clearer light or stronger comfort or more realistic hope than that which is communicated within our total experience by the Holy Spirit from Holy Scripture (*Psalm 119:10;, Romans 15:4 and 13*).

O that we discerning
  its most holy learning,
Lord, may love and fear you –
  evermore be near you!

God's Word and Creativeness

Words can confuse and hurt; they can reveal simplistic attitudes and uncomprehending, if well-meaning, responses. Hence, in counselling, the primary importance of really *listening*; for some schools of psychotherapy this is extended further to the principle of *non-directive* counselling.... But wise words can also clarify and heal. "A word aptly spoken is like apples of gold in settings of silver" (*Proverbs 25:11*). Derek Kidner comments "the whole simile is of uncertain interpretation, but at least its components carry associations of attractiveness, value and craftsmanship".

The Book of Proverbs, he reminds us, has a lot to say about words — all of great relevance to counselling.

Words at their best: are *honest* (*Proverbs 24:26, 27:5-6,*

28:23), they are *few* (17:28; 13:3; 11:12-13; 10:19), they are *calm* (17:27; 18:13; 15; 1; 25:15), they will be *apt* "a truth that makes no impression as a generalisation may be indelibly fixed on the mind when it is matched to its occasion and shaped to its task" (15:23; 10:20 and 32).

What we can *give to life*, to other people, is so often best expressed in words — words that commend and clarify God's words, words that communicate comfort from person to person and from God (1 Thessalonians 4:18), words which, derived from Scripture and aptly applied, can correct, teach, guide, train and show the way forward towards a fulfilling, God-glorifying future (2 Timothy 3:16 to 4:2). But not all the Christian counsellor's words will be preachy! Advice perfunctorily punctuated by Bible verses can be stultifying, even discouraging.

There is nothing magically therapeutic about *holy* words just because they're quoted *verbatim* from the Bible (even from the sacrosanct Authorised Version). But an honest, brief, calm, apt sharing of some biblically-derived insight which has been helpful to the listener may well prove helpful to the client.... Sometimes a poem echoing scriptural truth captures the need of the moment and sheds light, sometimes a ray of illumination from a novel, or an expository comment from a Christian writer.... But of course, a straight-forward relevant quotation from Scripture, passage or a single verse, *can* speak more powerfully and healingly than any other words.

And these principles are poignantly valid when we're really stuck and our *attitude*, the position we take is all-important, for ourselves and those near us.

God's Word and the Attitude We Need
Logos-light from God's Word can penetrate the deepest

darkness and kindle courage and hope and communicate the peace of God which transcends all understanding.

Towards the end of his last book, *Fear No Evil* David Watson, terminally ill, quoted the example of Martin Niemoller who "was incarcerated in a Nazi concentration camp for many years but was allowed the Bible as his one possession". Niemoller wrote "the Bible: what did this book mean to me during the long and weary years of solitary confinement and then for the last four years at Dachau cell-building? The Word of God was simply everything to me — comfort and strength, guidance and hope, master of my days and companion of my nights, the bread which kept me from starvation, and the water of life which refreshed my soul. And even more, 'solitary confinement' ceased to be solitary." David Watson adds "this is the constant experience of those who have dared to take God at his word, despite all the odds against them."

"David wrote the last pages of his book during the first week of January 1984. On January 8th he preached at St Michael's, Chester Square, from Jude verses 20 to 25" — "but you, dear friends, build yourselves up in your most holy faith and pray in the Holy Spirit. Keep yourselves in God's love as you wait for the mercy of our Lord Jesus Christ to bring you to eternal life."

David said "the last couple of months have seen some pretty sweeping changes in my own life. I have had to cancel all my engagements outside London and after travelling for many years I would have found that very difficult if it had not been for God so clearly calling me back to this love relationship with him. Even death itself is not a threat."

"On January 15th he preached again at St Michael's, this time on Psalm 91, which he found 'highly relevant'. —

He who dwells in the shelter of the Most High,

Who abides in the shadow of the Almighty,
Will say to the Lord, "my refuge and my fortress;
My God in whom I trust'".

"On Monday the 30th January he said to David MacInnes, 'I am completely at peace. There is nothing that I want more than to go to heaven. I know how good it is.' David Watson died peacefully very early on the morning of February 18th."

"To him who is able to keep you from falling and to present you before his glorious presence without fault and with great joy — to the only God our Saviour be glory, majesty, power and authority, *through Jesus Christ our Lord*, before all ages, now and forevermore! Amen" (*Jude 24-25*).

Hearing and Obeying — Height Theology

Logos as God-speaking — his Word written or proclaimed — requires a response of obedience; as divine imperative it commands submission to its authority. To adapt Frankl's terms: the *objective quality*, inherent in meaning and values, accounts for their *obligative quality*.

God's Word illustrates this principle much more clearly and forcefully: according to Scripture, God demands that his verbal revelation be heard and obeyed as a rule for the whole of human life. Thus, the commandments given directly to Moses ("And God spoke all these words") are introduced (in *Deuteronomy 5:1*) by the solemn *"Hear, O Israel ...* learn them and be sure to follow them"; very significantly, this urgent injunction (*Shema Yisrael*) also precedes the seminal command to love God (*Deuteronomy 6:4f*) — they are to love the one, true God with their total being, his commandments being both upon their hearts and permeating their whole way of life.

The link between obedience and hearing (or disobedience and deafness) is made in many places for the simple reason that the Hebrew word for "obey" means, literally, "hearken to". Similarly, in the New Testament the Greek verb translated "to obey" (*hypakouo*) is a compound of *akouo*, which also means "hear". The precise meaning of *hypakouo* is "hear under" — thus conveying the idea of submission to authority. (Interestingly, our English words obey/obedience are derived from the Latin *Ob-audire* (to hear): "obedience" means literally "in the way of, hearing".)

Disregard-*cum*-disobedience related to God's Word forfeits his blessing.

Thus God rebukes and punishes his people (see *Jeremiah 7:20f*) for rebellion against him which has resulted from their non-attention to his Word: "I gave them this command: obey me, and I will be your God and you will be my people. Walk in all the ways I command you, that it may go well with you. *But they did not listen or pay attention; instead, they followed the stubborn inclinations of their evil hearts.* They went backward and not forward … day after day, again and again I sent you my servants the prophets. But they did not listen to me or pay attention." (We note that rejection of his Word through the prophets is equivalent to rejection of God.)

The psychological importance of hearing-and-obeying God's Word (true *logotherapy*) is plain. Each one of us, time and time again, is faced with *choice*: to change for the better by listening to and obeying the guidance found in Holy Scripture or, by ignoring or rejecting it, to stay stuck where we are or to regress — "to go backward not forward".

Someone has written "blaming our faults on our nature does not change the nature of our faults". We are *responsible* — before God and before others — for seeking to fulfil the divine purpose for our lives. Arguably, such responsibility is the essence of our humanness.

In this sense we may "Christianise" Frankl's existential

maxim concerning the kind of person we remain or become: "bad" (perhaps wicked) or "good" (holy, in the biblical sense): "Man has both potentialities within himself: which one is actualised depends on decisions but not on conditions".

To quote again from Deuteronomy — pre-eminently the book containing God's written "commands, decrees and laws" — these are summed up in the following words "I have set before you life and death, blessings and curses. So choose life, so that you and your children may live and that you may love the Lord your God, listen to his voice, and hold fast to him. *For the Lord is your life" (Deuteronomy 30:19-20).*

Henri Nouwen comments "choose life, that's God's call for us, and there is not a moment in which we do not have to make that choice. Life and death are always before us. In our imaginations, our thoughts, our words, our gestures, our actions ... even in our non actions.

This choice for life starts in a very interior place — underneath very life-affirming behaviour that can still harbour death-thoughts and death-feelings ... and choose curse instead of blessing. Jealousy, envy, anger, resentment, greed, lust, vindictiveness, revenge, hatred ... they all float in that large reservoir of our inner life. Often we take them for granted and allow them to be there and do their destructive work. But God asks us to choose life and to choose blessing.

We cannot always do this alone; often we need a caring guide or a loving community to support us. But it is important that we both make the inner effort and seek the support we need from others to help us choose life."

Supremely, this surely means, for Christians, that we should seek to be *logotherapists* — helping each other to *identify* and to *understand* relevant Scriptures, to *re-order* our thoughts and attitudes in conformity with them, and to live them out in practical *obedience*.

Often such a response will go against the grain of our human nature.

"Choosing life instead of death demands an act of will that often contradicts our impulses ... how then can we let our wills dominate our impulses? The key word is *wait* ... we must distance, take time to think, talk it over with friends, and wait until we are ready to respond in a life-giving way. Impulsive responses allow evil to master us, something we always will regret. But a well-thought-through response will help us to "master evil with good" (see *Romans 12:14-21*).

"Height-psychology" such as this is healthily complementary (surely a necessary corrective) to the pessimistic determinism of Freudian depth psychology and the over-optimistic humanism of Rogerian lateral psychology.

But the really good news is that God has fulfilled his promise to his people made under the old covenant to cleanse us morally and spiritually, to put his law in our minds and write it on our hearts, and give us a new motivation: "I will put my Spirit in you *and move you* to follow my decrees and be careful to keep my laws". (See *Jeremiah 31:33; 32:40; Ezekiel 36:25-27*).

This wonderful fulfilment was *accomplished* by the Lord Jesus Christ himself who, by his own unfailing obedience "unto death" (*Philippians 2:8; cf Hebrews 5:8; 10:5-10*) brought acceptance with God and fellowship with God to all who believe in him (*Romans 5:15-19*).

The fulfilment is *applied* in our experience by the Holy Spirit, who enables us to obey the gospel-command to put our faith in Christ, and move forward in grateful submission to his authority (*Acts 6:7; Hebrews 5:9; 1 Peter 1:22; cf John 6:29 and 1 John 3:23*).

For, in the final analysis, true obedience must have its focus in Jesus Christ who is at the very heart of verbal revelation — the sum and substance of Logos-written: the golden thread running through the whole Bible.

CHAPTER 9

IMMANUEL

"We have seen his glory ... full of grace and truth"
John 1:14

Humanity's supreme *Signal of Transcendence* is Jesus Christ himself. His incarnation, his earthly ministry, and his exaltation all signify transcendency. He came into this world "from above"; on earth, he embodies and displays the glory of the Father; raised from death he has returned to the right hand of God.

In foregoing chapters I have sought to explore experiential and practical applications of three major doctrines derived from the Bible (regeneration, redemption, revelation) as they connect with "depth", "lateral" and "height" psychology respectively. All three doctrines have their focus and fulfilment in Jesus Christ: they illuminate different but linked aspects of *knowing* him, the perfect Man. Regeneration speaks of his life *in* us; as the redeemed community we are united by his life *among* us; as the focus of God-given revelation, we are drawn to him, now exalted to the highest place, *above* us.

The question is not, can depth, lateral and height psychology form a permissible approach to the consideration of the personhood of Jesus; but rather, what light does the personhood of Jesus, revealed in Holy Scripture, throw upon those psychological categories? In what ways does a biblical Christology support, modify or invalidate these?

Again, *Depth Psychology and Regeneration* as foundational will be considered first.

Christ and Depth Psychology

Christ by highest heaven adored,
    Christ, the everlasting Lord,
Late in time behold him come,
    Offspring of a virgin's womb!
Veiled in flesh the Godhead see!
    Hail, the incarnate Deity!
Pleased as man with man to dwell,
    Jesus, our Immanuel.

"Jesus Christ was born *into* this world, not *from* it. He came into history from the outside of history; he did not evolve out of history. Our Lord's birth was an advent.... He is God Incarnate, not man becoming God, but God coming into human flesh, coming into it from outside. His life is the Highest and the Holiest entering in at the lowliest door. Our Lord entered history by the Virgin Mary. By that entry into our world, Jesus Christ was constituted as one of the human race, but without its guilt" *(The Psychology of Redemption —* Oswald Chambers).

Freud's model of personality based on psychoanalysis and comprising *Id, Ego and Superego* is just that, a model. As such, it has always been a suspect theory in the view of some other professionals. For example, Professor Lewis Wolpert (Professor of Medicine as applied to Biology at University College, London) writes "I cannot take seriously claims that psychoanalysis should be treated as a science. The ideas are so vague and thus so all-inclusive that it is not possible to test whether they are right or wrong ... one only needs to look at the competing schools of analysis — Laconian, Freudian, Kleinian, Jungian — to see that their differences can never be resolved, since they are not based on science but just different interpretations of similar stories" (from *The Independent 5 May 2000*).

As a starting point for a consideration of Jesus it is therefore most certainly theologically questionable. More to the point: it proves to be inapplicable, as any attempt to employ Freud's key expressions with reference to Christ demonstrates.... If we *were* to posit an *"Unconscious"* (in a Freudian sense) within Christ's personhood, it is clear that its contents would have been pure — because of his supernatural conception. Being conceived by the Holy Spirit, the embryo growing in Mary's womb and born, full term, as a baby, and developing as an infant, was untainted by the entail of original sin.

Similarly, his *"superego"* would have been formed primarily by the inflow, throughout the whole of his earthly life, of the life of God — and secondarily, by the early security, training and teaching he received from God through the agency of Mary and Joseph. This would mean that his *"ego"* or "self" was expressed in attitudes, deeds and words which were utterly holy, and therefore self-consistent. All that he was reflected his deity; everything he said and did was at the Father's prompting.

In other words, Freud's three-fold model cannot be applied to him: he was one single, whole, unified person demonstrating deity in humanness: "for God was pleased to have all his fullness dwell in him" *(Colossians 1:19).*

The biblical accounts amply substantiate this conclusion. We read that through his childhood "Jesus grew in wisdom and stature, and *in favour with God and man*" as he submitted dutifully to the parenting of Mary and Joseph *(Luke 2:51-53).*

Plummer comments "His was a perfect humanity developing perfectly, unimpeded by hereditary or acquired defects.

It was the first instance of such a growth in history, and the first time a human infant was realising the ideal of humanity" (from *Commentary on Gospel of Luke — Norval Geldenhuys*).

This truth, evidenced through his whole life, is borne out by his own consciousness of sinlessness e.g. "Can any of you prove me guilty of sin? If I am telling the truth, why don't you believe me?" (*John 8:46; and see also 14:30; 15:10*).

These are momentous claims. Only someone who was God-incarnate could so confidently appeal to his own moral perfection.

Again: (with reference to the "inflow" of God's will into his ministry) "When you have lifted up the Son of Man, then you will know that I am the one I claim to be and that I do nothing on my own but speak just what the father has taught me. The one who sent me is with me; he has not left me alone, for I always do what pleases him" (*John 8:28-29.*) See also *6:38* "I have come down from heaven not to do my will but to do the will of him who sent me".

The conclusion is clear: the personality of Jesus was *totally* undefiled and positively pure. He was free of that heart-corruption of which he himself spoke (free of Freud's dark sex/aggression incubus); moral goodness, truth and beauty filled his being and flowed from him — the perfect human being.

Not only in a Freudian sense, but also from an Adlerian perspective, was Jesus Christ free of defect — for, clearly, no "will-to-power" was present in him; in fact, the very reverse: "being in very nature God, (he) did not consider equality with God something to be grasped, but made himself nothing, taking the very nature of a servant, being made in human likeness" (*Philippians 2:6*).

Based on these words we can surmise that, at a deeper

level — echoing Jung's approach, inadequate though it is — the deepest contents of his personhood related to memory, would have been derived from his pre-incarnate existence within the Trinity.

Theologians remind us that when "the Word became flesh, this does not mean that the *Logos* ceased to be what he was before. As to his essential being the Logos was exactly the same before and after the incarnation". The New Testament declares that it was while he was upholding all things by the word of his power that he died for our sins (*Hebrews 1:3*).

Of his self-awareness in this regard there is also ample evidence in his own words e.g. "I came from the Father and entered the world and now I am leaving the world and going back to the Father" (*John 16:28*); "And now, Father, glorify me in your presence with the glory that I had with you before the world began" (*John 17:5; see also John 8:38 and 58; Luke 10:18*). We can perhaps affirm then, that in becoming fully identified with our collective humanity, past and present, he became linked to our "collective unconscious" *but* with untainted virtue, "like the current of fresh water in an ocean of salt" (as J Stafford Wright put it).

In biblical terms, he was the new, the second, Adam from heaven — pure, sinless and "life-giving".

The Church Fathers went to the heart of the matter when they proclaimed, "What Christ did not assume he could not heal". He did assume our nature, in its entirety, and as our undefiled Representative, he could now take upon himself, voluntarily, the liability of humanity's sin, our sin, in our place — the Just One standing in for the unjust; the Innocent for the guilty; the Sinless for the sinful. This would entail nothing less than a substitutionary, propitiatory death — a death which would secure, for believers, peace with God and the peace of God. "Having been made like us in every way he could make atonement for the sins of the people" (*Hebrews 2:17*).

It must be stressed that death, for him, was not an unavoidable necessity. It was in obedience to the Father and out of his love for us that he died on the cross, thus robbing death of its hellish terror, and delivering us from guilty dread. "Since the children have flesh and blood, he too shared in their humanity so that by his death he might destroy him who holds the power of death — that is the devil — and free those who all their lives were held in slavery by the fear of death" (*Hebrews 2:14-15*).

May we, therefore, put the matter in this way: not just his *ego*, but his *whole being*, was filled with pure obedience (to the Father) and pure love (for us). That purity of obedience and love was not unassailed.

All through his life, and especially throughout his three years' public ministry he was opposed by Satan. Though never succumbing to the power of evil — sometimes blatantly overt, sometimes sinisterly hidden — he was "tempted in every way, just as we are."

The fierce personal battles he fought against the powers of darkness, and the strain upon him of moving steadily forward in God's will, are documented. "During the days of Jesus' life on earth, he offered up prayers and petitions with loud cries and tears to the one who could save him from death, and he was heard because of his reverent submission. Although he was a son, he learned obedience from what he suffered and, once made perfect, he became the source of eternal salvation for all who obey him" (*Hebrews 5:7-9*).

In Gethsemane he suffered the symptoms of both depression and anxiety at their darkest and most acute. "He took Peter, James and John along with him, and he began to be deeply distressed and troubled. 'My soul is overwhelmed with sorrow to the point of death' he said to them" (*Mark 14:33-34*).

This terrible soul-distress with its accompanying physical anguish was compounded by oppression — for this was "Satan's hour", when darkness reigned and hell's malevolence well-nigh crushed him.

But he did not break. Though the agony of his ordeal, endured with earnest prayer, caused his sweat "to be like drops of blood falling to the ground" he moved forward towards the *via dolorosa* and the cross with an obedience, and a love, "made perfect through suffering". He is now "crowned with glory and honour *because* he suffered death so that by the grace of God he might taste death for everyone" (*Hebrews 2:9-10*).

Death was thus robbed of its power to terrify, for he endured it victoriously in our place. The cry "It is finished" was a shout of triumph, not a dying groan of defeat. His last words, loud and clear, on the cross, "Father, into your hands I commit my spirit" should remind us of earlier words concerning his sacrificial death for his sheep, "No-one takes (my life) from me, but I lay it down of my own accord. I have authority to lay it down and authority to take it up again" (*John 10, 18*) Believers may now face death without guilty dread, unappalled, uncowed. Its sting has been drawn, its power broken. By faith-identification with the risen Christ we have already passed from death to life, from the depths of hell to the height of heaven.

Christ's Life in Us — Regeneration

Experiential assurance of the salvation-truths flowing *fundamentally* from the incarnation, is a fruit of regeneration. Or, to put it another way, it comes through Christ's birth *in us* — something which the atonement has made possible.

Paul uses this analogy in writing to the Galatian churches (*4:19*) "My dear children for whom I am again in the pains of childbirth until Christ is *formed in you*". Clearly, such a continuing transformation towards Christ-likeness must begin with an initial receiving of his life within. (The verb Paul uses has a medical connotation, when it means "the formation of an embryo").

Oswald Chambers again: "Just as our Lord came into human history from the outside, so he must come into us from the outside. Have we allowed our personal lives to become a 'Bethlehem' for the Son of God?"

This emphasis corrects a commonly-held view that the religious life (the "God-life") arises inside us. William James in his discussion of varieties of religious experience stipulated an inner "reservoir" (rather like Freud's Unconscious) which "contains, for example, all our momentarily inactive memories and it harbours the springs of all our obscurely motivated passions, impulses, likes, dislikes and prejudices.... *In it arise whatever mystical experiences we may have and ... it is also the fountain-head of much that feeds our religion*" (my italics). This, in essence, was his explanation of sudden "spiritual" transformation (conversion) — an uprush "into ordinary consciousness of energies originating in the subliminal parts of the mind."

There are echoes here of the Jungian concept of "God-within", which claims that a process towards wholeness, individuation, (outworked conversion) is something that rises up out of our unconscious life into our conscious life and acts as an integrating force between these two aspects of the psyche. The fact is, however, that "we cannot enter the realm of the Kingdom of God" (nor *know* intimate relationship with God) "unless we are born from above, by a birth totally unlike natural birth" (*John 3:5*).

In parallel with the transcendent source of our Lord's earthly life and ministry, the Christian's regeneration is also from "outside". We are born again "from above". "People have the idea that because there is good in human nature (and, thank God, there is a lot of good in human nature) that therefore the Spirit of God is in every man naturally, meaning that the Spirit of God in us will become the Christ in us if we let him have His way. Take that view if you like, but never say it is the view of the New Testament. It is certainly not our Lord's view. He said to Nicodemus, you should not be surprised at my saying "you must be born again.... The conception of new birth in the New Testament is of something that enters us, not of something that springs out of us." (*Oswald Chambers: The Psychology of Redemption*).

Through Christ's birth in us we enter a life of hope and inspiring challenge. Believers are no longer bound or dragooned by sin (or the destructive impulses of Depth Psychology), nor shackled by shame, guilt and fear. The future is not irrevocably pre-programmed by "the flesh" and its "works" (*Galatians 5:19-21*). We are *born again*: "Christ dwells in our hearts through faith" (*Ephesians 3:17*). That does not mean that we *cannot* sin, it means that if we co-operate with the life of God in us, we *need not* sin. The mainspring of our human nature is different. "You ... are controlled not by the sinful nature but by the Spirit, if the Spirit of God lives in you" (*Romans 8:9*).

Christ and Lateral Psychology

"I relate, therefore I am".

Our need for relationship, community, is built into the human psyche because the Holy Trinity, from whom our existence is derived, is essentially a relationship — of three persons in one. The Christian psychiatrist Jack Dominian, in his book *One Like Us*, an interesting "psychological interpretation of Jesus", makes the same point with reference to Christ and love among Christians. Jesus often asserts "a unique relationship of oneness between himself, the Father and the Holy Spirit" (*John 14:16-17, 26; 15:26*).

"In the relationship of the Father, Son and Holy Spirit we have the ultimate revelation of the nature of God. Just as John says in his first epistle that God is love, so we can say with equal veracity that God is relationship, a dynamic reality. Jesus was aware that his identity was embedded in relationship and the heart of this relationship is love, which he commands us to have for one another". He prays that the life-together of believers may reflect the relational unity existing between him and the Father: "that all of them may be one, Father, just as you are in me and I am in you" (*John 17:20-21*).

Unity and love are to be the hallmarks of the Christian community.

Christ's earthly life and relationships. As a young boy, Jesus lived at home in Nazareth where he was dutifully submissive to Mary and Joseph, growing "in wisdom and stature, and in favour with God and man". Mary, like every godly Jewish mother, would have been the source of her son's first education — a task shared in due time by Joseph.

Alfred Edersheim, the Jewish-Christian scholar writes, "There could not be national history, nor even romance, to compare with that by which a Jewish mother might hold her child entranced. And it was his own history — that of his tribe, clan, perhaps family; of the past indeed, but yet of the present, and still more of the glorious future. Long before he could go to school, or even Synagogue, the private and united prayers and the domestic rites whether of the weekly Sabbath or of festive seasons, would indelibly impress themselves upon his mind" (*The Life and Times of Jesus The Messiah*).

Such upbringing would have been experienced by Jesus, with his "brothers and sisters" — children born to Joseph and Mary later.

And this background of every day family-life in a small-town community, and familiarity with the countryside, clearly formed the base of much of his later teaching: "the happy games of children, festive gatherings, marriage processions, funeral rites, the exactions of tax collectors, the oppression of the widow by unjust judges — together with his observant love of nature — all these, and much else features in his teaching. He would also have known, with his half-brothers and sisters, Mary's tender love and care, appreciating the close bonds of family-life — hence his deep understanding of the joys — and sorrows of ordinary people occasioned by illness and bereavement/separation — as evidenced in the home of Lazarus".

Dominian writes "the results of the hidden world of Jesus' childhood are seen in his adulthood". And he suggests that because, like every infant and growing child, Jesus needed his mother, the quality of her response to his human emotional and physical needs (he hungered, thirsted, and needed comforting) did much for his own sensitive response to the needs of others.

The relationship with the apostles was far from impersonal: the bonds between them were affectionate; they were friends — as John's gospel makes clear. "You are my friends if you do what I command. I no longer call you servants, because a servant does not know his master's business. Instead, I have called you friends, for everything that I learned from my Father I have made known to you" (*John 15:14-15*). "It was one of his greatest achievements that he created a fellowship out of that strange group of men and women whom he called to him — the inner group of the Twelve and a larger group of disciples. It was a significant achievement that he could draw together a Simon the Zealot, fired with a passion for home rule for Palestine, with a Matthew the tax-gatherer who, because he earned his living from the Roman invader, must have seemed a traitor to Simon. But Jesus called these political opposites, and knitted them into a fellowship of loyalty to him; *and in that loyalty they found love for one another.*

So again, he called John, young, sensitive, mystical in outlook, and knit him into a fellowship with Peter, rough, outspoken, impetuous. In common loyalty to him, they found themselves in fellowship with one another. And Mary Magdalene 'from whom he had cast out seven devils' — poor soul, was she a woman of the streets as tradition would have it? She was drawn into the circle, together with Joanna who moved in court circles — so St Luke tells us (*8:2-3*). Political barriers, personal barriers, social barriers — all fall before the personality of Jesus, and a fellowship is created focused in him" (*The Prayers of the New Testament — Donald Coggan*).

So it was that during his earthly ministry Jesus is encountered as a life-affirming, people-loving breath of fresh air in a society oppressively overshadowed by a dreary religion and a pagan civil power. Crowds of ordinary people gathered and listened to him with delight (*Mark 12:37*) — amazed at his teaching because of his authoritativeness in contrast to the cautious, quote-heavy, pettifogging of their scribes.

On a personal level, possessed with an inner security derived from his intimate connectedness to the Father he could express his emotions — anger, grief, compassion, humour; uncowed by any compulsion to conform to political, social or "ecclesiastical" correctness he could freely declare divine truth and make God *real* to his spiritually hungry hearers.

Though a man of sorrows and familiar with suffering he could yet speak to others of the joy which was his and open their eyes to the beauty of nature, sharing with them the pleasure it gave him.

Castigated by the Pharisees for mixing with the socially marginalised and irreligious he declared that these were the very people who most needed to hear of the seeking, redeeming love of God (*Luke 15*) He himself was a way-in to the sheepfold of God's care and protection for all who hear his voice and follow him; he had come that they may have life, and have it to the full (*John 10, 7-30*) It is worth recalling, again, that all the metaphors he employed for entering, and belonging in, the new community he was establishing were of a corporate nature: a believer is pictured as a sheep in a flock, a child in a family, a citizen in a kingdom, a branch in a vine.... But he himself is the key to each word-picture: the shepherd, the elder brother, the king, the vine.... And yes, in Paul's words: the head of the body.

The result, then, of the "lateral" impact of Christ's ministry was the formation of a new community focused in him. And the open secret of their continuing unity was love: "As the Father has loved me, so have I loved you. Now remain in my love ... love each other as I have loved you."

Christ's Life Among Us — The Redeemed Community

The exalted Son of God through whom and in whom we have a shared redemption is "head of the body, the Church (the redeemed community); he is the beginning and the first-born from among the dead, so that in everything he might have the supremacy" (*Colossians 1:18*). Christ is the "second Adam" through whom a new branch of humanity is brought into existence; he is the very "fount" of the new community's life.

As its "risen Head" he is in organic union with all its members: they share a common life with him. This is the "lateral" significance of Christ-centred redemption continued after his bodily departure.

Pentecost led swiftly to a great enlargement of the redeemed community. "The fellowship of the incarnate Jesus has now become the fellowship of the Holy Spirit, and the withdrawal of his physical presence has made no difference to its continuance: indeed, it has opened up the way to its extension and its deepening" *(Donald Coggan).* Christ is still the magnetic force who draws people to himself and in flowing through them by his Spirit binds them together and empowers them. He may be absent physically, but the members of the fellowship find that, under the Spirit's ministry the historic Christ becomes a contemporary companion — known intimately as personal Saviour and Friend, and as their inner life.

For just as, in his earthly life, Jesus, in addition to relating to crowds had time for individuals, so now. His insight and sympathetic compassion continue –

> Though now ascended up on high,
>   He sees us with a brother's eye;
> He shares with us the human name
>   And knows the frailty of our frame.
>
> Our fellow-sufferer yet retains
>   A fellow-feeling of our pains:
> He still remembers in the skies
>   His tears, his agonies and cries.
>
> *(R Harrison)*
> *(Hebrews 2:14-18; 4:14-15)*

On earth he was, arguably, the supreme Person-Centred Therapist. But he was so much more. He not only comforted and affirmed people by his accepting, empathic, congruent love for them: he called them to lift their eyes above their personal needs, and look into his face and put their faith in him. He presented himself as more than a therapist, more than a healer: he was the *Redeemer*. True healing and wholeness come not primarily from self-fulfilment, but from putting God first. In his only saying to be repeated in all four Gospels he declares "Whoever tries to keep his life will lose it, and whoever loses his life for my sake (and the Gospel's) will (find it and) preserve it" (*Matthew 10, 39; Mark 8:35; Luke 9:24; John 12:25*). Self-actualisation as an end in itself is self-defeating. We are made for higher ends: "to glorify God, and fully to enjoy him forever." Together. In this endeavour we are assured of sympathy for our weaknesses and strengthening grace from the one who has trod that royal road before us, and is now exalted to the highest place.

> With boldness therefore at his throne
>> Let us make all our sorrows known:
> To help us in the darkest hour,
>> We ask for Christ the Saviour's power.

This is not an individualistic thing. As members of a redeemed community Christians need each other for mutual care and encouragement, and they function most effectively (for God's glory) as a united force standing firm in one spirit and of one mind (*Philippians 1:27; Ephesians 6:10-20*). To this end, they will fulfil the law of Christ by carrying each other's burdens and gently restoring those who stray by sinning (*Galatians 6:1-2*).

There is a reverse process related to such fellowship of

the Holy Spirit: it is derived from the love of the Father and the grace of the Son but our fellowship with them is fuelled by our fellowship with other Christians.

This fact underlines the truth that Christian fellowship is not an end in itself: it is for the sake of fellowship with God. Whether on earth, or in heaven (i.e. both here and hereafter) "the fellowship practised by the redeemed will have as its God-appointed goal the deepening of the fellowship which each of them enjoys with the Redeemer" (*God's Words — J I Packer*). Hence, in exhorting the Hebrew Christians to keep on keeping on, to maintain the freshness of their faith (which was flagging) the writer urges them: "Let us hold unswervingly to the hope we profess, for he who promised is faithful. And let us consider how we may spur one another on towards love and good deeds. Let us not give up meeting together, as some are in the habit of doing, but let us encourage one another" (*Hebrews 10, 23-25*).

Christians, no less than secular humanists, want to promote human happiness and fulfilment in this life, and they share with others a concern to respond in an enlightened way to humanitarian needs, and to environmental problems. With Carl Rogers and his followers, they see the poignant need for many to "become a person" — to have personality-potential released and positive, affirming relationships developed.

But we want to proclaim, firmly, thankfully, joyfully, persuasively that, in these terms, Jesus Christ is the supreme humanist and that it is through faith in him and following him that we can become truly human. Lateral psychology finds its effective fulfilment in and through him.

Christ and Height Psychology

Jesus Christ, *Logos-Incarnate* is the personal sum-and-substance of revelation — of (a) *Logos-immanent* and (b)

Logos-written.

(a) "He is the image of the invisible God, the firstborn over all creation … all things were created by him and for him. He is before all things, and in him all things hold together" (*Colossians 1:15-17*).

(b) "You diligently study the Scriptures because you think that by them you possess eternal life. *These are the Scriptures that testify about me,* yet you refuse to come to me" (*John 5:39-40*). "The words I say to you are not just my own. Rather it is the Father, living in me, who is doing his work." "The words I have spoken to you are Spirit and they are life" (*John 14:10, see verse 24, and 3:34; 8:28; 12:49; 6:63*).

It is very significant that *as such* Jesus Christ, *Logos-Incarnate*, is now raised from death and exalted to the right hand of God. By this fact God authenticates him for all time as the apex of revelation. "The divine act of raising Jesus from the dead was an unconditional validation of everything he was in his incarnate life on earth … the Father's 'Amen' … to the saving work: that by his death on the cross Jesus had indeed saved eternally all those whom the Father had sent him to save."

It also covered "the moral character and life of the Lamb of God. Jesus spoke of his sign-acts in the course of his ministry as works that the Father had given him to do, and it was his claim that he had finished this work (*John 5:19 and 36; 17:4*): did he perform all the Father's works and leave nothing undone or imperfectly done? And finally, was Jesus true to his vocation as the Word of the Father so that he declared all the truth the Father sent him to declare, nothing half-said and taught nothing that had any admixture of untruth?

It is in this sense that the resurrection is an uncondi-

tional divine validation of the teaching as much as of the saving efficacy of Christ.

This great Lord Jesus came from outside and voluntarily and deliberately attached himself to the Old Testament, affirmed it to be the Word of God and set himself, at cost, to fulfil it (e.g. *Matthew 26:51-54*). This fact of facts cuts the ground from under any suspicion that the *doctrine* of biblical authority rests on a circular argument such as, 'I believe the Bible to be authoritative because the Bible says it is authoritative'. Not so! It was Jesus who came 'from outside' as the incarnate Son of God, Jesus who was raised from the dead as the Son of God with power, who chose to validate the Old Testament in retrospect and the New Testament in prospect, and who is himself the grand theme of the 'story-line' of both Testaments, the focal-point giving coherence to the total 'picture' in all its complexities.

There is an old jingle which is certainly simple and verges on the simplistic, but our forebears were fundamentally right when they taught that: the Old Testament is Jesus predicted; the Gospels are Jesus revealed; Acts is Jesus preached; the Epistles, Jesus explained; and the Revelation, Jesus expected. *He is the climax as well as the substance and centre of the whole. In him all God's promises are Yea and Amen (2 Corinthians 1:20)*" (*Look To The Rock — Alec Motyer*).

Nothing can be added to that! As Height theology, dealing with revelation, it cannot be bettered.

Christ's Life Above Us — Christian Logotherapy
Pursuing the parallelism of Christ's life, and ours derived from him, both having a transcendent origin, it follows that the life of Christ implanted in us by regeneration is the life of the now risen Christ.

He "easters in us". To know Christ by faith is to know,

experientially, "the power of his resurrection" by which we are being changed into his likeness and energised to do his will. "In the distinctive New Testament usage, resurrection signifies not the reanimation of corpses but the transformation of the whole person into the image of Christ by the power of the indwelling Spirit, in spite of the intervention of death" (*Dictionary of New Testament Theology* — *Vol 3 Resurrection Ed: Colin Brown*).

We live in an age where death reigns. "The dust of death" covers our world, and we are part of our world.... But "Christ Jesus ... has destroyed death and has brought life and immortality to light through the Gospel" (*2 Timothy 1:10*). "The Christian is destined to gain an immunity to that principle of decay and deterioration which characterises humanity in Adam, through sharing the endless life of God" (*Colin Brown* ibid). Jesus says, "I am the resurrection and the life. He who believes in me will live, even though he dies; and whoever lives and believes in me will never die" (*John 11:25*).

Our resurrection after physical death is, clearly, a future event; but the resurrection-life of Jesus can be enjoyed in the present because of the Spirit of life which indwells us. Eternal life begins *now*. The transformation is underway.

The drawing-power of Jesus in glory, connecting with his risen life within us, becomes the motive force for Christian living. "Since, then, you have been raised with Christ, set your hearts on things above, where Christ is seated at the right hand of God. Set your minds on things above, not on earthly things. For you died, and your life is now hidden with Christ in God. When Christ, who is your life, appears, then you also will appear with him in glory" (*Colossians 3:1-4*).

This emphasis upon the *transcendent*, future-orientation of the Christian life has far-reaching psychological implications. No longer, for the Christian, is the downward drag of forces revealed by Depth Psychology dominant. Nor need we be lamed by the undermining pressures of self-rejection exacerbated by the disconfirming attitudes, imagined or real, of others. Ugly and damaging drives/impulses, words and deeds, still threaten to rear their heads, even in the regenerate; an inappropriately negative self image, which distorts relationships, may also threaten to persist. But these can now be progressively expelled through "knowing Christ and the power of his resurrection."

God's "pull" upon our lives, focused in the risen, exalted Christ, becomes stronger than sin's residual obstructiveness and the strangely stultifying push of self-actualisation.

"Forgetting what is behind and straining towards what is ahead, I press on towards the goal to win the prize for which God has called me heavenwards in Christ Jesus" (*Philippians 3:13-14*).

On a broader canvas this Christian height psychology has sharp relevance to the "cabin'd, cribbed and confined" worldview within contemporary society and its mundane pre-occupation with *this* age — with current priorities and moral "standards" which are so often bounded by consumerism and economic considerations.

It rebukes that secularisation of theology by which the Gospel is interpreted as a social panacea, an ethical school of thought, or merely a subjective beneficial experience. "Early Christianity thought in terms of the long perspective for it recognised not only the earthly, but also the supra-worldly, the eternal.... The Gospel is the declaration that God brought something wholly new into this age, that *through Christ* he brought the new age among us — an age begun in our midst, but to be fulfilled in glory." "Basic to this view (of Paul) are two facts: one, that in this world we belong to death's domain" (where Christ-defying self indulgence, a reverse of true moral standards, and earth-bound motivations dominate — *Philippians 3:18-19*); "the other, that through Christ, God has burst in upon this world with the dominion of life, *calling us by the Gospel to enter it with him*" (*Commentary on Romans — Anders Nygren*).

Far from being a daunting or discouraging prospect, the challenge of such spiritual endeavour is stimulating and heart-lifting because its motivating energy comes from Christ himself. And the "goal" and the "prize" are surpassingly worthwhile. In *Philippians 3:14*, (quoted above) these are left undescribed. "Paul tells us neither what the goal is nor what the prize will be.

Yet suddenly the earthly scene with all its strivings, sufferings and sacrifices is suffused with heavenly glory. One scriptural picture after another fills and elevates the mind: the Lord's own 'well done!'; 'the crown of righteousness, which the Lord, the righteous judge, will award to me on that Day;' 'the unfading crown of glory', gift of the chief Shepherd; the privilege (above all) that his servants should worship him, see his face and have his name written on their foreheads; the blood-cleansed robes and the unending presence of the Lord. All this and, in addition, 'what no eye has seen, nor ear heard, nor the heart of man conceived, what God has prepared for those who love him'. That is the goal and the prize!" *(The Message of Philippians — Alec Motyer)*.

As an evangelist and church-planter and writer, Paul had no illusions about his imperfectness. On a personal level he *had* come a long way: he had exchanged a self-satisfied "righteousness" for the righteousness of Christ; he had grown in his knowledge of Christ and the experienced power of his resurrection; he had proved the strengthening companionship of Christ in times of suffering and cross-bearing; and he was confident that whatever lay before him, smooth or rough, he would one day share the eternal glory of resurrection and glorification with his master.

But he knew that he had not yet "arrived". There was still a long way to go along "the road less travelled". So much *more* to learn of Christ and to do for Christ and, above all to become for Christ. He was not impelled by fear or self-aggrandisement, but by a desire to serve Jesus Christ. The Son of God had taken hold of him; Paul now wanted to *press on* — the verb is vigorous — to live out the purpose for which Christ had made him his own. He can never feel content with a partial attainment; not because of an inner psychologically-explicable drivenness, but because of the divine "pull" upon his heart and life (*Philippians 3:7-14*). There is a lot of truth in Robert Browning's lines

"Ah, but a man's reach should exceed his grasp,

Or what's a heaven for?"

Depression, related to problems in our past, and discouragements derived from present circumstances, and anxiety about our tomorrows, and strained relationships, are debilitating. The "future grace" of God is energising. Paul could have felt disqualified and disequipped to serve Christ by his past failings and mistakes, by the present pressures upon him and the possible pitfalls on the path ahead. But he moved into his future with buoyant resolution *in response* to the "heavenward calling of God in Christ Jesus".

So his is now a "purpose-driven life". The lines of Bishop J B Monsell's hymn (below) are more profound than perhaps they first appear, because they capture the complementarity of Christ-centred call *and* enabled response. Here are the first two verses:

Fight the good fight with all thy might;

Christ is thy strength, and Christ thy right.

Lay hold on life, and it shall be
Thy joy and crown eternally.

Run the straight race through God's good grace,
Lift up thine eyes, and seek his face;
Life with its path before thee lies;
Christ is the way, and Christ the prize.

I suggest that the principles drawn out in preceding paragraphs amount to *Logotherapy* of the highest order! — For they are derived from a "height theology" which has resonances (though certainly not identity) with Frankl's "height psychology" — and his use of *"logos"*.... But because they are centred in Jesus Christ, *Logos-incarnate*, they are infinitely more relevant to the innate human longing to find, and connect with, Meaning. Personal faith in the risen, exalted Son of God who is the Way, the Truth and the Life, imports into our lives his "all-sufficient grace": grace which both satisfies and stimulates.

To adopt Frankl's three areas of meaningfulness: *experientially*, Christ immeasurably enhances the pleasure derived from all that is "true... noble ... right ... pure ... lovely ... admirable ... excellent ... and praiseworthy" — in nature, and in our fellow human beings and their achievements. Secondly, the Spirit of Christ within us touches into life and into *creative expression*, the latent potentialities, aptitudes and talents with which God has gifted us –whether in acts of practical kindness or works of art.... And the *attitudinal* benefits from Christ-centred logotherapy?

Believers are linked by their faith with a Saviour who has drained the cup of pain and endured the deepest darkness, and triumphed. Now, from "the throne of grace" he is able with total sympathy to sustain, as no-one else can, all who come to God through him (*Hebrews 4:14-16; 5:7-9; 7:25*).

Berger's *signals of transcendence* form, in his view, a counterpoint to "the onset of secularisation": they linger on in the human psyche as a "rumour of God", despite the receding of religion. A rediscovery of the supernatural through an openness to signals of transcendence will lead to "an over-coming of triviality … the true proportions of our experience are rediscovered. This is the comic relief of redemption: it makes it possible for us to love and to play with a new fullness … this is no way implies a remoteness from moral challenges of the moment … but one of the best things that can happen to us is to recall that, to use Dietrich Bonhoeffer's suggestive term, all historical events are "penultimate", that their ultimate significance lies in a reality that transcends them and that transcends all the empirical coordinates of human existence."

Biblically, that reality of transcendence has its focus in the risen, exalted Christ, who will one day return, and establish a final, ultimate glorious new heaven and earth, the home of righteousness (*Revelation 21:1-7; 2 Peter 3:13*) The "rumour of God" finds its *actuality* in the Person of Christ who is "the radiance of God's glory and the exact representa-tion of his being" *(Hebrews 1:3).* In him, all *signals of transcendence* have their apotheosis….

Frankl's insistence upon the fundamental nature of our "Will-to-Meaning", our reaching out to transcendent values and purposes, is indeed vindicated, for Christians, *in Christ.* And his *logotherapy* can find validity and effectiveness when linked to the risen Son of God — *Logos-incarnate* exalted, and coming again.

When John the Apostle was given a personal revelation of the glorified Christ, he wrote "When I saw him, I fell at his feet as though dead. Then he placed his right hand on me and said: 'do not be afraid. I am the First and the Last. I am the Living One: I was dead, and behold I am alive forever and ever!" (*Revelation 1:17-18*).

The Risen Lord

My wife and I were seated among spring flowers and blossoming trees, facing the Garden Tomb in Jerusalem. As many readers will know, this may well have been the actual sepulchre where the body of the crucified Jesus was laid. We had just finished reading together the resurrection narratives from all four gospels. Breaking the sunlit silence Hilary said quietly, "How wonderful it must have been for him...."

It was a new thought for me. I was reflecting on what Easter morning must have meant to Mary and Peter and John ... not *him*. But how right Hilary was. It was profoundly moving to picture him walking out of the sepulchre into the early morning sunlight, the cool air on his face, the grass and soil under his feet, blessed by birdsong and refreshed by the scent of flowers ... it was all over: the darkness, the pain, the blood, the horror.

With resurrection life surging through his healed body he walked into the garden. The scene was vivid in our minds, in our imaginations. We almost *saw him* there, smiling at us. I shall never forget that moment; nor Hilary's words: "How wonderful it must have been for *him*."

A few years later, through my son, I came across John Updike's "*Seven Stanzas at Easter*": for me, a brilliant theological/poetic evocation of that shared hour in the Garden, and of the sheer physical/spiritual reality of the resurrection:

Make no mistake: if he rose at all
    It was as His body;

If the cells' dissolution did not reverse, the molecules
    Reknit, the amino acids rekindle,
The Church will fall.

It was not as the flowers,
    Each soft Spring recurrent;
It was not as His Spirit in the mouths and fuddled
    Eyes of the eleven apostles;
It was as His flesh: ours.

The same hinged thumbs and toes,
    The same valved heart
That — pierced — died, withered, paused, and then
    Regathered out of enduring Might
New strength to enclose.

Let us not mock God with metaphor,
    Analogy, sidestepping, transcendence;
Making of the event a parable, a sign painted in the
    Faded credulity of earlier ages:
Let us walk through the door.

The stone is rolled back, not papier-mâché,
    Not a stone in a story,
But the vast rock of materiality that in the slow
    Grinding of time will eclipse for each of us
The wide light of day.

And if we will have an angel at the tomb,
    Make it a real angel,
Weighty with Max Planck's quanta, vivid with hair,
    Opaque in the dawn light, robed in real linen
Spun on a definite loom.

Let us not seek to make it less monstrous,
> For our own convenience, our own sense of beauty,
Lest, awakened in one unthinkable hour, we are
> Embarrassed by the miracle,
And crushed by remonstrance.

Christ is now ascended, back with his Father and ours in the glory of heaven as our representative, our brother. Risen with him, we shall one day be with him where he is. Therefore, says Paul, let your hearts respond to the "heavenward call of God in Christ Jesus". While you live, keep "straining towards what is ahead ... pressing on towards the goal...."; and die climbing. Heaven's glory beckons.

And yet ... it will not always be the distant scene that is of primary comfort to us in the here and now; not the indescribable, awesome, glory of that great white throne and the new Jerusalem with its golden streets and river of life, the swelling sound of angelic choirs, nor even a new heaven and a new earth, filled with the beauty of righteousness.

This is a wonderful heart-lifting prospect, of course, and we are to encourage one another with the sure expectation of it all. But until then, as we, like Pilgrim, walk through the wilderness of this world, it is the *present* companionship of the Man of Galilee which often moves us deeply: the Jesus of Easter morning, who comes to meet us, as he met with Mary and as he met with Hilary and me outside the empty tomb.

Most poignantly is this so when, in grief, we confront darkness ... but Jesus is *there* and through our tears speaks to our hearts of "the irrelevance of death". Evangeline Patterson reminds us of this in her beautiful poem "*Deathbed*":

Now, when the frail and fine-spun
    Web of mortality
Gapes, and lets slip
    What we have loved so long
From out our lighted present
    Into the trackless dark.

We turn, blinded,
    Not to the Christ in Glory,
Stars about his feet,

But to the Son of Man,
    Back from the tomb,
Who built fires, ate fish,
    Spoke with friends, and walked
A dusty road at evening.

Here, in this room, in
    This stark and timeless moment,
We hear those footsteps

And
    With suddenly lifted hearts
Acknowledge
    The irrelevance of death.

CONCLUSION

The models and approaches of depth, lateral, and height psychology dissolve before the reality of the presence and grace of Jesus Christ. Face to face with him, *all* metaphors give way to Truth and Reality. In him, we actually encounter God, in human form. He makes known to us, makes real in our present experience, *Yahweh* — the divine name: the essence of all that God is and will be. "I have revealed your Name to those whom you gave me out of the world ... in order that the love you have for me may be in them and I myself may be in them."

Christ is not only *in us* as our new life and as our hope — the certain guarantee — of glory, he is also *with us* as a living Friend who will never leave us or forsake us, he is also *among us* as our common Lord and Saviour and Brother, and he is *above us* as our Representative and King, gone to prepare a place for us in the Father's house, that where he is there shall we also be. He himself is our true destiny.

"O Lord of life, send my roots rain". An old hymn expresses well the gratitude which Christians feel for God's refreshing Word and, above all, for the Redeemer of whom it speaks:

> Father of mercies, in your word
>   what endless glory shines!
> For ever be your name adored
>   for these celestial lines.
>
> Here may the blind and hungry come
>   and light and food receive;

here shall the humble guest find room
    and taste and see and live.

Here the redeemer's welcome voice
    spreads heavenly peace around,
and life and everlasting joys
    attend the glorious sound.

Here springs of consolation rise
    to cheer the fainting mind,
and thirsty souls receive supplies
    and sweet refreshment find.

Divine instructor, gracious Lord,
    be now and always near:
teach us to love your sacred word
    And view our Saviour here.

(Anne Steele 1760)

SCRIPTURE INDEX
Page numbers for this book are in brackets

Luke

2:51-53 (p.268); *9:24* (p.280); *10:18* (p.270); *12:7,32* (p.31); *12:24,27* (p.242); *15* (p.278); *23:34* (p.202)

John

1:1-3, 14 (p.238); *1:14* (p.266); *3:3-7* (p.109-10, 125, 273); *3:16-21* (p.194); *3:34* (p.282); *5:19-20* (p.192) *5:36* (p.282); *5:39-40* (p.282); *6:29* (p.264); *6:38* (p.269); *6:63* (p.282); *7:37-39* (p.46, 125,132); *7:41,49,52* (p.181); *8:28-29* (p.269, 282); *8:31-36* (p.200); *8:38,58* (p.270); *8:46* (p.269); *10:18* (p.272); *10:7-30* (p.278); *11:25* (p.56, 284); *12:25* (p.280); *12:49* (p.282); *13:1-7* (p.231); *13:34* (p.130); *14:1* (p.31); *14:6* (p.256); *14:16-17,26* (p.275, 282); *14:24* (p.282); *14:26* (p.275); *14:30* (p.200, 269); *15:10* (p.269); *15:14-15* (p.276); *15:26* (p.275); *16:28* (p.270); *16:33* (p.31); *17:4* (p.282); *17:5* (p.270); *17:20-21* (p.275)

Acts

2:42-47 (p.168, 182); *2:47* (p.182); *4:32* (p.181); *5:17-32* (p.231); *6:7* (p.264); *10:9-16* (p.231); *12:12-16* (p.231); *14:15* (p.126); *21:37-40* (p.231); *26:18* (p.126)

Romans

1:18-32 (p.201); *1:18-2:16* (p.235); *1:20-239*); *5:1-2,11* (p.203); *5:8* (p.203); *5:15-19* (p.264); *7:14-25* (p.93); *7:18-19* (p.172, 173); *7:23-24* (p.172); *8:7-8* (p.172); *8:9-11* (p.138, 274); *8:15-17* (p.136); *8:28* (p.13); *8:35-37* (p.1); *10:4* (p.186); *10:14-15* (p.235); *11:33f* (p.256); *12:2* (p.85, 135, 164); *12:14-21* (p.264); *13:10* (p.131); *15:4,13* (p.34, 87, 258); *15: 4-5,13* (p.25); *15:26* (p.181)

1 Corinthians

2:4 (p.67); *4:11f* (p.128); *4:6, 18, 19* (p.256); *8: 1-3* (p.257); *10: 16-17* (p.180); *13* (p.168)

2 Timothy
1:10 (p.284); *3:5* (p.55); *3:14-17* (p.255); *3:16* (p.48); *3:16-4:2* (p.259)

Titus
3:1-8 (p.139)

Hebrews
1:3 (p.235, 239, 270, 289); *2:9-10* (p.272); *2:14-15* (p.122, 271); *2:17* (p.270); *2:18* (p.137); *4:14-16* (p.137, 289); *5:7-9* (p.271, 289); *5:8* (p.264); 5:9 (p.264); *6:19-20-106); 7:25* (p.289); *10:5-10* (p.264); *10:23-25* (p.281); *11:1* (p.226)

James
1:5-8 (p.139); *1:17-18* (p.125,139); *1:19-21* (p.134); *1:18, 21* (p.239)

1 Peter
1:3-5 (p.136); *1:6f* (p.137); *1:22-23* (p.168, 264); *1:22-25* (p.131, 164, 239); *1:23,25* (p.124); *2:9* (p.174); *2:21-25* (p.202)

2 Peter
1:21 (p.48); *3:13* (p.289

1 John
3:8 (p.12); *3:17* (p.182); *3:23* (p.264); *4:7* (p.129,168); *4:10* (p.203); *4:18* (p.204); *4:21* (p.130)

Jude
20-25 (p.260-1)

Revelation
1:17-18 (p.252, 290); *3:7* (p.252); *21:1-7* (p.289)

MAIN INDEX

ALSO BY DEREK OSBORNE
From White Tree Publishing

No, not a children's book! An affectionate, optimistic look at church life involving, as it happens, Roddy and his friends who live in a small town. Problems and opportunities related to change and outreach are not, of course, unique to their church!

Maybe you know Miss Prickly-Cat who pointedly sits in the same pew occupied by generations of her forebears, and perhaps know many of the characters in this look at church life today. A wordy Archdeacon comes on the scene, and Roddy is taken aback by the events following his first visit to church. Roddy's best friend Bushy-Beard says wise things, and he hears an enlightened Bishop . . .

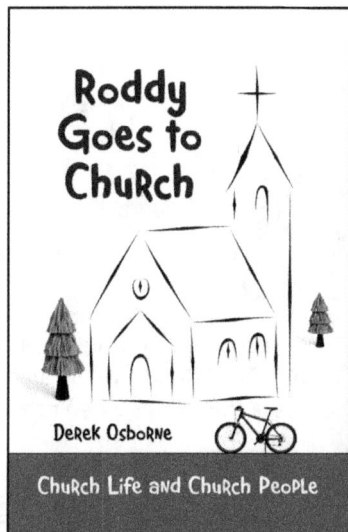

Bishop David Pytches writes: *A unique spoof on church life. Will you recognise yourself and your church here? ... Derek Osborne's mind here is insightful, his characters graphic and typical and the style acutely comical, but there is a serious message in his madness. Buy this, read it and enjoy! David Pytches, Chorleywood*

ISBN: 978-09927642-0-3
46 pages 5.5 x 8.5 inches paperback only, UK £3.95
Available from bookstores and major internet sellers

(See front of this book for more retail outlets for this title)

BOOKS BY J STAFFORD WRIGHT

From White Tree Publishing

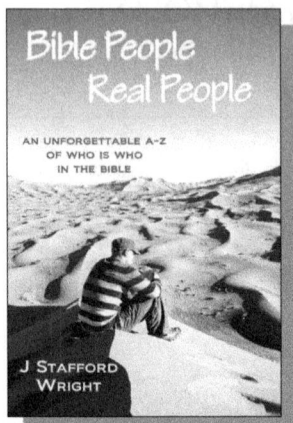

BIBLE PEOPLE
REAL PEOPLE

In a fascinating look at real people, J Stafford Wright shows his love and scholarly knowledge of the Bible as he brings the characters from its pages to life in a memorable way.

✓ Read this book through from A to Z, like any other title.
✓ Dip in and discover who was who in personal Bible study.
✓ Check the names when preparing a talk or sermon.

The good, the bad, the beautiful and the ugly — no one is spared. This is a book for everyone who wants to get to grips with the reality that is in the pages of the Bible, the Word of God.

With the names arranged in alphabetical order, the Old and New Testament characters are clearly identified so that the reader is able to explore either the Old or New Testament people on the first reading, and the other Testament on the second.

Those wanting to become more familiar with the Bible will find this is a great introduction to the people inhabiting the best selling book in the world, and those already familiar with the Bible will find everyone suddenly becomes much more real — because these people *are* real. This is a book to keep handy and refer to frequently while reading the Bible.

Paperback ISBN 13: 9-780-9525-9565-6
310 pages 6 x 9 inches £9.95, US $14.95
Available from bookstores and major internet sellers
Searchable Kindle e-Book ISBN: 978-0-9932760-7-1
Previously published as *Dictionary of Bible People*

MAKES A GREAT GIFT!

CHRISTIANS AND THE SUPERNATURAL

BY J STAFFORD WRIGHT

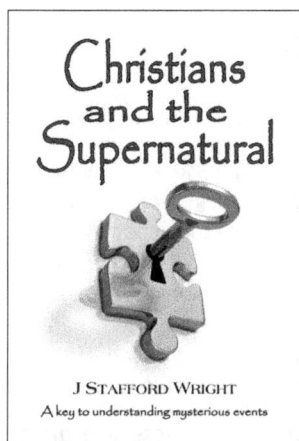

Christians and the Supernatural

J STAFFORD WRIGHT

A key to understanding mysterious events

There is an increasing interest and fascination in the paranormal today. To counteract this, it is important for Christians to have a good understanding of how God sometimes acts in mysterious ways, and be able to recognize how he can use our untapped gifts and abilities in his service. We also need to understand how the enemy can tempt us to misuse these gifts and abilities, just as Jesus was tempted in the wilderness.

In this single volume of his two previously published books on the occult and the supernatural (*Understanding the Supernatural* and *Our Mysterious God*) J Stafford Wright examines some of the mysterious events we find in the Bible and in our own lives. Far from dismissing the recorded biblical miracles as folk tales, he is convinced that they happened in the way described, and explains why we can accept them as credible.

The writer says: *When God the Holy Spirit dwells within the human spirit, he uses the mental and physical abilities which make up a total human being . . . The whole purpose of this book is to show that the Bible does make sense.*

And this warning: *The Bible, claiming to speak as the revelation of God, and knowing man's weakness for substitute religious experiences, bans those avenues into the occult that at the very least are blind alleys that obscure the way to God, and at worst are roads to destruction.*

Paperback ISBN 13: 9-780-9525-9564-9
222 pages 5.25 x 8 inches £8.95 and US $12.95
Available from bookstores and major internet sellers
Also available as an e-Book in most formats
ISBN 13: 978-0-9932760-4-0

A PREVIOUSLY UNPUBLISHED BOOK

THE SIMPLICITY OF THE INCARNATION

BY J STAFFORD WRIGHT

Foreword by J I Packer

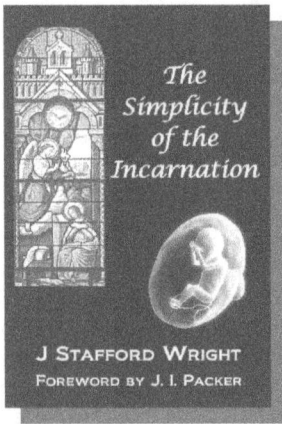

"I believe in ... Jesus Christ ... born of the Virgin Mary." A beautiful stained glass image, or a medical reality? This is the choice facing Christians today. Can we truly believe that two thousand years ago a young woman, a virgin named Mary, gave birth to the Son of God? The answer is simple: we can.

The author says, *"In these days many Christians want some sensible assurance that their faith makes sense, and in this book I want to show that it does."*

In this uplifting book from a previously unpublished and recently discovered manuscript, J Stafford Wright investigates the reality of the incarnation, looks at the crucifixion and resurrection of Jesus, and helps the reader understand more of the Trinity and the certainty of eternal life in heaven.

This book was written shortly before the author's death in 1985. *The Simplicity of the Incarnation* is published for the first time, unedited, from his final draft.

Paperback ISBN: 9-780-9525-9563-2
160 pages 5.25 x 8 inches £7:95 and US $11:95
Available from bookstores and major internet sellers
Also available as an e-Book in most formats
ISBN 13: 978-0-9932760-5-7

A PREVIOUSLY UNPUBLISHED BOOK

LOCKED DOOR SHUTTERED WINDOWS
A NOVEL BY J STAFFORD WRIGHT

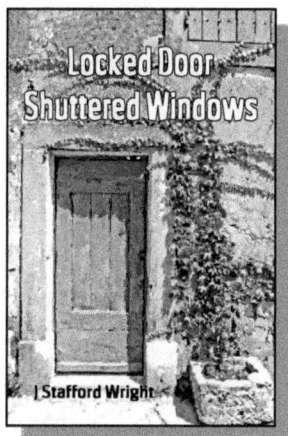

What is inside the fascinating house with the locked door and the shuttered windows? Satan wants an experiment. God allows it. John is caught up in the plan as Satan's human representative. The experiment? To demonstrate that there can be peace in the world if God allows Satan to run things in his own way. A group of people gather together in an idyllic village run by Satan, with no reference to God, and no belief in him.

J Stafford Wright has written this startling and gripping account of what happens when God stands back and Satan steps forward. All seems to go well for the people who volunteer to take part. And no Christians allowed!

John Longstone lost his faith when teaching at a theological college. Lost it for good — or so he thinks. And then he meets Kathleen who never had a faith. As the holes start to appear in Satan's scheme for peace, they wonder if they should help or hinder the plans which seem to have so many benefits for humanity.

Paperback ISBN: 978-0-9927642-4-1
206 pages PAPERBACK 5.25 x 8.0 inches £6.95 and US $11.95
Available from bookstores and major internet sellers
Also available as an e-Book in most formats
ISBN 13: 978-0-9932760-3-3

English Hexapla — The Gospel of John

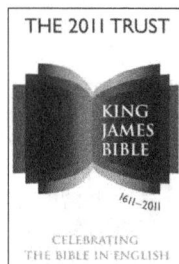

Published to coincide with the 400th anniversary of the Authorized King James Version of the Bible, this book contains the full text of Bagster's assembled work for the Gospel of John. On each page in parallel columns are the words of the six most important translations of the New Testament into English, made between 1380 and 1611. Below the English is the original Greek text after Scholz. To enhance the reading experience, there is an introduction telling how we got our English Bibles, with significant pages from early Bibles shown at the end of the book.

Here is an opportunity to read English that once split the Church by giving ordinary people the power to discover God's word for themselves. Now you can step back in time and discover those words and spellings for yourself, as they first appeared hundreds of years ago.

Wyclif 1380, Tyndale 1534, Cranmer 1539, Geneva 1557, Douay Rheims 1582, Authorized (KJV) 1611.

English Hexapla — The Gospel of John
Published in paperback only by White Tree Publishing
PAPERBACK ISBN: 978-0-9525956-1-8
Size 7.5 x 9.7 inches paperback
UK £6.95, US $9.95.

Further details on these and other Christian books for young readers as well as adults can be found by entering *White Tree Publishing* in the relevant search box on the websites of internet book sellers. Titles are available in paperback and/or e-Book format.

WHITE
TREE
PUBLISHING

www.ingramcontent.com/pod-product-compliance
Lightning Source LLC
LaVergne TN
LVHW051453080426
835509LV00017B/1754